CRITIQUE OF HEGEL'S
'PHILOSOPHY OF RIGHT'

Cambridge Studies in the History and Theory of Politics

CRITIQUE OF HEGEL'S 'PHILOSOPHY OF RIGHT'

BY

KARL MARX

TRANSLATED FROM THE GERMAN BY
ANNETTE JOLIN AND
JOSEPH O'MALLEY

EDITED
WITH AN INTRODUCTION
AND NOTES BY

JOSEPH O'MALLEY

Assistant Professor of Philosophy
Marquette University

CAMBRIDGE
AT THE UNIVERSITY PRESS
1970

Published by the Syndics of the Cambridge University Press
Bentley House, 200 Euston Road, London N.W.1
American Branch: 32 East 57th Street, New York, N.Y. 10022

Library of Congress Catalogue Card Number: 74–112471
Standard Book Number: 521 07836 9

Printed in Great Britain by
Alden & Mowbray Ltd at the Alden Press, Oxford

Contents

Editor's Preface

The translation of Marx's *Kritik des Hegelschen Staatsrechts* (§§ 261–313) is based on the German edition in *Karl Marx/Friedrich Engels/Werke* (Institut für Marxismus–Leninismus beim Zentralkomitee der Sozialistischen Einheitspartei Deutschlands, Band I, Berlin, Dietz Verlag, 1964), pp. 203–333; and photocopies of the original manuscript (No. A4, Marx–Engels Archives, Internationaal Instituut voor Sociale Geschiedenis, Amsterdam). The editions of Rjazanov (Frankfurt a/M and Berlin, 1927), Landshut (Stuttgart, 1953), and Lieber and Furth (Stuttgart, 1962) were also consulted. In the translation, all departures from the text of the *Werke* edition follow the reading of Lieber and Furth on the basis of an examination of the manuscript photocopies, and all such departures are noted. The passages from Hegel's *Rechtsphilosophie* are in the English version of T. M. Knox (*Hegel's Philosophy of Right*. Oxford, The Clarendon Press, 1962) by permission of The Clarendon Press, Oxford. This is the standard English version of Hegel's work, hence the decision to allow Knox's rendition of Hegel to govern the present translation of Marx. The translation of Marx's 'Zur Kritik der Hegelschen Rechtsphilosophie. Einleitung' is based on the German edition in *Karl Marx/Friedrich Engels/Werke*, Band I, pp. 378–91. The English translations of Bottomore (New York, 1964) and Easton and Guddat (Garden City, 1967) were consulted. This 'Introduction' by Marx is included in the present volume because of its special relationship to the earlier, and lengthier *Critique*.

It is a pleasure to acknowledge the help of the following persons in the preparation of the translations, Introduction and notes: Drs Gerhard König and Manfred Kliem of Dietz Verlag, Berlin; Messrs H. P. Harstick and Götz Langkau of the Internationaal Instituut voor Sociale Geschiedenis, Amsterdam; Dr Maximilien Rubel of the Centre d'Etudes Sociologiques, Paris; Dr Georg Eckert of the Friedrich–Ebert–Stiftung, Bonn; Mr C. Pels of Velsen, Holland; Dr Loyd Easton, Ohio Wesleyan University; Dr James Collins, St Louis University; and Drs Denis and Rosa Savage, Marquette University and Cardinal Stritch College respectively. I am especially indebted to Dr Shlomo Avineri of The Hebrew University, Jerusalem, for acquainting me with the importance of Marx's critique of Hegel's *Rechtsphilosophie* and the need for its translation, and for his continuing counsel; and to Annette Jolin, the co-translator of this text.

My debt to other scholars in the field is evidenced in the footnotes to the Introduction and the texts and in the Bibliographical Note at the end of the Introduction. The typescript of the translations, Introduction and notes was prepared by Mrs Kay Camele and Mrs Barbara Neal. The work of translating Marx's *Critique of Hegel's 'Philosophy of Right'* was supported through a research grant and a summer Faculty Fellowship granted by the Marquette University Committee on Research.

Milwaukee   J. O.
September 1969

Editor's Introduction

I

The work translated here is Karl Marx's critical commentary on Paragraphs 261–313 of Hegel's major work in political theory, the *Grundlinien der Philosophie des Rechts oder Naturrecht und Staatswissenschaft im Grundrisse*.[1] The manuscript of Marx's work, which he left unpublished during his lifetime, now resides in the International Institute of Social History, in Amsterdam; it carries neither title nor date. It is usually referred to as the *Kritik des Hegelschen Staatsrechts*; in English, the *Critique of Hegel's 'Philosophy of Right'* or, more conveniently, the *Critique*. The manuscript is in the form of a notebook (19×32 cm.) whose front cover and first four pages are lost. The missing pages probably contained Marx's commentary on Paragraphs 257–60 of Hegel's work. The loss of the cover, on which Marx probably recorded the date of composition, has given rise to differences on this matter among the commentators. Two early editors, Landshut and Mayer, date the *Critique* from 1841–2. However, best evidence indicates that it dates from the period March–August 1843, and that it was almost certainly composed in its entirety in the summer of that year. This would make the place of composition Kreuznach (am Nahe), to which Marx, then twenty-five, had retired in the spring of that year to pursue research in political theory and history, and where he was married, on 19 June, to his childhood sweetheart, Jenny von West-phalen. The work was probably composed at the summer home of the bride's mother, where the couple honeymooned.[2]

Marx had planned to do a critique of Hegel's *Philosophy of Right* for over a year. He first mentioned the project to his editor–friend, Arnold Ruge, in a letter dated 5 March 1842; it was to be an essay for a collection

---

[1] The standard English version is *Hegel's Philosophy of Right*, transl. with notes by T. M. Knox (Oxford, 1942, with subsequent corrected editions). Hegel published this work in 1821, and used it as the text for his lectures in political philosophy at Berlin from 1821 until his death on 7 November 1831. Marx based his commentary on the edition of Eduard Gans, *G. W. F. Hegels Werke*, Vollständige Ausgabe, Band 8. 1. Aufl. (Berlin, 1833).

[2] On the date of composition, see esp. Bert Andréas, 'Marx et Engels et la gauche hégélienne', *Annali*, Instituto Giangiacomo Feltrinelli (Milan, 1964/5), vol. 7 (1965), pp. 355, 356, n. 1; also Manfred Friedrich, *Philosophie und Œkonomie beim jungen Marx* (Berlin, 1960), p. 56, n. 22. These commentators accept the judgment of

of miscellaneous writings which Ruge planned to edit and publish, because of Prussian censorship, in Switzerland. The purpose of the essay, according to the same letter, was 'to fight against the constitutional monarchy, as a self-contradictory and self-destroying hybrid'. Marx subsequently contributed two other pieces to Ruge's collection, which appeared in two volumes under the title *Anekdota zur neuesten deutschen Philosophie und Publizistik* (Zurich und Winterthur, February 1843). One of these was a lengthy criticism of the latest Prussian censorship directives, which Marx wrote in February 1842; the second, written about the same time, was a short piece signalling the importance of Ludwig Feuerbach's criticism of speculative philosophy and theology. But Marx never submitted his essay on Hegel's *Philosophy of Right*; in fact, it appears that the work as originally projected was never written. This may have been due to a lack of time available to Marx for such work; for after March 1842 he began to work seriously at journalism; and we know, for example, that these new responsibilities caused him to abandon another projected essay, this one on the history of religious art, for which he had done considerable research. On the other hand, his failure to write the *Critique* when originally planned may have been due to his lack of a methodology suitable for a systematic criticism of Hegel's political philosophy; for as it turned out, a key element in the methodology employed by Marx in the *Critique* was provided by an essay by Feuerbach which first appeared, of all places, in Ruge's *Anekdota*. More on this later.

In any event, when Marx finally carried out his plan to criticize the *Philosophy of Right* he did not produce an essay, but instead filled some 150 manuscript pages copying out paragraph-by-paragraph Hegel's doctrine on the internal constitution of the state, and subjecting it to lengthy and painstaking analysis. The result was a piece of writing at once brilliant and prolix, whose uneven style, shifting tone, and spontaneous doctrinal statements faithfully reflect the different moods, the flashes of inspiration, and in fact the personality of the author himself. Of the whole *corpus* of Marx's writings, the *Critique*, largely because we have it just as it first flowed from his pen, especially exemplifies what Wilhelm Liebknecht meant when he observed that 'if Buffon's phrase holds good

---

David Rjazanov, who cites two references in Marx's later writings (see p. xi below), and also the similarity between passages toward the end of the *Critique* and comments by Marx in his research notebooks which he dated 'Kreuznach, July and August, 1833'. Cf. Rjazanov's remarks in *Karl Marx/Friedrich Engels/Historisch-kritische Gesamtausgabe* (hereafter *MEGA*) (Berlin and Frankfurt a/M, 1927–32), vol. I, 1/1 (1927), pp. lxxi–lxxv, 402; and *ibid.* 1/2 (1929), pp. xxiv–xxx. (See also below, p. xxxix, n. 3 and the 'Note on the manuscript', pp. lxiv–v.)

of anyone, it holds good of Marx: "the style is the man"—Marx's style is Marx himself".[1]

When he finished the *Critique* in the fall of 1843 Marx intended to revise his manuscript immediately for publication. He wrote an essay, entitled 'Zur Kritik der Hegel'schen Rechts-Philosophie. Einleitung' as an introduction to the proposed revision. He published this essay in the *Deutsch-französische Jahrbücher* (February 1844), co-edited by himself and Ruge in Paris, where he had gone with his wife into self-imposed exile in October 1843. In the same issue of the *Jahrbücher*, the only issue ever to appear, he also published an essay entitled 'Zur Judenfrage' in which he developed and applied some of the leading themes of the Hegel *Critique*. But shortly thereafter he abandoned his plan to revise the *Critique* itself, giving as his reason the complexity of the work; and though he referred to it twice in later writings in terms suggesting its importance in the development of his thought, he apparently made no subsequent effort to prepare it for publication. After his death in March 1883 the manuscript remained undiscovered among his papers until 1922, when David Rjazanov, who was then attempting to establish the contents of the full Marx–Engels *Nachlass*, found it in the Berlin archives of the German Social-Democratic Party. It was then published for the first time, edited by Rjazanov, in the first volume of the *MEGA* (1927).[2]

Rjazanov cites two references in Marx's later writings as part of his evidence for the 1843 date of composition. The first of these references is in Marx's Preface to his *Zur Kritik der politischen Œkonomie* (1859). There Marx recounts his background and the events leading up to the writing of this book. He refers to a critical revision of Hegel's *Philosophy of Right* which he undertook shortly after resigning as editor-in-chief of the *Rheinische Zeitung* (he took the step officially on 18 March 1843) as his first attempt to resolve his doubts about the play of material interests in political society. His second reference is in the Authors Afterword to the second German edition of *Das Kapital*, vol. 1 (January 1873). There Marx discusses the difference between his and Hegel's use of the dialectic, and mentions a critique of the mystifying side of the Hegelian dialectic

---

[1] *Karl Marx: His Life and Work. Reminiscences by Paul Lafargue and Wilhelm Liebknecht* (New York, 1943), p. 39.

[2] On the discovery of the manuscript, see David Rjazanov, 'Neueste Mitteilungen über den literarischen Nachlass von Karl Marx und Friedrich Engels' (German transl. by Carl Grünberg), *Archiv für die Geschichte des Sozialismus und der Arbeiterbewegung*, vol. XI (1925), pp. 385–400, esp. 391–2. Details of the first and subsequent editions of the *Critique* are given below in a special note in the Appendix to the Introduction, p. lxiii.

which he had produced nearly thirty years earlier. In addition to providing evidence about the date of composition of the *Critique*, these references suggest something of the complexity of the work which caused Marx to give up the job of revising it for publication. Its complexity is a result of the multiple aims which Marx brought to the work.

Marx's original aim in producing a critique of *The Philosophy of Right* was to attack the constitutional monarchy. This suggests that he intended from the beginning to go beyond an evaluation of Hegel's political philosophy to an evaluation of existing political institutions as well; and, moreover, to do both through a critical examination of *The Philosophy of Right*. We shall see later how he could conceive of criticizing both Hegel's philosophy and existing institutions at once. For the moment we should note that Marx's later reference to the *Critique*, in his Preface of 1859, indicates that in executing the work he had an additional aim beyond the two originally proposed, namely, to clarify for himself the relationship between the existing political institutions and the economic workings of society. This additional aim was the result of his experience, as correspondent then editor of the *Rheinische Zeitung* through 1842 and early '43, of concrete social and political issues. This experience first raised in his mind questions about the importance of economic factors in political society, and led him to conclude that he lacked the specific kind of knowledge necessary for effective social criticism—knowledge of the anatomy and historical genesis of modern political society. Both his work on the *Critique of Hegel's 'Philosophy of Right'* and the research he pursued simultaneously at Kreuznach were intended to provide at least the beginnings of this knowledge. The notebooks he compiled at Kreuznach constitute the record of this research. There are five of these notebooks, totalling some 250 pages of excerpts, with his occasional comments, from twenty-four books in political theory and history. The relationship between these researches and the *Critique* itself becomes especially evident in the second half of this work, as Marx begins more and more to introduce historical data into his commentary on Hegel. His use of historical data is a special feature of the critical methodology Marx employs in the *Critique*.

A final point which is relevant to the explanation of the complexity of the *Critique* is Marx's own view of its scope. From his later reference to the work in the second German edition of *Das Kapital*, which we noted above, and from a number of passages in the *Critique* itself, it is evident that Marx considered it to be more than a criticism of Hegel's political philosophy. In fact, he claimed to have exposed and criticized, through his examination of *The Philosophy of Right*, the essential features—and errors—of Hegel's philosophy in general. The *Critique* was not the last effort of Marx in this direction; he renewed the effort in his *1844 Economic and Philosophic Manuscripts*, composed in Paris, though in this work he concentrated on Hegel's *Phenomenology of Spirit*. But it seems clear, again from his reference in *Das Kapital*, that he considered the *Critique* to be important, and perhaps definitive, as an evaluation of Hegelian philosophy itself.

To summarize the complex character of the *Critique* we can say that it was Marx's first effort to expose and criticize Hegel's philosophy in general and his political philosophy in particular; and through this effort both to criticize existing political institutions and, with the help of research in political theory and history, to clarify the relationship between the political and economic aspects of society.

The reader may judge for himself whether the *Critique* succeeds in all these aims. Marx himself evidently felt that it had succeeded so well that more than a single publication was required in order to present its results. Hence he abandoned the plan to revise the *Critique* and publish it as a single work:

In the *Deutsch-französische Jahrbücher* [i.e., in the Introduction to the proposed revision of the *Critique*] I announced a critique of jurisprudence and political science in the form of a critique of the Hegelian philosophy of law. Preparing this for publication, I found that the combination of criticism directed solely against speculation with criticism of various subjects would be quite unsuitable; it would impede the development of the argument and render comprehension difficult. Moreover, the wealth and diversity of the subjects to be dealt with could have been accomodated in a single work only in a very aphoristic style, and such aphoristic presentation would have given the impression of arbitrary systematization. Therefore, I shall issue the critique of law, morals, politics, etc., in separate, independent brochures, and finally attempt to give in a separate work the unity of the whole, the relation of the separate parts, and eventually a critique of the speculative treatment of the material.[1]

Marx wrote these words in August 1844 in the Preface to his *Economic and Philosophic Manuscripts*, which constitute the first draft of the various separate brochures that were to grow out of the *Critique*. But these, too, remained unpublished, and in fact unfinished during Marx's lifetime. He had hardly finished writing the words just quoted when he undertook, with Engels, the task of composing *Die Heilige Familie*, written while pursuing further his research in the literature of political economy. However, the program set down in the passage cited was not abandoned. The reference to a work which would attempt to give the unity of the whole appears to foreshadow that work which is most often, and correctly, characterized as the first statement of Marx's mature theory of history and

---

[1] *MEGA* I, 3 (1932), p. 33; English transl. Loyd Easton and Kurt Guddat, *Writings of the Young Marx on Philosophy and Society* (hereafter Easton and Guddat) (Garden City, 1967), p. 284.

society: Part One of *Die deutsche Ideologie*.[1] In fact, the *Critique of Hegel's 'Philosophy of Right'* developed into the whole program of research and writing which occupied Marx for the remainder of his life. More immediately, however, it represents the first of several works produced by Marx during a crucial period in the development of his thought. The period in question began with his retirement to Kreuznach in the spring of 1843, and it ended with the completion of *Die deutsche Ideologie* which was written jointly with Engels and finished sometime late in 1846.[2] Some remarks on the subject of Marx's intellectual development will clarify the significance of this period in his life, as well as the importance of the *Critique* as marking a point of transition in the development of his thought.

II

Marx's adult life was governed from beginning to end by a deeply-felt dedication to social criticism aimed at social revolution. We see his early sense of this vocation expressed in a graduation exercise done in his final year in the *Gymnasium*, 1835: 'The main principle which must guide us in the selection of a vocation is the welfare of humanity...Man's nature makes it possible for him to reach his fulfillment only by working for the perfection and welfare of his society.'[3] The subsequent course of Marx's life, seen in retrospect, allows us to take this youthful declaration seriously.

As applied to Marx, the term 'criticism' has three-fold significance: it means self-clarification, the clarification of others, and political action. If one is to revolutionize human society in the interests of its perfection and welfare one must understand its nature, workings and failures, one must impart this understanding to others, and one must somehow effect the translation of this understanding into organized political action which will transform society in the interest of the common good. The unity of theory and *praxis* for Marx meant the inseparability of these three efforts in genuine social criticism. Social scientist, teacher, political

---

[1] See also, in one of Marx's notebooks of 1845, what appears to be a list of topics to be treated in a book projected but never written; the list includes practically every point of political significance touched on in the *Critique*; see *Karl Marx/ Friedrich Engels/Werke* (hereafter *Werke*) (Berlin, 1953–), vol. III, p. 537.

[2] For dates of composition of Marx's early works I rely on Maximilien Rubel, *Bibliographie des Œuvres de Karl Marx. Avec en appendice un Répertoire des Œuvres de Friedrich Engels* (Paris, 1956), with *Supplément* (1960); and the work of Andréas, already cited.

[3] *MEGA* I, 1/2, p. 167; in English, Easton and Guddat, p. 39.

organizer—this is the three-fold vocation of the critic in the full Marxian sense.

Marx's intellectual life was a function of this single, complex vocation; it does not display a sharp division into two parts, as was once commonly supposed. There appears to be no basis for the view that the young and the old Marx represent two distinct periods in which his doctrinal principles, his theoretical and practical concerns and his intellectual positions were radically opposed. His own major posthumously published writings —among them especially the *Critique* and his preliminary draft of *Das Kapital*—provide the textual evidence against such a view. On the basis of this evidence it has been shown that Marx's intellectual and doctrinal development was, in Rubel's words, 'organic', that it did not involve his rejection in later years of any essential, earlier-held positions, and that within this development the early and the late writings remain fundamentally consistent in presenting a unified social and political theory.[1]

We can appreciate both the development and the continuity in Marx's intellectual life if we see it in terms of his dedication to social criticism. Marx came to appreciate fully the intellectual and practical demands of his vocation only by stages and as a result of particular experiences. As his appreciation of these demands grew, the focus of his research and writings shifted. In other words, his intellectual and doctrinal development was a function of the development in his awareness of the knowledge and action required for effective social criticism.

Marx's first serious efforts at social criticism took the form of journalism during 1842 and early '43. These are recorded for the most part in his lengthy article on censorship in the *Anekdota*, and in his writings on a variety of social and political questions in the *Rheinische Zeitung*. Here,

---

[1] See esp. Maximilien Rubel, *Karl Marx: Essai de biographie intellectuelle* (Paris, 1957) (hereafter Rubel, *Essai*); and Shlomo Avineri, *The Social and Political Thought of Karl Marx* (Cambridge, 1968) (hereafter Avineri, *The Social and Political Thought*); cf. by the same author, 'Marx's Critique of Hegel's "Philosophy of Right" in its systematic setting', *Cahiers de l'Institut de Science Economique Appliquée* (August 1966), pp. 45–81; also Iring Fetscher, 'The Young and the Old Marx', in *Marx and the Western World*, edited by Nicholas Lobkowicz (Notre Dame and London, 1967), pp. 19–39; and Gajo Petrović, *Marx in the Mid-twentieth Century* (Garden City, 1968), pp. 31 ff., esp. pp. 35–51. Both Fetscher and Petrović rely on a textual comparison of Marx's *1844 Economic and Philosophic Manuscripts*, *Das Kapital* i (1st edition 1867), and the preliminary draft of the latter, first published in Russia in 1939–41 under the title *Grundrisse der Kritik der politischen Œkonomie (Rohentwurf)*, *1857–58* (hereafter *Grundrisse*, with subsequent references being to the 1953 edition by Dietz Verlag, Berlin).

his approach to criticism is characterized by his apparent conviction that social reform could be achieved by educating the public, and especially the régime, about the shortcomings of the existing socio-political order by appealing to a philosophical understanding of the nature and purpose of political society. The theoretical aspect of criticism was identified with social philosophy, and the practical aspect with public education through the medium of the popular press.

Two experiences caused him to lose confidence in the ability of such a program to generate social reform. First, he saw official reaction in the form of censorship effectively silence the critical press, which for him represented the voice of reason in society; this led him to conclude that efforts at public education alone could not bring about social reform; they must be combined with a program of practical, political organization. Second, he saw the power of economic interests within political society effectively frustrate the pursuit of the common good; and this led him to conclude that a philosophical understanding of society, however valid, does not of itself constitute an adequate theoretical basis for achieving the revolutionary aims of criticism; an understanding of the economic factors in political society is also required.

This recognition of his own theoretical shortcomings, especially in regard to the importance of economic interests in political society, marked the end of the first phase in Marx's intellectual development. His subsequent intense efforts to remedy these shortcomings and to achieve the essentials of an adequate theoretical basis for effective social criticism constitute the second, and decisive phase (from spring 1843 to late 1846). This period is best characterized as one of intense self-clarification accompanied by his first efforts at political organization. From this period date his first attempts to achieve the knowledge, first in political theory and history, then in political economy, necessary to complement his philosophic conception of society and to provide the basis for an effective revolutionary program. In this period he also had his first encounter with the industrial proletariat, which led him to identify it as the material force in society which would be the vehicle for social revolution once it was informed by the spiritual force of his own social theory. Henceforth, education as an integral part of social criticism would be directed less at the public and the régime and more at the economically, socially and politically dispossessed; and its aim would be to bring these people to full consciousness of their interest and potential role in the revolutionizing of society. Workers' organizations would be the means both for education and for the achievement and exercise of political power aimed at the radical transformation of the existing economic, social and political order.

By the end of 1846 Marx had become fully aware of the demands of his vocation. He had clarified in his own mind the essentials of the theory of society which was one of the demands, and had begun the work of political organization, combining the educative aspect of criticism and the pursuit of political power, which was another of the demands. The remainder of his active life was devoted to the continuing effort to pursue all these aspects of his vocation.

The theory of society which he formulated was set within the framework of a theory of history and was based on a conception of man as *homo laborans* and *zoon politikon*. Man is part of Nature, which is identified as the sum total of reality. Man consciously transforms his environment in response to the immanent dynamism of his needs. The transformation of his environment by man is called 'production'; it is always pursued within a social context; and it is only within the framework of this social activity that the individual man is able to realize his own potential as a rational being. History is described as a sequence of forms of production analyzable in terms of the particular ways in which men have related to the environment, the ways in which they have marshalled and developed the productive forces available to them, and have related to one another in the application of these forces to the task of meeting their needs. His historical sketch traces the European experience up to the point where the dynamic development of the most recent form of social production, capitalism, creates a world-wide system of production and exchange which breaks down national and regional isolation and brings the whole world of men into working relationships with one another. At this stage, the significance of historical development ceases to be limited to the western world: history becomes world history, and it points to the establishment of a universal community of men each benefitting from the creativity of all the others within a historically transformed, humanized environment in which the development of human life is under man's own rational control. This, in brief, is the doctrine of Part 1 of *Die deutsche Ideologie*. It summarizes the results of Marx's efforts at self-clarification in the period 1843–6, and its genesis is only clearly traceable in the unpublished writings of the period, beginning with the *Critique of Hegel's 'Philosophy of Right'* and the contemporaneous Kreuznach notebooks in political theory and history (1843), through his Paris notebooks in political economy and the *Economic and Philosophic Manuscripts* (1844), the *Theses on Feuerbach* and the Brussels and Manchester notebooks in political economy (1845–6), to *Die deutsche Ideologie*. The theoretical positions and the ideals asserted in this latter work continued to govern all Marx's subsequent labors. From 1847 to 1878, when the illnesses which eventually claimed his life first put an end to his productive years of research, writing and political action, he continued to pursue his threefold task: deepening through incessant research his understanding of human history and society; attempting to impart this understanding to others in a series of historical, political and economic writings which culminated in *Das Kapital,* his final and unfinished effort at a comprehensive exposition of the nature and dynamism of modern society; organizing the working class, the material force which was to be the mediating element in the creation of a truly human society. Thus, the final thirty years of Marx's productive life represent a continuation of the program established between 1843 and 1847, and his doctrinal development in these final thirty years builds upon and refines, without essentially changing, the basic social theory found in *Die deutsche Ideologie.* As the first major work undertaken in that early, crucial period of his theoretical self-clarification, the *Critique of Hegel's 'Philosophy of Right'* occupies a special place in the development of Marx's mature doctrine. I shall indicate some of the essential features of the *Critique,* both as a work of criticism and as a doctrinal statement; my specific concern will be to clarify the critical methodology which the work embodies and the main points of doctrinal difference between Marx and Hegel. To prepare for this, we must examine the events in Marx's life and his doctrinal positions prior to the composition of the work.

III

Karl Marx spent his earliest years in the Rhenish town of Trier (Trèves) on the Moselle River. He was born on 5 May 1818, the third of nine children and the oldest son to survive past infancy, of Heinrich (born Hirschel) and Henrietta Pressburg Marx.[1] Marx's father was a lawyer who, in 1816, had broken with the religious tradition of his family, passing from Judaism to Lutheranism in order to enjoy the practical, social benefits afforded by such 'emancipation'; in 1824 he had his children baptized as Lutherans also. Young Karl appears to have matured early under the influence of his father, with whom he enjoyed a warm relationship, and of a family friend whom he later called 'my fatherly friend', the Baron Ludwig von Westphalen. Both men judged young Karl to be

[1] On Marx's early life, see Boris Nicolaievsky and Otto Maenchen-Helfen, *Karl Marx: Man and Fighter,* transl. G. David and E. Mosbacher (London, 1936), pp. 1–60. A basic biographical source is *Karl Marx: Chronik seines Lebens in Einzeldaten* (hereafter *Karl Marx: Chronik*), Zusammengestellt vom Marx-Engels-Lenin Institut Moskau (Moscow, 1934).

unusually gifted, and both imparted to him something of their own intellectual values and attitudes. From his father he inherited a regard for the ideals of the humanism of the Enlightenment, and from von Westphalen, a liberal political spirit imbued with the ideas of Saint-Simon—whose doctrines permeated the intellectual circles of the German Rhineland of the 1830s—together with a love of classical and romantic literature. Young Marx did not, however, imbibe anything of the patriotic attitude toward the Prussian monarchy—under whose hegemony the Rhineland had been placed in 1815 by the Congress of Vienna—which his father held in a lukewarm way, and which von Westphalen combined enthusiastically with his highly cultured liberalism.

Young Marx completed his formal secondary education in the Friedrich Wilhelm Gymnasium in Trier in August 1835, and that fall began to study law at the University of Bonn, where he showed a taste both for scholarship and fun (one of the earliest likenesses we have of him appears in an engraving of the Bonn drinking club of students from Trier). In October 1836 he transferred to the University of Berlin, registering for law, philosophy and history, and he remained there until the spring of 1841, at which time he submitted a thesis ('The Difference between the Democritean and Epicurean Philosophy of Nature') to the faculty of philosophy of the University of Jena, which earned him a doctoral diploma in April of that year. His university transcripts show only one formal course in philosophy (logic, at Berlin in the summer semester of 1838); but we know from other sources that he undertook, between 1837 and 1841, a heavy program of reading in the works of Aristotle, Spinoza, Leibnitz and Hume, a history of the Kantian school, and the *corpus* of Hegel's writings.[1]

In Berlin Marx found an intellectual atmosphere which stimulated his nascent impulse for social criticism. He quickly moved into the circle of the *Doktorenklub*, a group of young university teaching assistants and radical intellectuals who engaged in spirited, critical discussion of religion and politics within the framework of Hegelian philosophy, which no longer enjoyed official approval but was still the dominant intellectual force and the focus of all theoretical controversy. This was his introduction to the thought of Hegel, whose philosophy, he wrote to his father, he

---

[1] Marx's academic records at Bonn and Berlin are in *MEGA* I, 1/2, pp. 194–5, 247–8; the other sources for his philosophical studies from this period are his long letter to his father from Berlin, dated November 1837, and the excerpt notebooks he compiled in connection with his readings at Berlin. The letter is in *MEGA* I, 1/2, pp. 213–21; English transl. in Easton and Guddat, pp. 40–50; for his Berlin notebooks, see *MEGA* I, 1/2, pp. 104–5, 107–13.

soon came to know from beginning to end. In this company the political liberalism he brought with him from the Rhineland acquired a more radical cast; for the common theoretical position of the members of the *Doktorenklub* was an interpretation of Hegel's philosophy as a revolutionary call to transcend the social and political *status quo*, and their practical political attitude, especially toward the Prussian régime, was an enthusiastic endorsement of this aim. Marx had no difficulty in adopting this political view; and, in the beginning at least, he shared his colleagues' interpretation of Hegel, in whose philosophy he sought the theoretical tools for a rational transformation of society. But while persisting in the revolutionary aim, it appears that his early enthusiasm for Hegel gave way rather quickly to an ambivalent attitude of mixed respect and distrust; only rarely is Hegel directly cited in Marx's journalistic writings of 1842 and early '43, and then only with qualified approval; a high regard for Hegel's abilities as an abstract thinker, which is evident in Marx's writings both early and late, did not prevent Marx from maintaining, even prior to the *Critique*, a suspicious attitude toward Hegel's views on social and political theory. In the *Critique* we see what looks like earlier ambivalence toward Hegel give way to overt and genuine hostility, the bitterness of which suggests the depth of Marx's disappointment at finding Hegel to be not a champion of social revolution but an arch-conservative whose political philosophy is an elaborate justification, even a benediction, of the *status quo*.

The legacy of Marx's Berlin years is not limited to the radicalization of his political views and his introduction to the thought of Hegel. He also gained at Berlin a healthy respect for discipline and technique in fashioning and applying the theoretical tools of social criticism. The lectures of Eduard Gans and Karl von Savigny, under whom he studied law, appear to have been most influential in this respect. The lectures of Gans, who had been a favorite disciple of Hegel and whose edition of *The Philosophy of Right* Marx later used in writing the *Critique*, served as a model of rational, critical analysis of legislative institutions and procedures; while it was apparently von Savigny who introduced Marx to the historical method of analyzing social and political institutions. And though Marx subsequently excoriated the 'Historical School of Law', which was identified with von Savigny, for its failure, or refusal, to judge the moral worth of historical institutions against the criterion of human nature, he nonetheless adopted as an integral part of his own scientific methodology the Savignian technique of clarifying the significance of existing institutions through an account of their historical genesis. Marx's first systematic use of this historico-genetic technique was in the *Critique*, where he goes so far as to assert that it is essential to true, philosophical criticism;[1] subsequently he used it in the elaboration of his overall theory of history, where his primary aim remained the clarification of the realities of the historical present.[2]

Marx hoped to pursue the dual career of teacher and journalist, lecturing in logic at the University of Bonn and collaborating with Bruno Bauer, a Berlin colleague, in the publication of a critical journal, tentatively titled the 'Journal' or 'Archive of Atheism'.[3] But Bauer was expelled from the faculty of theology at Bonn because of his strong atheist views, and with his friend's dismissal Marx gave up his plans for lecturing at the university and turned exclusively to writing. His first efforts were those eventually published by Ruge in the *Anekdota*. Then Marx plunged with characteristic enthusiasm and energy into his collaboration with the *Rheinische Zeitung*. His pre-*Critique* doctrine in social and political theory is found in these writings, which incorporate also his early views on the practical significance of philosophy.

He calls philosophy the activity of applying free reason, and divides it into two phases, theory and *praxis*. As theory philosophy is an ascetic activity carried on in solitude and systematic seclusion. To the popular mind it appears to be an overstrained and impractical occupation, a kind of magic whose incantations sound pompous and incomprehensible. It appears unrelated to ordinary life. But this is a misunderstanding. In fact, philosophers are the fruit of their times, and philosophies spring from the same spirit in man which gives rise to his practical works. Despite its appearance, philosophy is not outside the world; it simply has a different kind of presence in the world than do man's other rational activities. The world is its ground; it is the spiritual quintessence of its age. Moreover, the world is the object of its enquiry and concern; it is the wisdom of the world. This formula summarizes the essence of philosophy as theory, and establishes the basis of its reality as *praxis*; it also serves to distinguish it from religion, which he calls, with quiet hostility, the wisdom of the other world.

Philosophy as *praxis* is the activity of informed criticism. On the basis

[1] See translation, below, p. 92.
[2] On the influence of Gans, see Georges Gurvitch, 'La Sociologie du jeune Marx', in *La Vocation actuelle de la Sociologie* (Paris, 1950), esp. pp. 575–7, where it is also suggested that Gans brought to his lectures an enthusiasm for Saint-Simon which must have reinforced that element from Marx's earlier background; cf. Nicolaievsky and Maenchen-Helfen, *Marx: Man and Fighter*, pp. 30–1. On the generally neglected question of the influence of von Savigny on Marx, see Hasso Jaeger, 'Savigny et Marx', *Archives de Philosophie du Droit*, vol. XII (1967), pp. 65–89.
[3] *Karl Marx: Chronik*, p. 8.

of the understanding achieved in the solitude of the study and first expressed in incomprehensible language, philosophers view the world with critical eyes, measuring existence against essence, the actual against the ideal, 'is' against 'ought'. This is philosophy measuring the world and declaring it to be deficient. Philosophy becomes worldly, that is, a practical, creative element in the world, an active force in culture and society. The philosopher speaks only after study, appeals to reason not faith, teaches rather than dogmatizes, demands and welcomes the test of being doubted, promises truth, and aims at the achievement of a world 'become philosophical'.[1]

Needless to say, philosophy as the practical activity of criticism remains a thoroughly rational exercise: the measuring of existence against essence, of actuality against ideal, presupposes a grasp of the essential and ideal. But this grasp is achieved only through a study of what exists. 'True theory', Marx writes to Dagobert Oppenheimer in August 1842, 'must be developed and clarified in concrete circumstances and existing conditions'.[2] The criteria against which the world is to be measured are derived by philosophical enquiry from the world itself. In short, philosophy as theory finds the 'ought' implied within the 'is', and as *praxis* seeks to make the two coincide.

Philosophy so described is to be sharply differentiated from other intellectual approaches to human affairs. Marx rejects the positivism of the 'Historical School of Law', and asserts against it that the mere historical existence of an institution does not justify it morally. The positivist attitude, which is said to be rooted in scepticism, desecrates everything sacred to lawful, moral, political man. It is an irrational position, for reason can find in human institutions the structures of human rationality, and thus can measure actual, historical institutions against the demands of rationality.[3] Again, philosophy is not to be confused with exercises of imagination, which bring preconceived and fictitious ideals into the discussion of human life and institutions. Nor is true philosophy a speculative

---

[1] 'Der letiende Artikel in Nr. 179 der Kölnischen Zeitung' (hereafter 'Leitende Artikel') *Rheinische Zeitung* (hereafter *RhZ*) (July 1842); *Werke* I, pp. 97–101; also Marx's discussion of philosophy in the notes to his doctoral dissertation (1841), *MEGA* I, 1/1, pp. 64–5. On the dissertation itself as embodying a seminal statement of these themes, see the introductory remarks and references in Norman Livergood, *Activity in Marx's Philosophy* (The Hague, 1967), which also contains an English translation of the dissertation.

[2] *MEGA* I, 1/2, p. 280.

[3] 'Das philosophische Manifest der historischen Rechtsschule', *RhZ* (August 1842); *Werke* I, pp. 79, 80, 85; Easton and Guddat, pp. 98, 99, 104–5. On Marx's attack on the 'Historical School of Law', see Jaeger, 'Savigny et Marx'.

exercise, in the sense of an application of a ready-made schema of concepts to the task of understanding and judging the historical world of human affairs. Here it is Hegel, though he remains for the moment unnamed, whom Marx has in mind; and he counsels his readers to follow the lead of Ludwig Feuerbach, who emphasizes the primacy of immediate experience, in which philosophical reason can grasp things as they are and find the criteria for rational criticism.[1]

In all this Marx makes two fundamental claims: first, the historical world of human institutions has its own immanent and substantive rational and ethical content; and second, it is the task of philosophy, properly understood, to grasp this content and criticize this world for the purpose of improving it.

In becoming theoretical *praxis*, philosophy in Germany of the 1840s uses the popular press as its medium of expression. It gives up its solitude and ascetic existence and enters public life through the more conventional means of the newspaper and journal of social criticism. The philosopher becomes a journalist without ceasing to be a philosopher. Political society is the prime object of his attention. He brings his understanding of the foundations and purposes of society, law and the state to a public discussion of the deficiencies of the existing socio-political order.[2]

The institutions and codes of political society are the objective expression of human nature, a product of the actions of men which are rooted in the inclinations of their rational and social nature. Thus, the state is rooted in the natural ground of innate human capacities and inclinations; accordingly, demands for social and political harmony are based on natural premises: the justice of state constitutions is to be decided not on the basis of Christianity, not on the basis of the state's own nature and essence, not from the nature of Christian society but from the nature of human society. Neither religious considerations nor the abstractions of speculative philosophy underlie the true philosopher's demands for social justice. Marx accepts Hegel's idea that the state is the actualization of rational freedom, then goes on immediately to assert that since this is so the state must be derived from the rationale of freedom and developed from reason in human relations. Whence comes the general criterion for judging the existing political order: the state arises out of the exigencies of man's nature, and must express that nature and embody man's rational freedom. To the extent that it fails to do this, it is an unsatisfactory state. If the state

---

[1] 'Die Zentralisationsfrage' (unpublished, May 1842), *MEGA* I, I/I, pp. 230–1; Easton and Guddat, p. 108; 'Luther als Schiedsrichter zwischen Strauss und Feuerbach' (January 1842), *Anekdota* II, p. 208; Easton and Guddat, p. 95.

[2] 'Leitende Artikel', *Werke* I, pp. 97–8, 100.

is a product of man's inherent rationality and sociability, then the philosopher demands that it should be the state of human nature, that it should be adequate to meet the demands of human nature.[1]

Marx's position on the subject of law follows as a corollary of this general doctrine on the nature of the state. Once again Hegel, among others, is cited with approval: the superiority of modern political philosophy lies in its conception of the state as an organism in which legal, ethical, and political freedom must be realized. It is an organism, Marx adds, in which the individual citizen, in obeying the laws of the state, simply obeys the natural laws of his own reason, human reason.[2] The laws of the state, like the state itself, derive from the nature of man. They are in essence (or idea), and thus ought be in fact (actuality), nothing less than the internal laws of man's rational, social activity expressed in formal codification. The secular world is filled with natural, legal, ethical content to which the legislator is subject: 'The legislator...must consider himself a naturalist. He does not *make* laws; he does not invent them; he only formulates them. He expresses the inner principles of spiritual relationships in conscious, positive laws.' This judgment on the nature of legislation reappears almost *verbatim* in the *Critique*.[3]

Thus, just as organic political society, in originating in and meeting the demands of man's nature, is an expression of that nature, so too are the laws of political society, for they are the conscious expression of the will of the people, created with and through it.[4] This in turn provides the general criterion for judging the existing laws of the state. Human activity, not formal law, is paramount. If laws are to be the conscious reflections of man's life, then to be valid and genuine they must reflect the needs and capacities of the people. They must not fetter human life, but yield to it; that is, they must change as the needs and capacities of the people change. Only in this way can law be actually identified with human freedom.[5]

Such are the fundamental positions of Marx's early (pre-*Critique*) social and political philosophy. It is a doctrine which consistently emphasizes the primacy of the individual, rational, social members of the state, over

[1] 'Leitende Artikel', *Werke* I, pp. 102, 103.
[2] *Ibid.*, *Werke* I, p. 104; Easton and Guddat, p. 130.
[3] 'Der Ehescheidungsgesetzentwurf', *RhZ* (November–December 1842), *Werke* I, pp. 316, 318; Easton and Guddat, pp. 138, 140. Cf. in the *Critique* below, pp. 58, 120. According to Jaeger, 'Savigny et Marx' p. 77, this conception of legislation is basically Savignian.
[4] *Ibid.*, *Werke* I, p. 319; Easton and Guddat, p. 141
[5] 'Debatten über die Pressfreiheit', *RhZ* (May 1842), *Werke* I, p. 58.

against the institutions and laws of the state. The natural capacities, needs and inclinations of men constitute both the origin and the purpose of the state: the state derives from them, being their product and their expression in the form of institutions; and the state's *raison d'être*, the realization of rational freedom, is precisely their fulfillment.

In the light of these considerations on the nature and role of philosophy and the political criteria which philosophy establishes, the deficiencies of the existing social–political order which Marx immediately faces—the Prussian State of the 1840s—are all too obvious to him. State censorship, exercised in ignorance and with caprice by bureaucrats, suppresses the organs of rational criticism, thereby silencing the very voices best qualified to guide the state to its proper end.[1] Prussian provincial law (*Landrecht*) consistently violates the criterion for valid law by ignoring the natural, legal, and ethical content of human social life, treating this not according to its innate principles but rather as intrinsically lawless matter, then attempting to shape, modify, and arrange this spiritless and lawless matter for an external purpose.[2] The legislators violate, in specific cases, the traditional customs of the people, customs which transcend national boundaries and are said to be rooted in a common and popular consciousness of right which conforms to the nature of things.[3] Finally, contrary to the idea of a rational state, there are in existing society groups of people who effectively fall outside the state's organizational framework—a deficiency evidenced by the state's inability if not unwillingness to apply its administrative power to the alleviation of economic misery.[4]

His recognition of this latter deficiency must have caused Marx to question once again the relationship between economic interests in society and the workings of its political institutions. He had already concluded some weeks earlier that the interests of landed private property, rather than a concern for the public good, had governed legislative proposals, thus in effect transforming the state into a means for the successful pursuit

[1] 'Bemerkungen über die neueste preussische Zensurinstruktion. Von einem Rhein-länder' (February 1842), *Anekdota* I, pp. 56–88. His own struggles with the censors, which eventually brought on his resignation from the *RhZ* and the suppression of the paper, provided Marx with at least part of the experience which underlies his long and bitter attack on the bureaucracy in the *Critique*; see esp. pp. 44–8 below.

[2] 'Der Ehescheidungsgesetzentwurf', *Werke* I, p. 316; Easton and Guddat, p. 138.

[3] 'Debatten über das Holzdiebstahlgesetz', *RhZ* (October–November 1842), *Werke* I, pp. 112, 119.

[4] 'Rechtfertigen des —— Korrespondenten von der Mosel', *RhZ* (January 1843), *Werke* I, pp. 172–99; the relevant passages are in English in Easton and Guddat, pp. 143–8. Cf. 'Debatten über die Holzdiebstahlgesetz', *Werke* I, p. 119.

of private, economic interest.[1] Indeed, an examination of the legislature itself, in its constitution as an assembly of Estates, shows that it derives not from the need of the state but from the need of special interests against the state, and that its principle is not the representation of political reason but of the egoism of private interests, which is the absolute antithesis of political reason. And Marx concludes that the representation of political intelligence and the general interest in such an assembly is, therefore, a contradiction and an absurd claim.[2]

The increasingly radical tone of the articles carried in the *RhZ*—especially those of Moses Hess retailing the idea of such men as Fourier and Weitling—drew the charge in late 1842 that the paper was flirting with communistic ideas. In answering the charge Marx admitted by implication his own lack of knowledge regarding both the fundamental question of the influence of economic factors in political life and the particular communistic ideas in question; and he declared his intention to submit these ideas to the thorough criticism they deserve.[3]

Thus, as his year of political journalism drew to a close in early 1843, two things had become increasingly clear to Marx: first, the existing socio-political order was far short of—indeed, in some respects it was the antithesis of—a rational state; and second, its reform could not be effected without a clearer understanding of the operation of economic forces within it.

Marx expressed the first of these conclusions in his letters to Ruge in the spring of 1843: the actual world, he writes, is a perverted world; existing political society is a despotism and tyranny in which the monarch, ruling by caprice in a state where man is despised and dehumanized, is the equivalent of the whole political system and is the only political person. But the state, he asserts, is too serious a thing to be made into a harlequinade. Then, reaffirming a principle already asserted in the *RhZ*—representation of the whole of the people by the people—he writes:

Freedom, the feeling of man's dignity will have to be awakened in these men. Only

---

[1] 'Debatten über die Holzdiebstahlgesetz', *Werke* I, pp. 126, 130, 143–4.
[2] 'Die Beilage zu Nr. 335 und 336 der Augsburger Allgemeine Zeitung über die ständischen Ausschüsse in Preussen' (hereafter 'Die ständischen Ausschüsse'), *RhZ* (December 1842), *MEGA* I, 1/1, p. 332. It is not, therefore, surprising that these two related issues, namely, the influence of landed private property and the character of the Estate-legislature, receive such extended and detailed treatment by Marx in the *Critique*: they were the very issues in which a connection between economic interests and the deficiencies of the existing political structure first became evident to him, and this in the final months of his tenure with the *RhZ*.
[3] 'Der Kommunismus und die Augsburger Allgemeine Zeitung', *RhZ* (October 1842), *Werke* I, pp. 105–8.

this feeling, which disappeared from the world with the Greeks and with Christianity vanished into the blue mist of heaven, can again transform society into a community of men to achieve their highest purposes, a democratic state.[1]

This condemnation of the Prussian monarchy voiced in the spring of 1843 did not represent a significant advance in Marx's thinking. A year earlier, as we have seen, he had written to Ruge of the need to fight against the constitutional monarchy, which he described then as a self-contradictory and self-destroying hybrid. In this respect, then, his year on the *RhZ* had served mainly to confirm the earlier judgment by providing concrete evidence of the deficiencies of the state in the context of particular social problems.

Marx's second conclusion, however, represented a significant advance, for it marked his realization of the need for new theoretical work, and it established the program of study and writing to be pursued at Kreuznach. In other words, criticism had at this point measured the gap between 'is' and 'ought' with regard to political society; now additional understanding was required if the two were to be made to coincide. When news of the impending suppression of the *RhZ* reached him, Marx recalled in 1859, he welcomed it as an opportunity to retire to the study. In the space of the next five months he read the twenty-four works in political theory and history, filled the 250 pages with excerpts from these, and produced his 150-page *Critique of Hegel's 'Philosophy of Right'*.

IV

Marx employs three critical techniques in the course of the *Critique*. The first, which is borrowed from Ludwig Feuerbach, is generally referred to as the transformative method of criticizing Hegelian speculative philosophy; the second is straightforward textual analysis and explication; the third is the historico–genetic method of criticism, which, as we noted earlier, was probably inspired by von Savigny. Marx combines these three techniques in such a way that they become steps in a single overall critical procedure which has the effect of combining a criticism of Hegel's philosophical doctrine with a criticism of the existing social and political order. Transformative criticism focuses on the form and character of Hegel's philosophy as a mystical and pantheistic view of reality; its purpose is to divest of its mystical form the empirical content of Hegel's doctrine, to expose Hegel's account of the existing political order, an account which Marx judges to be essentially accurate when stripped of its

[1] *Werke* I, pp. 338–40; Easton and Guddat, pp. 206, 207–8; cf. 'Die ständischen Ausschüsse', *MEGA* I, I/I, p. 334.

speculative trappings. Textual analysis and explication then expose the internal contradictions in Hegel's account of existing political society, contradictions which, on the premise that Hegel's account is accurate, can be said to reflect the internal contradictions of existing political society. Finally, historico–genetic criticism further clarifies these contradictions by tracing, with the help of historical research, the genesis of the modern state. With the exception of this last step, Marx's critical operations are carried out wholly within the doctrinal framework of *The Philosophy of Right*. The key to Marx's complex critical procedure is his judgment that within the peculiar philosophic form of *The Philosophy of Right* Hegel accurately depicts existing political society. It is this judgment which allows Marx to effect a criticism of political and social actualities via an immanent critique of Hegel's *Rechtsphilosophie*.

As Marx himself put it:

The criticism of the German philosophy of right and of the state, which was given its most logical, profound and complete expression by Hegel, is at once the critical analysis of the modern state and of the reality connected with it, and the definitive negation of all the past forms of consciousness in German jurispridence and politics, whose most distinguished and most general expression, raised to the level of a science, is precisely the speculative philosophy of right.[1]

In short, Hegel's *Philosophy of Right* is not only the highest expression of German philosophico–political consciousness, but a completely faithful account of the modern state.

Marx borrowed the technique of transformative criticism from Ludwig Feuerbach, whom he first encountered at Berlin, and whom he considered both then and later to be the most serious of Hegel's philosophical successors. In a short essay in the *Anekdota*, which we cited earlier,[2] Marx called Feuerbach the purgatory through which speculative philosophy would have to pass if it was to attain the status of truth. Later, in his *1844 Manuscripts*, Marx would write that positive humanistic and naturalistic criticism begins with Feuerbach, whose writings are the only writings since Hegel's *Phenomenology of Spirit* and *Logic* containing a real theoretical revolution.[3]

Two of Feuerbach's works influenced Marx in this respect: *Das Wesen des Christentums* (*The Essence of Christianity*) and, more importantly, the

---

[1] 'Zur Kritik der Hegel'schen Rechts-Philosophie. Einleitung'; pp. 136–7 below.
[2] 'Luther als Schiedsrichter zwischen Strauss und Feuerbach'; see n. 1 to p. xxiii above.
[3] *MEGA* I, 3, p. 34; Easton and Guddat, p. 285; and in *MEGA* I, 3, p. 151; Easton and Guddat, p. 316: 'Feuerbach is the only one who has a serious critical relation to Hegel's dialectic, who has made genuine discoveries in this field, and who above all is the true conqueror of the old philosophy.'

'Vorläufige Thesen zur Reform der Philosophie' ('Provisional Theses for the Reform of Philosophy'). The first was published in 1841; it contained Feuerbach's critique of religion, the gist of which was his inversion of the traditional theological view which conceives of God as the primary subject and man as a being who is dependent on God, and in whom the divine qualities are expressed or objectified. Feuerbach's doctrine declares man to be the true subject and God to be man's projection, an objectification of man's own essential perfections. Instead of God being conceived as the subject and man the predicate, man is now declared to be subject and God predicate. After establishing this subject–predicate (or subject–objectification) conversion, Feuerbach went on to trace the genesis of the concept of God in the human psyche—a procedure which is alluded to by Marx in the *Critique* as rational criticism, that is, criticism which shows the genesis of the object being criticized.[1]

In his 'Provisional Theses for the Reform of Philosophy', which first appeared in Ruge's *Anekdota* and thus came into Marx's hands just before he started the *Critique*, Feuerbach made explicit his technique of the subject–predicate conversion utilized earlier in *The Essence of Christianity*, and presented it as a general method of criticizing speculative philosophy and its most perfect form, Hegelian philosophy. The truth about God and man had been shown by converting the religious subject and predicate; if now one wishes to find the truths hidden in the peculiar, theological framework of Hegel's philosophy all one need do is systematically convert Hegel's philosophic subjects and predicates:

The method of the reforming criticism of speculative philosophy in general is no different from that already used in the philosophy of religion. All we need do is always make the predicate into the subject...in order to have the undisguised, pure and clear truth.[2]

What theology—and in parallel fashion speculative philosophy— regards as infinite and transcendent is actually the essence of the finite hypostatized and conceived to be an independent subject:

[1] See *Ludwig Feuerbachs Sämmtliche Werke* (hereafter *Sämmtliche Werke*) (Leipzig, 1883), vol. VII, pp. 26–7, 48 ff.; in English, *The Essence of Christianity*, transl. George Eliot (New York, 1957), pp. xi, 12 ff. Cf. in the *Critique*, p. 92 below.
[2] 'Vorläufige Thesen zur Reform der Philosophie', *Anekdota* II, pp. 62–86; I cite here the edition in *Sämmtliche Werke*, vol. II, pp. 244–68; the text above, p. 246. The passage parallels exactly a conclusion voiced in *The Essence of Christianity*: 'We need only...invert the religious relations—regard that as an end which religion supposes to be a means—exalt that into the primary which in religion is subordinate, [and] at once we have destroyed the illusion, and the unclouded light of truth streams in upon us.' *Ibid.*, pp. 274–5.

The infinite of religion and philosophy is and was never anything other than some finite thing, some determinate thing, but mystified; that is, a finite and determinate thing postulated as being not finite, not determinate. Speculative philosophy is guilty of the same error as theology, namely, the error of making the determinations of what is actual or finite into determinations or predicates of the infinite, this through the negation of the determinacy in which they are, and which they are.[1]

This speculative error is what characterizes German idealist philosophy, the governing concepts of which, culminating in Hegel's concept of the Absolute, result precisely from this mystifying procedure. Against this, transformative criticism reasserts the primacy of the finite, specifically the primacy of man himself, who is the actual subject of those powers, qualities, and capacities which speculation attributes to mystical subjects such as the Monad and the Absolute:

All speculation over right, will, freedom, personality without man, outside of or completely above man, is speculation without unity, necessity, substance, ground or reality. Man is the existence of freedom, the existence of personality, the existence of right. Thus man alone is the ground and basis of the Fichtean "I", the ground and basis of the Leibnitzean Monad, the ground and basis of the Absolute.[2]

Thus, transformative criticism of speculative philosophy is an extension of Feuerbach's original criticism of religion. The extension is natural and valid because speculative philosophy is itself a refinement of religion; speculative philosophy is really theology: 'The secret of theology is anthropology, but the secret of speculative philosophy is theology— speculative theology [which] transfers the divine being to this world as represented, determined, and realized in it.'[3] Feuerbach's 'Provisional Theses' establish this relationship between religion and Hegelian philosophy, which is called the perfected form of speculative philosophy, thus branding the latter, like the former, an instance of human self-alienation— that is, an example of man elevating the perfections which are properly predicted of himself to the status of independent subjects:

Feuerbach's great achievement is [to prove] that philosophy is nothing more than religion brought to and developed in reflection, and thus is equally to be condemned as another form and mode of the alienation of man's nature.[4]

Neither Feuerbach nor, following him, Marx doubted that Hegel's philosophy was essentially theological in character, and that what Hegel

---

[1] 'Vorläufige Thesen', *Sämmtliche Werke*, vol. II, p. 253.
[2] *Ibid.*, p. 267.   [3] *Ibid.*, p. 244.
[4] *MEGA* I, 3, p. 152; Easton and Guddat, p. 316. Marx's failure to qualify philosophy with the epithet 'speculative', in this passage from the *1844 Manuscripts*, is no mere slip of the pen. In fact, through 1844 and 1845 he tended more and more to gloss over his distinction, maintained earlier, between valid, or true philosophy and speculative philosophy. In the *Critique*, however, he still maintains the distinction.

called the Absolute was what the ordinary man calls God. Both were familiar enough with passages in Hegel where he identifies the object of his philosophy with that of religion, namely, eternal truth in its very objectivity—God, and nothing but God, and the explication of God; and in which he characterizes his philosophy as divine service which renounces all subjective brain-waves and opinions while engaging with God.[1] Neither man doubted the basically theological character of Hegel's philosophical standpoint, summarized in his *Science of Logic*, which reduces all particular philosophic inquiries to elucidations of particular aspects of the self-manifestation and self-realization of God or the Absolute. This is the standpoint of speculative philosophic thought, which Hegel calls the only truly scientific and rational mode of procedure:

The Absolute Idea alone is Being, imperishable Life, self-knowing truth, and the whole of truth. The Absolute Idea is the only object and content of philosophy. As it contains every determinateness, and its essence is to return to itself through its self-determination or particularization, it has various phases. It is the business of philosophy to recognize it in them... The derivation and cognizance of these particular modes is the further business of the particular philosophic sciences.[2]

Hegel alludes to this passage in his Preface to *The Philosophy of Right*, alerting his reader to the fact that this work proceeds speculatively and thus is one of the particular philosophic sciences mentioned in the *Logic*. *The Philosophy of Right* applies the concept of the Absolute to an account of man's social and political institutions, thereby elevating political theory to the level of speculative knowing and true philosophical science. In other words, in *The Philosophy of Right* man's social and political institutions are understood as particular modes of the Idea, and as various phases of its self-determination.[3]

Against this, Feuerbach asserts the claim which is consistent with transformative criticism: 'The beginning of philosophy is not God, not the Absolute, not being as the predicate of the Absolute or the Idea. The beginning of philosophy is the finite, the determinate, the actual.'[4] Where Hegelian speculation declares that the state is divine will as present-Spirit which unfolds into the real form and organization of a world,[5]

---

[1] G. W. F. Hegel, *Sämmtliche Werke*, ed. Glockner (Stuttgart, 1959), vol. xv, p. 37; quoted in Nicholas Lobkowicz, 'Marx's Attitude Toward Religion', in *Marx and the Western World* (Notre Dame and London, 1967), p. 315.
[2] *Hegel's Science of Logic*, transl. by W. H. Johnston and L. G. Struthers (London and New York, 1961), vol. II, pp. 466–7.
[3] *Hegel's Philosophy of Right*, transl. by T. M. Knox (Oxford, 1962), p. 2; cf. Knox's comments, *ibid.*, pp. viii–ix, and p. 298, n. 4.
[4] 'Vorläufige Thesen', pp. 252–3.   [5] Hegel, *Sämmtliche Werke*, vol. VII, p. 350.

transformative criticism asserts instead that man is the ἐν χαὶ πᾶν of the state. The state is the realized, developed, totality of the human essence.[1] The thought is congenial to Marx who, as we have seen, expressed a similar view of the state in his writings of 1842 and early '43; indeed, Marx's sole reservation concerning Feuerbach's 'Provisional Theses' was that Feuerbach did not pursue further his application of transformative criticism to the sphere of politics. For it is precisely in the sphere of politics, he writes to Ruge in March 1843, that philosophy can be fulfilled.[2]

In the *Critique* Marx moves immediately to attack the speculative character of Hegel's political philosophy. Beginning with his lengthy comment on Hegel's Paragraph 262 he carries through what was only tentatively begun by Feuerbach in the 'Provisional Theses'. He notes that Hegel, true to the method of speculative knowing, derives the institutions of existing political society from '*die wirkliche Idee*'. The state is the Idea in its moment of fulfillment as infinite actual mind, while the family and civil society—which are the other two social spheres delineated in Hegel's political theory—are the finite phase in the achievement of this fulfillment. Central to the issue are the implications of Hegel's use of '*wirkliche*', with its multiple connotations of actual, working and effective when speaking of the Idea; for it is the Idea which is conceived by Hegel to be the efficacious principle or acting subject, which operates according to its own immanent teleology. Correlatively, Hegel reduces actual human deeds and institutions to the status of 'allegorical' existences, particular modes of the Idea and phases of its self-determination. They are merely phenomenal beings, appearances of the Idea, receptacles for its manifestation and actualization; they are incarnations of an alien reality, thus do not have substantive being, form, meaning or purpose of their own. This, in sum, is Hegel's logical, pantheistic mysticism: he makes the Idea the creative, mystical subject and empirical actualities its products and predicates.[3]

The Philosophy of Right is permeated with this mysticism. Thus, for example, Hegel reduces the patriotism of individuals and the organism of the state to different aspects of the inner self-development of the Idea, generates the constitution out of the organism, refers to the purposes and powers of the state as modes of existence and incarnations of the essence of will, characterizes the monarch as the incarnation of the idea of sovereignty, and describes the legislature as the existence (*Dasein*) of public affairs. Thus Hegel inverts the true order of things: he always makes the

---

[1] Feuerbach, 'Vorläufige Thesen', p. 267.   [2] *Werke* XXVII, p. 417.

[3] See translation, below, pp. 7–9. 'Allegory' here means 'ascribing to any empirical existent the meaning of actualized Idea', translation, below, p. 40.

true subject into the predicate and the true predicate into the subject, such that the conditions are established as the conditioned, the determining as the determined, the producing as the product of its product.[1] And this inversion constitutes the essential character of the Hegelian method; while the inverted view of reality which results from it is the mystery of *The Philosophy of Right* and of Hegelian philosophy in general.[2]

An immediate effect of this speculative and mystical mode of procedure is that empirical reality is given a mystical aura. For although empirical reality is emptied of intrinsic value and meaning—in other words is mystified—it is at the same time assigned the meaning of phenomenon of the Idea. This preserves intact the features of the empirical order while allegorically ascribing to them an ideal quality. To speak of these features as they are is one thing; to speak of them as objective moments of the Idea is something else. In both cases what is spoken of is the same; the difference, Marx notes, lies not in the content, but in the way of considering it, or in the manner of speaking. By its way of considering things speculative philosophy invests the old empirical content with a new form, and consequently by its manner of speaking about them it creates the impression of something mystical and profound, for it makes a deep mystical impression to see a particular empirical existent established by the Idea, and hence to encounter at all levels an incarnation of God. The comment is inspired by Feuerbach's aphorism in the 'Provisional Theses': 'That which is as it is—and thus the truth truly expressed—seems superficial, while that which is as it is not—and thus the truth untruly and pervertedly expressed —seems profound.'[3]

Marx is not charging Hegel with empirical inaccuracy; the truth about existing political society is to be found in *The Philosophy of Right*, though expressed inaccurately by virtue of the speculative inversion of subject and predicate. Marx's charge of pseudo-profundity is directed against Hegel's way of considering and manner of speaking about political society. It is the philosophical form, not the empirical content of *The Philosophy of Right* which is under attack; and Marx is careful to maintain the distinction between the two, form and content, because of his conviction—often repeated in the course of the *Critique*—that within his speculative framework Hegel accurately depicts the existing institutions of

[1] See translation, below, pp. 9, 10–11, 13–15, 16–17 and 23–4, 42, 61–2.
[2] See translation, below, p. 9; cf. *Die heilige Familie*, *Werke* II, p. 62; *The Holy Family*, in English in Easton and Guddat, p. 373.
[3] See translation, below, pp. 8, 39–40; 'Vorläufige Thesen', p. 254. Cf. in *The Holy Family* Marx's tongue-in-cheek explanation of 'The Mystery of Speculative Construction'; *Werke* II, pp. 61–2; Easton and Guddat, pp. 371–3.

political society. What is crucial is to disengage the empirical content from the philosophical form of *The Philosophy of Right*. Applying transformative criticism is the crux of the disengagement; it strips the mystical aura away from the depicted institutions. But it is necessary as well to clarify the way in which Hegel establishes a relationship between the empirical content and the speculative form of his doctrine. Hence Marx's painstaking analyses of certain key paragraphs in *The Philosophy of Right* in which Hegel deductively links empirical institutions to the mystical Idea.[1] Once this link is shown to be an illusion generated by fallacious argument, the empirical matter can be treated in its own terms—that is to say, divested of the mystical aura and taken as an accurate account of substantive realities which have their own intrinsic value and meaning, and thus are open to direct critical confrontation. At this point the criticism of Hegel's philosophy ceases to be simply that, and becomes simultaneously a criticism of the social and political actualities mirrored in Hegel's pages.[2]

Marx finds, in the first place, that Hegel's logical development proceeds not from a consideration of the specific character or nature of actual social and political institutions, but from a consideration of the abstract categories of his *Science of Logic*. This makes *The Philosophy of Right*, like Hegel's 'Philosophy of Nature' (in his *Encyclopedia of the Philosophical Sciences*), an exercise in Hegelian logic—that is, Hegelian metaphysics—only with the names of empirical actualities substituted for the categories of the *Logic*. Logic, says Marx, not political philosophy, is Hegel's real interest in *The Philosophy of Right*. The work is simply a parenthesis to the *Logic*, an effort to give the *Logic* a political body instead of exposing the logic of the political body itself.[3]

Moreover, the link constructed by Hegel between the point of departure and the conclusions of his arguments, that is, between the abstract categories of his *Logic* and the institutions of political society, is purely verbal. Hegel introduces the empirical data into his pattern of abstractions, and links the two together by simply inserting terms like 'hence' at key points on his development. Thus, the relationship he establishes between the empirical and ideal orders is illusory and sophistic. In *The Philosophy of Right* Hegel is a sophist.[4] Marx repeats the same charge later, in *The Holy Family*:

[1] Especially §§ 269–74, 279; see translation, below, pp. 11–20, 23–5.
[2] Cf. Jean Hyppolite, 'La conception hégélienne de l'Etat et sa critique par Karl Marx', in *Etudes sur Marx et Hegel* (Paris, 1965), p. 120; Shlomo Avineri, *The Social and Political Thought*, p. 16.
[3] See translation, below, pp. 10, 12, 18–19, 64.
[4] See translation, below, pp. 12–13, 20, 25, 27, 123.

Hegel knows how to present with sophistic mastery...an actual presentation, a presentation of the matter itself, within his speculative presentation. This actual development within a speculative development misleads the reader into taking the speculative development as actual and the actual as speculative.[1]

Marx was fully aware of the seductive character of Hegel's philosophy. He had experienced it himself as a student at Berlin when, in a period of personal intellectual turmoil, and despite his initial repugnance at its grotesque and craggy melody, he had plunged into a study of Hegel's philosophy from beginning to end.[2] Hence the care with which he now procedes in the *Critique* to clarify in his own mind the peculiarities of Hegel's argument: it is essential to distinguish what is true from what is sophistic in Hegel's doctrine. What is at stake is not simply an appreciation of the peculiarities of Hegel's philosophical *modus operandi*, but in addition, and more importantly, the establishment of a valid philosophical basis for social and political criticism. So long as one remains within the speculative intellectual framework one cannot assume a truly critical position *vis-à-vis* existing political society. The reason is that speculative thought is by its very nature uncritical thought. Empirical actualities are understood to be appearances of the Absolute; as such, they must be accepted regardless of any apparent irrationality in their makeup. As Marx puts it in *The Holy Family*:

It is brilliantly clear how speculation...sophistically trying to avoid rational and natural dependence on the object, falls into the most irrational and unnatural subservience to the object, whose accidental and individual properties it must construe as absolutely necessary and universal.[3]

In the *Critique* Marx shows how Hegel comes to adopt this subservient attitude toward existing political institutions, and thus in effect to become a political conservative. Hegel recognizes and points out the apparent irrationalities, the internal contradictions, of existing political society. 'We recognize his profundity', writes Marx, 'precisely in the way he always begins with and accentuates the antithetical character of the determinate elements (as they exist in our states)'.[4] But because he takes the empirical world to be the manifestation of the Idea or Absolute Essence, and the determinate elements of political society to be particular modes of existence of the Idea, Hegel is committed *a priori* to the principle that the empirical order is, in the last analysis, rational. Because of this he is driven to great lengths of intellectual sleight-of-hand in order to resolve

---

[1] *Werke* II, p. 63; Easton and Guddat, p. 373.
[2] *MEGA* I, 1/2, pp. 218–19.   [3] *Werke* II, p. 63.
[4] See translation, below, p. 55, parentheses in the original.

empirical contradictions. He accomplishes this by acknowledging the presence of contradictions in the phenomenal order while claiming that they are overcome or transcended in the Idea. In other words, contradictions in the order of existence are dissolved in the order of essence, that is, in the thought-world of the Idea. This, says Marx, is Hegel's chief mistake: for him, contradictions lie only in the realm of existence (phenomena), but not in the realm of essence (Idea) which is mystically conceived as separate. But, Marx argues, the truth is that the realm of essence is not separate from that of existence, and contradictions are found in the realm of existence because there are essential contraditions there, or in other words, because there are contradictions in the essential structure of the existent:

Hegel's chief mistake consists in the fact that he conceives of the contradiction in appearance as being a unity in essence, i.e. in the Idea; whereas it certainly has something more profound in its essence, namely an essential contradiction.[1]

Within the mystical framework of speculative thought, contradictions are relegated to the level of phenomena and dissolved in thought as logical moments which are transcended in the Idea, while contradiction and conflict persist within the constitution of the existing state. Hegel clearly sees the empirical conflict, but contents himself with the appearance of its dissolution, and passes it off for the real thing.[2] In taking the actual, or existent, to be phenomenalized Idea, the speculative philosopher is prone to accept in an unqualified way the maxim that the actual is rational, and thus in matters of political life to accept uncritically the most irrational actuality, even though he sees it as it is:

Hegel is not to be blamed for depicting the nature of the modern state as it is, but rather for presenting what is as the essence of the state. The claim that the rational is actual is contradicted precisely by an irrational actuality, which everywhere is the contrary of what it asserts and asserts the contrary of what it is.[3]

As a result of his uncritical acceptance of the social and political *status quo* and his efforts to justify it as rational, Hegel is repeatedly driven to internal, doctrinal self-contradictions which he himself senses but cannot escape. These contradictions become all the more evident once transformative criticism has stripped the mystical aura from his description of

---

[1] See translation, below, p. 91; the specific context is Marx's assertion that the contradictory character of the political state is most manifest in the contradictory character of the legislature as treated by Hegel; cf. pp. 82–92 below.

[2] See translation, below, p. 76.

[3] See below, p. 64. On the essentially uncritical character of Hegel's political philosophy, which is directly traceable to his 'mysticism', see also below, pp. 39, 42, 61, 83–4.

political society, and are easily demonstrated by straightforward textual commentary. Thus it is easy for Marx to show, for example, that in order to justify the institution of entailed landed property (primogeniture) as a political good, Hegel contradicts his earlier assertion that the principle of the family is love; for love of one's children is violated by an institution like primogeniture which limits inheritance to the eldest son. Again, and for the same doctrinal purpose, viz. maintaining the political desirability of primogeniture, Hegel openly contradicts his own earlier assertion that property as such is essentially alienable as subject to the will of its owner; for the entailed landed property cannot be divided or sold by its owner, but only passed on to his eldest son whose ownership is subject to the same limiting condition; thus Hegel ends up by giving his philosophical blessing to an institution in which property is inalienable and the owner becomes the property of his property. In primogeniture it is the property, the inalienable landed estate, which inherits the man. Such doctrinal inconsistencies faithfully reflect the irrationality of existing political society. Hegel's doctrinal account of primogeniture, for example, is in conflict with his doctrine on the family because the actual institution of primogeniture in fact violates family life, and his accounts of primogeniture and of property conflict because landed private property in fact violates human social life. But, once again, Hegel's mysticism, his conception of an irrational *status quo* as incarnate Idea, leads him inevitably to accept these irrational conditions as being ultimately rational and thus justified, and this counter to his own, sometimes sounder philosophical instincts.[1] Thus in sum, speculative thought is criticized as being in essence a theological view of reality which, on its theoretical side, asserts the primacy of the ideal while conceiving of the empirical order as an intrinsically valueless receptacle for the appearance of the ideal, and which, from a practical point of view, leads to an uncritical acceptance of empirical evils. This criticism becomes an integral theme in Marx's subsequent writings.[2]

[1] See translation, below, pp. 40, 98–102; also pp. 59, 87–8.
[2] For example, on Hegel in the *1844 Manuscripts* (*MEGA* I, 3, pp. 167–8; Easton and Guddat, pp. 332–3); in *The Holy Family*, where the philosophical efforts of the 'Young Hegelians' are condemned as a low-grade version of Hegel's theories of consciousness and history (*Werke* II, pp. 88–90; Easton and Guddat, p. 382; cf. *MEGA* I, 3, pp. 257, 265, 301, 314, 345); in a series of fragmentary revisions of a paragraph in the Preface to *The German Ideology*, Part One of which may be read as a critique of Hegelian historiography (*Werke* III, p. 14; English transl. C. Dutt *et alii* (London, 1965), p. 24); in *The Poverty of Philosophy* against Proudhon's 'speculative' political economy (*Werke* IV, pp. 127–8, 135; English transl. anon. (Moscow, n.d.), pp. 102–3, 111; cf. Marx's letter of 28 December 1846 to P. V.

Nothing could be more opposed to this uncritical Idealism than a truly philosophical criticism which aims at changing the *status quo* because and in so far as it fails to meet the standards of rationality. True philosophical criticism not only shows the contradictions as existing, but clarifies them, grasps their essence and necessity, and comprehends their own proper significance.[1] Essential to this is a genetic account of the contradictions in question, that is, an account of the way in which the existing contradictory social and political order has come about. Feuerbach had pointed out the perverted character of the world of religion, then had further clarified it through psychogenetic criticism. Marx has now, with the help of Hegel's *Philosophy of Right*, come to see more clearly the perverted character of the world of politics. But this is a world not of mental realities or imaginary beings, but of historical institutions whose internal contradictions are most clearly shown by historico–genetic criticism. How God comes about is a matter for psychological investigation; how an irrational social–political order comes about is a matter for historical investigation. Once Marx has subjected Hegel's earlier paragraphs on the internal constitution of the state to transformative criticism (especially §§ 261 through 286) and then added to this the sort of textual commentary which highlights Hegel's doctrinal contradictions, he begins increasingly to apply to his commentary the results of his historical research. Thus the

Annenkov, in *Werke* IV, pp. 552, 549–50; English *ibid.*, pp. 174, 178). Just as Hegel's 'mysticism' led him to give privileged status to an irrational political order, so Proudhon gives privileged status to the modern 'bourgeois' form of economic society—an 'alienated form of social intercourse'—conceiving it to be the empirical actualization of the eternal and natural laws of production and exchange, precisely the uncritical attitude of modern political economists like Destutt de Tracey, Adam Smith, James Mill and David Ricardo (*Werke* IV, pp. 139–40, 552; cf. *MEGA* I, 3, pp. 536–7; Easton and Guddat, p. 265 ff.). Because of the relationship he saw to exist between 'speculative' thought and an uncritical attitude toward the *status quo*, Marx in the opening sentence of *The Holy Family* calls speculative idealism the most dangerous enemy of real humanism (*Werke* II, p. 7; English transl. R. Dixon (Moscow, 1956), p. 15). Finally, there is the statement in *Capital* I: 'My dialectic method is not only different from the Hegelian, but is its direct opposite. To Hegel, the life-process of the human brain, i.e., the process of thinking, which under the name of 'the Idea,' he even transforms into an independent subject, is the demiurgos of the real world, and the real world is only the external, phenomenal form of 'the Idea' . . . The mystifying side of Hegelian dialectic I criticised nearly thirty years ago, at a time when it was still the fashion . . . In its mystified form, dialectic became the fashion in Germany, because it seemed to transfigure and to glorify the existing state of things.' (*Werke* XXIII, p. 27; English transl. S. Moore and E. Aveling (Chicago, 1932), p. 25.)

[1] See translation, below, p. 92.

Critique develops from an immanent critique of Hegel's philosophical doctrine to a critique of the actual social–political *status quo*, with the latter increasingly assuming the character of an historical account.[1]

In his research Marx focuses on three historical developments: the evolution of political institutions, the emergent division between civil and political life, and the relationship between private property and the political state. Toward the end, it is the political significance of private property that comes to dominate his interest. Once again, it is in all cases the paragraphs of Hegel that provide the point of departure for Marx's comments, but he increasingly goes outside the framework of Hegel's philosophy in general, and of the *Philosophy of Right* in particular, bringing in from sources in the literature of political history the evidence for his critical judgments. An early discussion in the *Critique* of the relationship between civil and political life, for example, is obviously carried on within the conceptual framework of Hegel's *Philosophy of History*; but subsequent discussions of the same relationship—the first with special reference to the Middle Ages, the second comparing medieval and modern political society—suggest increasing reliance on historical research as the basis for analysis and judgment.[2] Indeed, once he has pointed out, on historical grounds, the falsity of certain positions of Hegel, Marx at times appears in his commentary less concerned with confronting Hegel than with giving voice to his own new historical discoveries.[3]

[1] Cf. the remarks of Rjazanov in the Introduction to *MEGA* I, 1/2, xxv ff.

[2] Cf. translation, below, pp. 32–3; and pp. 72–3, 80–4. See Avineri, *The Social and Political Thought*, pp. 19 ff.

[3] See translation, below, pp. 55, 57, and 107–11. As I noted earlier, it is the appearance of results of this research in the latter part of the *Critique* which Rjazanov cites as evidence for the 1843 date of composition. In *MEGA* I, 1/1, pp. lxxiv–lxxv he quotes Marx's lengthy comment in his Kreuznach *Exzerptheft* IV, dated by Marx 'July–August 1843', on Leopold Ranke's book on the Restoration in France; and he relates this to Marx's comments on the French Chamber of Peers in the *Critique* (pp. 113–14 below). Rubel (*Essai*, pp. 77–8, esp. n. 60) notes Rjazanov's remarks and further points out the similarity of Marx's comment on Ranke with yet another passage in the *Critique* (pp. 83–4 below).

Marx's comments on the French Chamber of Peers in the *Critique* also appear to be related to his study of C. G. Jouffroy, *Das Princip der Erblichkeit und die französische und englische Pairie; ein Beitrage zur Geschichte*, excerpted in Kreuznach *Heft* V, which carries no date but was evidently also written in the period July–August 1843 (*MEGA* I, 1/2, pp. 134–5). For further parallels between the *Critique* and material in the *Exzerpthefte*, cf. Marx's discussion (pp. 110–11 below) of German and Roman property rights in the *Critique* and the description of materials in *Heft* V (*MEGA* I, 1/2, p. 133); also Marx's comment in the *Critique* on the differentiation of *assemblée constituante* and *assemblée constituée* (p. 58 below) and material in *Heft* II (see item no.

Thus, Marx's extensive historical research contributes both to his critical appraisal of Hegel's political theory and to the further formation of his own distinctive social and political doctrine. A particular historical development provided the context of Marx's doctrinal dispute with Hegel on the question of social and political institutions. I referred to it above as the emergent division between civil and political life. This was the phenomenon characteristic of modern political society, a feature of the evolution of the modern political state, which Rousseau first heralded in his distinction between *homme* and *citoyen*: the existence of two distinct spheres of aims, rights and responsibilities, the separated spheres of private and public interest. Rousseau had pointed to the existence of such a duality in modern society, and thus in the life of its members, and had asked how modern man could be restored to a unified condition, how the dualism of private and public, or civil and political life could be overcome. This question, which he himself left unanswered, was his legacy to subsequent political theorists. Both Hegel and Marx were his heirs in this regard; the effort to understand and to resolve the dualism of private and public life was their common problem.[1] In the *Critique*, both the criticism which Marx levels against Hegel's institutional conclusions in *The Philosophy of Right*, and the counter-proposals he himself makes, are stated primarily in terms of this common problem. Marx demolishes through criticism the institutional structures which Hegel presents as the answer to Rousseau's question, and takes the first steps toward the formation of his own alternate answer—his own vision of a society adequate to man's social nature, and a program for its achievement. This is the subject of the next section.

V

As we have seen, the assertion that man is a naturally social being and that social and political institutions are expressions of man's social inclinations

6 in Marx's topic index to the latter; *MEGA* I, 1/2, p. 123).

In *MEGA* I, 1/2, pp. xxiv ff., Rjazanov comments at length on the significance of the Kreuznach *Exzerpthefte* and their relationship both to the *Critique* and to Marx's two essays in the *Deutsch-Französische Jahrbücher* (February 1844)—i.e., his 'Einleitung' to the *Critique*, and 'Zur Judenfrage'. Both he and Rubel have called attention to the importance of Marx's notebooks in general, and to the need for further work, especially on the later notebooks, to make the contents available to scholars and students. On this, see the relevant items in Rubels' *Bibliographie des Œuvres de Karl Marx* (and *Supplément*) cited earlier, and his 'Les Cahiers de lecture de Karl Marx', *International Review of Social History*, vol. I, no. 3 (1957), pp. 392–420.

[1] See Karl Löwith, *From Hegel to Nietzsche*, transl. David E. Green (New York, 1967), Part Two, Ch. I, 'The Problem of Bourgeois Society', pp. 232 ff.

was a feature of Marx's political journalism in 1842–3. This doctrine, which he further developed in his early writings up to and including *The German Ideology*, served as the basis of his attack in the *Critique* on modern political society and Hegel's philosophical treatment of it in *The Philosophy of Right*. The basic operative notion is that man is a *Gattungswesen*, a species-being. Marx follows Feuerbach in using the notion of species-being to characterize man. This notion specifies man as a conscious being, and it has immediate implications regarding man's social nature.

To say that man is a species-being is to say that he can apprehend in thought not only his own individual self, but also his own species-character, his own essential nature. Human consciousness differs from animal consciousness by reason of the fact that it includes an awareness of the self as being a member of a species, as sharing a common nature with others, as being one kind of being among other kinds of beings. Human consciousness thus includes, among other capacities, the ability to define and to classify, and therefore to be scientific. Feuerbach's analysis of religion builds on the notion of man as species-being: man's ability to objectify his essential perfections is what allows his projection of them into a being existing beyond nature. Man could have created God only because he, man, is a species-being.[1] At the same time, it is man's ability to be aware of himself as sharing a common nature with others that is the basis in human consciousness for the existence of specifically human society; and it is this aspect of man's species-character that Marx develops.

Throughout his early writings Marx employs a set of technical philosophical expressions which derive from the notion of man as a species-being. For example, in the *Economic and Philosophic Manuscripts of 1844*, which is the closest thing to a treatise in philosophical anthropology which Marx ever wrote, he speaks of man's species-life (*Gattungsleben*), species-spirit (*Gattungsgeist*), species-character (*Gattungscharakter*), species-activity (*Gattungstätigkeit*), species-capacity (*geistiges Gattungsvermögen*), species-relationship (*Gattungsverhältnis*), species-consciousness (*Gattungsbewusstsein*), and species-powers (*Gattungskräfte*). It is in these terms that Marx discusses such subjects as the freedom that man enjoys in his productive activity, human artistic capacities, and the sexual relationship between man and woman. In brief, these expressions signify for Marx the kind of life, spirit, character, activity, capacities, relationships, consciousness and powers which he takes to be essentially *human*.[2]

---

[1] See Feuerbach, *Sämmtliche Werke*, vol. VII, pp. 34 ff.
[2] *MEGA* I, 3, pp. 87–9, 113, 117, 156, 536.

The same notion of man as a species-being lies behind Marx's reference in the *Critique* to the family and society as species-forms (see translation, below, p. 27), and his reference to the species-will in relation to the determination and execution in political society of public affairs (pp. 58, 65). The expression species-will refers to the will of the individual man as a social being, rather than to any sort of collective or general will; it refers to a rational inclination which is a feature of man's universal nature, the political inclination, the will to communal life which involves full participation in the determination and execution of the affairs of the community. Marx notes that the question of the fulfillment of man's species-will is closely related to the idea of the state: man is a political as well as a social being; that is to say he *consciously* performs social functions.[1] Accordingly, where the state is in fact what it ought to be—or in the language of the pre-*Critique* writings, where existing political society lives up to its ideal—the state represents the full realization of man's capacity for conscious social life and activity, that is, it fulfills man's species-will or political inclination.[2]

Marx's use of the expression species-forms in the *Critique* also derives from the notion of man as species-being. It is used to characterize the social formations with which Marx, following Hegel, is immediately concerned, viz. the family, society and the state. Marx calls these species-forms because they are essential to man's life in as much as they derive from man's innate social inclinations and are the way in which he exercises and expresses them. Further (and here we see an enduring feature of Marx's social philosophy), these social formations—which he speaks of in the *Critique*, again following Hegel, as moral or artificial persons—are a necessary condition for man's development as an individual, fully social being. For while it is true that man is by nature social, it is also true that he requires a structured social fabric in which to develop as a truly human being: society, community and family are, he writes, 'precisely those species-forms in which the actual person brings his actual content to existence, objectifies himself, and leaves behind the abstraction of "person *quand-même*" '. And again: 'In fact, the abstract person brings his personality to its real existence only in the artificial [or moral] person, society, family, etc.'[3] This idea reappears in Marx's subsequent writings. In the *Economic and Philosophic Manuscripts* it appears in a brief but remarkable discussion of the development in the individual person of humane sensibilities;[4] and in *The German Ideology* it appears in an account of the genesis of

---

[1] See translation, below, pp. 117–18, 119. [2] Cf. pp. 65 and 118–19 below.
[3] See translation, below, pp. 27, 39. [4] *MEGA* I, 3, pp. 119–21.

human speech and individual consciousness.[1] Later, it receives concise formulation in Marx's unpublished Introduction (1857) to his *Contribution to the Critique of Political Economy*, where he states that 'man is in the most literal sense of the word a *zoon politikon*, not only a social animal, but an animal which can develop into an individual only in society'.[2]

What governs these discussions is a special notion of the relationship between the individual social being on the one hand, and society on the other: society is the *sine qua non* for the humanization of the individual man; and the character of the individual member of society will be a function of the character of society itself. At the same time, however, the character of society will be an expression of the character of its members, for society itself is the actual social or communal nature of its members. Such a conception of the relationship of the individual and society underlies Marx's use, in the *Critique*, of the term *Gemeinwesen* (communal being) to signify both the individual and society. The individual is *ein Gemeinwesen*, and the social complex within which he lives and acts is *das Gemeinwesen*.[3] Marx expands on this notion in a gloss on James Mill, which appears in one of his unpublished notebooks of 1844, bringing together this double sense of the term *Gemeinwesen* and the notion of man's social species-character:

The exchange of human activity within production itself as well as the exchange of human products with one another is equivalently the species-activity and species-spirit whose actual, conscious, and authentic existence is social activity and social satisfaction. As human nature is the true communal nature, or communal being (*Gemeinwesen*) of man, men through the activation of their nature create and produc a human communal being (*Gemeinwesen*), a social being (*gesellschaftliche Wesen*) which is no abstractly universal power opposed to the single individual, but is the nature or being (*Wesen*) of every single individual, his own activity, his own life, his own spirit, his own wealth . . . Men as actual, living, particular individuals, not men considered in abstraction, constitute this being. It is, therefore, what they are.[4]

Marx pursues the theme further in the *Economic and Philosophic Manuscripts* declaring that the very existence of the individual man is to be understood as a social activity, and that, because of this, one must avoid postulating society as a kind of abstract thing which confronts the individual:

[1] *Werke* III, pp. 30–1.
[2] In Karl Marx, *Grundrisse*—(Berlin, 1953), p. 6; English version in *A Contribution to the Critique of Political Economy*, transl. N. I. Stone (Chicago, 1904), p. 268. In the same text Marx reiterates the point, made in *The German Ideology*, that the development of language pre-supposes an existing social structure.
[3] See translation, below, pp. 79, 81.
[4] *MEGA* I, 3, pp. 535–6; a slightly different English rendition is in Easton and Guddat, pp. 271–2.

The individual is the social being (*gesellschaftliche Wesen*)...Individual human life and species-life are not different things...Though man is a unique individual—and it is just his particularity which makes him an individual, a really individual communal being (*Gemeinwesen*)—he is equally the whole, the ideal whole, the subjective existence of society as thought and experienced. He exists in reality as the representation and the real mind of social existence, and as the sum of human manifestations of life.[1]

Thus society is a complex of relationships among men, and of institutions which embody, express and regularize these relationships; it derives its existence from the nature of man himself whose species-activity is the exchange both of activities and of products, and whose species-spirit finds satisfaction only in such exchange. Man is essentially social, and society is precisely the actualization of his social nature. The being of society is not to be distinguished from the being of its members; nor is the essence of man in its actuality to be distinguished from the ensemble of social relationships of which he is the focus and subject, and which, taken as a whole, constitute the matrix of his life as an individual. In his individual existence he embodies his society.[2] In more explicitly metaphysical terms, which Marx himself uses, the individual man is the subject and society the predicate, or again, man himself is the substance in question, and society is the accidental, or contingent thing.[3]

Given Marx's view of the nature of human society and its relationship to the individual man, the question of the existence of opposed spheres of interests, aims and duties within society becomes crucial. He asserts that the individual and society are one in essence and being (though distinguished as subject, or substance, and mode) and that hence the interests, aims and duties of the individual should not in any fundamental way be opposed to the interests and aims of society as accomplished social existence and the sum of human manifestations of life. If actual human, that is, political, society shows the existence of opposed spheres of interest—individual and particular on one hand, general and universal on the other—then this existence of opposed spheres constitutes an aberration as measured against the social nature of man. It means that the lives of the individual men who constitute society are aberrant versions of what man's social life ought to be. Men's lives will be either contradictory or one-sided; contradictory if they manage somehow to live and act simultaneously or by turns in the opposed spheres, one-sided if they live wholly within the

---

[1] *MEGA* I, 3, pp. 116–17; English transl. T. B. Bottomore, *Karl Marx: Early Writings* (New York, 1964), p. 158.

[2] Cf. Marx's 'Theses on Feuerbach', *Werke* III, p. 534.

[3] See translation, below, p. 40.

sphere of private interest and pursuits. In neither case can there be a fulfillment of man's social species-being. In neither case is man in his social existence a unified whole. Rousseau's question, framed against the development of modern political society, was precisely 'How can something right and whole be made of the modern bourgeois?'[1]

Marx came to appreciate fully the nature of the problem through his reading of *The Philosophy of Right*, in which Hegel struggles with the same problem, and through his historical research into the genesis and nature of the modern state. It is no mere coincidence that one of the first works he examined and excerpted at Kreuznach in the course of his critical analysis of *The Philosophy of Right* was *Le Contrat Social*.[2] Through both his research into political theory and history and his analysis of Hegel, whose account of modern political society, as we have noted, he accepted as empirically accurate, Marx was led to acknowledge as fact the dual character of modern life. Moreover, he was led to understand and to treat it in the same terms as Hegel.

Hegel himself had grappled with the problem long before composing *The Philosophy of Right* (1821). In the account of Jean Hyppolite, Hegel had approached the problem in his earlier writings within the framework of social history, contrasting the modern world with the city-state of classical antiquity, which he understood—as did many of his contemporaries—to have been a socio-political form in which no valid distinction could be made between man and citizen: the life of the individual man and the life of the city were identical; so too, were the individual and the general will; *l'homme* was immediately and identically *le citoyen*. This identity, however, is unknown in the modern world; and the great failure of the French Revolution was precisely its failure to effect a reintegration of man's social life within the political state. The separation of private and political life first occurred within the Roman Empire, with the withdrawal of the individual from the life of the city and his concommitant self-enclosure within a private, restricted sphere where his concerns centered on himself, his property and his work. The state, consequently, assumed the guise of an alien power, a form of alienation. Enclosed within his own limited sphere, and thus deprived of a sense of participation in the common and universal, the private man sought solace in a postulated realm of universality, a divine realm separate from the limited sphere of his individual and finite life. Thus, political and religious alienation developed *pari passu*. The failure of the French Revolution to suppress

---

[1] Löwith, *From Hegel to Nietzsche*, p. 235.
[2] See *MEGA* I, 1/2, pp. 120–1; also Marx's topic-index to his *Exzerptheft* II in *ibid.*, pp. 122–3.

both forms of alienation by overcoming the duality of *homme privé* and *citoyen* is evidence for the impossibility of a modern restoration of the ancient condition of socio-political unity. The strength and grandeur of the modern state—and its claim to rationality—must lie in its ability to be the accomplished organic unity of political life even while allowing within itself the fullest exercise of individualism and particularistic self-seeking.[1] Hegel's treatment of the state in *The Philosophy of Right* begins with this very assertion:

The state is the actuality of concrete freedom. But concrete freedom consists in this, that personal individuality and its particular interests not only achieve their complete development and gain explicit recognition for their right...but, for one thing they also pass over of their own accord into the interest of the universal, and, for another thing, they know and will the universal...The principle of modern states has prodigious strength and depth because it allows the principle of subjectivity to progress to its culmination in the extreme of self-subsistent personal particularity, and yet at the same time brings it back to the substantive unity and so maintains this unity in the principle of subjectivity itself.[2]

The point of departure of *The Philosophy of Right*, then, is the recognition of the historically conditioned existence of two principal, opposed spheres within political society, and the assertion that the rationality of the modern state depends on its being a synthesis of the two which is built upon their very opposition. In his Preface to the work, Hegel identifies the task of philosophy as the apprehension of the present and the actual, not the construction of an ideal world. What is pre-supposed is the rationality of the actual, the presence of the eternal in the temporal and transient. This is the starting point of true, that is, speculative, philosophy. As a work of philosophical science, *The Philosophy of Right*

is to be nothing other than the endeavour to apprehend and portray the state as something inherently rational. As a work of philosophy, it must be poles apart from an attempt to construct a state as it ought to be...To comprehend what is, this is the task of philosophy, because what is, is reason.

To show that the apparent opposition within modern political society is in fact overcome in the modern state is to show the rationality of the modern state, to show that the actual is rational. The speculative philosopher can celebrate the modern state because he can discern within its apparent contradictions the glimmering of eternal reason:

To recognize reason as the rose in the cross of the present and thereby to enjoy the present, this is the rational insight which reconciles us to the actual...[3]

---

[1] Hyppolite, 'La conception hégélienne', *Etudes sur Marx et Hegel*, pp. 124–5.
[2] § 260; English transl. Knox, pp. 160–1; also, the addition to this paragraph; *ibid.*, p. 280.
[3] *Ibid.*, Knox transl., pp. 10–12.

The institutional schema which Hegel presents in *The Philosophy of Right* is offered as a rational organic structure within which the dualism of modern socio-political life is finally overcome. I shall give a brief account of the general theoretical framework of his discussion, and of the particular institutions which he offers as agencies of socio-political unity; for Marx's criticisms are made within the same framework, and focus on these supposed agencies of unity.[1]

In Hegel, Rousseau's distinction *homme-citoyen* takes the form of the distinction *Bürger-citoyen*, the burgher meaning a man who is active in civil as distinct from political life, or a man who pursues his private and particular interests as distinct from the public and universal interests of the body-politic. The sphere of civil life, the life of the burgher, is civil society (*bürgerliche Gesellschaft*); the sphere of political life, the life of the citizen, is the state. The question of reconciling the spheres of particular and universal interest, of restoring the identity of *homme* and *citoyen*, is thus the question of the modern confrontation of civil society and the state.[2]

Hegel uses the expression civil society to designate that phase of human social life in which the needs and therefore the interests of the individual govern his relations with others. Thus understood, civil society is Hobbes's *bellum omnium contra omnes*, the battlefield where everyone's individual private interest meets everyone else's. Social relationship within civil society reduces in all cases to the relationship of an individual subject with needs to other individuals who are means to their satisfaction; the operative motives are egoism and selfishness; the burgher is man related to other men strictly as means to his own individual well-being.[3] This is the sphere of economic life, whose regularities are expressed in the laws of political economy, and whose content is the pursuit of selfish ends.[4]

---

[1] There is, of course, an extensive body of literature on Hegel's political theory. Among the secondary studies in English, see esp. Z. A. Pelczynski's 'Introductory Essay' in *Hegel's Political Writings*, transl. T. M. Knox (Oxford, 1962), pp. 5–137. A concise account of his doctrine in *The Philosophy of Right* is in J. N. Findlay, *Hegel: A Reexamination* (New York, 1962), esp. pp. 326–30 treating that section of the work directly criticized by Marx. Two additional studies done with special reference to Marx's criticism are H. Marcuse, *Reason and Revolution: Hegel and the Rise of Social Theory* (Boston, 1960), pp. 169–223; and L. Dupré, *The Philosophical Foundations of Marxism* (New York, 1966), pp. 39–66. These are in addition to the works of Avineri and Löwith, already cited.

[2] Löwith, *From Hegel to Nietzsche*, pp. 237 ff. Cf. Hegel's remark to § 190 of *The Philosophy of Right*, Knox transl., p. 127; and translator's note 46 to Hegel's § 187, *Ibid.*, pp. 355–76.

[3] Hegel's remark to § 289, Knox transl., p. 189.

[4] *The Philosophy of Right*, Knox transl., translator's note 41 to Hegel's § 182, p. 354.

But civil society is more than a conceptual category which signifies an aspect of man's social life; for that aspect of social life has come to exist as a concrete sphere within modern political society, a sphere of officially recognized, particular rights and interests, a sphere, finally, with its own proper institutions whose purpose is to safeguard and advance those rights and interests. The existence of civil society in this sense, that is, a distinct legal system and set of corporate structures whose common interest is care for particular interest, is a peculiarly modern phenomenon: 'The creation of civil society is the achievement of the modern world.'[1] Hegel's task in *The Philosophy of Right* is to demonstrate how the unity of social and political life is effected within the modern state despite the apparent duality of civil and political life which this achievement of the modern world implies. His claim is that this unity is effected within and by means of an institutional framework whose principle features are: (1) a monarch who comes to the throne by birth, and thus independently of political factions; (2) an extensive bureaucracy of salaried civil-servants, who constitute an estate or class whose aims are identical with those of the state itself; and (3) an Assembly of Estates, in which representatives of the crown and the executive power meet with representatives of the civil estates to deliberate and determine the way in which the aims of the state and of civil society shall be reconciled, and to translate their decisions into law.

The term 'estate' (*Stand*) has both a civil and a political significance for Hegel. Its civil significance is that 'of a group or class of men having a similar profession or occupation or enjoying the same legal, economic, or social status'. When used in a political context it appears in the plural (*Stände*) and signifies a representative body which mirrors in legislative deliberations 'the diversity of particular interests in the country'. Hegel argues from the etymology of the word to the validity of structuring the representative political legislature, the Assembly of Estates (or the Estates of the Realm), so as to mirror the class, or estate, divisions within civil society.[2] Hegel calls two of the civil estates 'unofficial' to distinguish them from the bureaucracy which is a distinct estate and which has immediate political significance. Each of the unofficial estates is represented

---

[1] Hegel's addition to § 182, Knox transl., pp. 266–7; cf. Hegel's §§ 157 and 188, *Ibid.*, pp. 110, 126.

[2] Pelczynski, 'Introductory Essay', pp. 82, 85; cf. Hegel's remark to § 303, Knox transl., p. 198; and Knox's foreword to his transl., p. vii. In keeping with this double significance of the term 'Estate' we shall, in what follows, use lower case when referring to the estates *qua* civil classes, and capitalize the E when referring to the Estates *qua* legislative body.

in its appropriate chamber of the legislature: the substantial estate, which embraces the agricultural class, and whose politically significant membership consists of the landed gentry and aristocracy is represented in the chamber of peers. The 'acquisitive' estate, which embraces the industrial and commercial class, the burghers *par excellence*, is represented in the chamber of deputies.[1]

It is within this general institutional framework that Hegel finds the principles of social–political unity. In brief, these reduce to four: the bureaucracy, the 'corporations', primogeniture in entailed landed property, and the Assembly of Estates as a whole.

The bureaucracy of civil servants, as we have already noted, is an estate with immediate political significance; that is to say, its aims as a particular class are said to be identical with the universal aims of the state, its business identical with the business of the state; hence its title as 'universal class' (*der allgemeine Stand*).[2] The two unofficial classes, however, require some kind of internal, institutional structure which can reconcile the particularism of their civil existence with a concern for the common weal which their representatives must show when participating in the deliberations of the Assembly of Estates. The institutions which are the basis for this reconciliation within the acquisitive and substantial estates are, respectively, the 'corporations' and entailed landed property governed by the principle of primogeniture. The corporation within the class of burghers and primogeniture within the class of landed aristocracy are, in addition to the bureaucracy as universal class, forces for socio-political unity in Hegel's account of the state.

Hegel uses the term 'corporation' to signify a wide variety of trade, professional and municipal organizations, conceived along the lines of the guild system, which are primarily economic but also political in character. The corporations organize the workings of civil society, especially the competitive activities of the acquisitive class, and champion the interests of civil society against the state. The political function of the corporation is two-fold: as a body of associates with a common economic or professional purpose its membership channels the egoism of the individual member into programs of co-operative action. Second, the corporation articulates the common aims of its members so that their consideration is assured in the deliberations of the legislature, where the

---

[1] I follow J. N. Findlay (*Hegel: A Reexamination*, p. 325) in designating this the 'acquisitive' estate. Hegel's formal division of the civil estates, or classes, designates this as 'the reflecting or *formal* [or business] class'; *The Philosophy of Right*, § 202, Knox transl., p. 131.

[2] Hegel, §§ 291, 303 of *The Philosophy of Right*.

interests of civil society must be balanced against the interests of the state. In short, the corporations mediate between the raw, particularistic egoism which characterizes civil society, and the concern for the common weal which characterizes the state.[1]

As noted earlier, primogeniture in entailed landed property is the system of inheritance where all the land of a noble family passes automatically and necessarily to the first-born son. This institution precludes the sale of any part of the property, and any division of it within the family; hence the property is preserved intact within the family, passing from generation to generation under the ownership of the successive eldest sons. The property is thus shielded both from the fluctuations of the market (to which the fortunes of the acquisitive class are subject) and from arbitrary interference by the government. It thus provides the members of the substantial class with a stable basis of economic independence which allows for the development of a disinterested political spirit. Accordingly, the institution of primogeniture within the substantial estate, like the corporation within the acquisitive estate, is a force for socio-political unity: it mediates between the egoistic spirit of civil society and the altruistic, public spirit of political life.[2]

It is the Assembly of Estates as a whole, however, which Hegel identifies as the agency *par excellence* for the achievement of socio-political unity in the modern state. Within the legislative body of the Estates representatives of the various civil and political elements—the crown, the bureaucracy, and the civil estates—meet to debate and determine the course of the nation–state. Its purpose is to safeguard the interests of civil society while furthering the interests of the body politic as a whole. Hegel describes it as a complex system of mediations within which is achieved the desired synthesis between the particularism of civil society and the universality of the state. As an institution it embodies and brings to fruition all the particular mediations between private and public interest already implied in the bureaucracy as universal class, the corporation-structured acquisitive class, and the substantial class subsisting on entailed landed property. It is in no sense, according to Hegel, to be construed as a body antagonistic to the crown, or to the executive's power in general; rather, the Estates and the government-*qua*-executive are 'complementary organs of one and the same body politic'.[3]

Such, in brief, is the institutional framework that Hegel presents as the answer to Rousseau's question; Hegel's schema is the means for trans-

---

[1] See Pelczynski, 'Introductory Essay', pp. 121–2. [2] Esp. Hegel's §§ 305–7.
[3] Pelczynski, 'Introductory Essay', p. 84.

cending the duality between private and public life and restoring in a uniquely modern way the unity of *homme* and *citoyen*. It is offered, moreover, as achieving the aim of *The Philosophy of Right*, viz. to apprehend and portray the state as something inherently rational in order to enjoy the present and be reconciled to the actual. For Marx, on the other hand, this same institutional framework, which he judges to be an accurate portrayal of Hegel's own Prussia, is an anachronistic and self-contradictory hybrid that epitomizes the historical bifurcation of man's social life and therefore of his social nature.

The political state, Marx notes, has indeed become separated from civil society. In terms reminiscent of Hegel's early doctrine on the simultaneous development of religious and political alienation, Marx declares that the modern political state exists as the religious sphere of human life in opposition to the mundane sphere of civil society; it is the religion of popular life, the heaven of its universality in opposition to the earthly existence of its actuality. Or again, the individual elements of modern society have in the political state the sphere of their universal character, that is, their religious sphere, the sphere of their species-being. This separation of civil and political life was completed in the French Revolution, which wiped out the vestiges of the medieval order, within which no real distinction existed between civil and political life. Now, however, with civil society and state separated as distinct spheres of man's social life, the citizen of the state and the member of civil society, the *citoyen* and the burgher, are also separated. Thus, in modern political society the individual man must effect an essential schism within himself. In *The Philosophy of Right* Hegel has fully expressed the strangeness of this development; he has not, however, eliminated the estrangement, or alienation, which it represents. Hegel's institutional conclusions actually constitute an uncritical acceptance of this estrangement in the guise of its resolution.[1]

But even while criticizing Hegel's institutional conclusions, Marx remains within the general framework of Hegel's doctrine. In fact, he formulates the basic features of his own social and political theory through a systematic rejection of the agencies for social–political unity offered by Hegel. For Hegel's bureaucracy he eventually substitutes the proletariat as universal class; in place of landed property under primogeniture he advocates the abolition of private property; and he demands in place of the Assembly of Estates the institution of universal suffrage as the medium *par excellence* for the abolition (*Aufhebung*) of the state–civil society duality.

---

[1] See translation, below, pp. 31–2, 77, 80, 107.

The last point is made explicitly in the *Critique*,[1] while the first two are prepared in the *Critique* and explicitly formulated in subsequent writings, beginning with the 'Einleitung' and 'Zur Judenfrage', both of which were composed immediately following the *Critique* and published in February 1844. All three points represent developments of themes which first appeared in Marx's writings before the *Critique* itself.

Marx took seriously Hegel's notion of a universal class, that is, a class within society whose interests are identical with the interests of society as a whole, and therefore of man himself as a naturally social, species-being. His own experience with the Prussian government, however, would hardly allow him to accept Hegel's identification of the bureaucracy as such a class. In his very first political writing, directed specifically against government censorship, he criticized Prussian bureaucratic officialdom as an organ within the body politic which pompously claims a monopoly on political wisdom while operating above the law, irresponsibly and in secret and without concern for any objective standards of behaviour, a hierarchical vicious circle within which the attempt is made to place unlawfulness at such a high level that it is no longer visible.[2] The same charges are repeated in the *Critique*, by which time Marx has had the benefit both of historical studies in the development of political bureaucracy and of further personal experience with the censors and the bureaucracy in general. His long and biting criticism condemns the bureaucracy as a closed corporation, a kind of civil society within the state, which transforms the universal aims of the state into another form of private interest. It is a 'pseudo-universal' class whose members disdainfully regard popular life as material to be manipulated in the pursuit of their own careers. Even Hegel is forced to recognize the spirit of the bureaucracy as that of business routine and the horizon of a restricted sphere.[3]

Marx combines his critique of the corporation with his critique of the bureaucracy: the corporation is the civil counterpart of the bureaucracy and the bureaucracy the political counterpart of the corporation, for both are institutionalized forms of one and the same mentality which asserts the primacy of individual and private interests as the only general interest. Thus, the burgher and the bureaucrat share the same mentality which maintains, in opposition to a rational social impulse, that the *bellum omnium contra omnes* is the natural social condition of man. At the same

---

1 See especially p. 121 below.
2 'Bemerkungen über die neueste preussische Zensurinstruktion' (February 1842); *Werke* I, pp. 15, 20, 24, 25; Easton and Guddat, pp. 81, 86–7, 91, 92.
3 See translation, below, p. 44–54.

time the bureaucracy and the corporation represent opposed forms of that same mentality, and thus constitute a special instance of the institutionalization of the duality between the state and civil society.[1]

Thus, Marx dismisses Hegel's claim that the bureaucracy represents the identity of the universal interest with the interest of a particular social class: in the bureaucracy this identity is imaginary and contradictory. In the *Critique* it remains to be seen whether a class can be found for which the identity is not imaginary, a class whose interests are identical with the interests of man's universal, social nature; a class, therefore, which can truly transform present society into one adequate to man's social nature. It is a clear indication of the rapidity with which Marx's thought developed during this period that by February 1844 he can identify the proletariat as the class within modern society which satisfies the criteria of the genuine universal class. The immediate occasion of this theoretical advance was his encounter with the French working class in Paris, where he emigrated shortly after completing the *Critique*; but, once again, this development is foreshadowed in his earlier writings. In October 1842, in the *Rheinische Zeitung*, he had alluded to the existence of a class possessing nothing which demands a share in the wealth of the middle class—a fact clearly evident in the streets of Manchester, Paris, and Lyons; and in October of the same year and again in January of 1843, also in the *RhZ*, he had deplored the fact that the laborers in the Rhineland constituted an impoverished sector of society effectively cut off from political participation and the economic benefits this might bring.[2] In these instances Marx was encountering at first hand a condition which was already attracting the attention of social theorists, viz. the existence of a social stratum which was at once essential to the economic workings of modern society yet excluded from its material and spiritual benefits. His familiarity with the literature devoted to this phenomenon and identifying the deprived social stratum as the proletariat is suggested in the *Critique*, where he speaks of a class, characteristic of modern society, which is marked by the lack of property and the need to labor. This class, he notes, is less a class of civil society than the basis upon which the spheres of civil society rest and move.[3] Yet, within

---

[1] See translation below, pp 45–6.

[2] 'Der Kommunismus und die Augsburger Allgemeine Zeitung', *Werke* I, p. 106; also 'Debatten über das Holzdiebstahlsgesetz', *Werke* I, p. 119, and 'Rechtfertigen des —— Korrespondenten von der Mosel' (see n. 4 on p. xxv above).

[3] See p. 81 below. Avineri argues convincingly that Marx was not introduced to the notion of the proletariat simply through the writing of Lorenz von Stein, as is usually supposed. For his treatment of the question see *The Social and Political Thought*, esp. pp. 53–7.

the *Critique*, the term proletariat does not appear; nor has Marx connected his implied demand for a class within existing society whose interests are truly universal—a class whose achievement of power implies the abolition of the bureaucracy—with this class whose chief characteristic is socio-economic deprivation.[1] Within five months, however, the connexion is made in unmistakable terms: the dissolution of the existing order of things will derive from

the formation of a class with radical chains, a class in civil society that is not of civil society, a class that is the dissolution of all classes, a sphere of society having a universal character because of its universal suffering and claiming no particular right because no particular wrong but unqualified wrong is perpetrated on it;... a sphere, finally, that cannot emancipate itself without emancipating itself from all the other spheres of society, thereby emancipating them; a sphere, in short, that is the complete loss of humanity and can only redeem itself through the total redemption of humanity. This dissolution of society existing as a particular class is the proletariat.[2]

The ability of the proletariat to play the historical role of a truly universal class derives from the universal character of its deprivation: its exclusion is not simply from the sphere of political life but from the sphere of human life itself. Its existence is the negation of all the benefits of human social life; its interests, therefore, coincide with the interests of man's social nature. The proletariat is repeatedly characterized in these terms in Marx's subsequent writings.[3]

[1] See p. 48 below. At this point one might also wonder at the lack of any direct reference by Marx to Hegel's account of the economic and social impoverishment of the laboring class, in §§ 241–5 of *The Philosophy of Right*; and especially since Marx's later descriptions of the plight of the proletariat are strikingly similar to Hegel's description of the plight of the impoverished 'rabble' (*Pöbel*). This lack might be explained if, as Lapine suggests, Marx definitely intended to extend his critique of *The Philosophy of Right* to Hegel's section on Civil Society (§§ 182–256); see Marx's references to a critique of this section on pp. 81, 82. If Marx did intend to carry through such a critique, he might have avoided direct references to Hegel's account of pauperization pending a detailed critical analysis of the paragraphs in question. The critique of Hegel's section on Civil Society was not undertaken, however, and early in 1844 Marx moved instead into his study of the political economists themselves. Cf. Nicolai Lapine, 'La première critique approfondie de la philosophie de Hegel par Marx', *Recherches Internationales à la lumière du marxisme* (Paris), Cahier 19, p. 63.

[2] 'Zur Kritik der Hegel'schen Rechts-Philosophie. Einleitung'; pp. 141–2 below.

[3] For example, in *The Holy Family* (*Werke* II, p. 38; English transl. Dixon (Moscow, 1956), p. 52), and in *Vorwärts* (10 August 1844), *MEGA* I, 3, p. 21; English transl. Bottomore, in *Karl Marx: Selected Writings in Sociology and Social Philosophy* (New York, 1964), p. 237. On the later appearance of this theme in *The Communist Manifesto* (1848) and the *Preamble* to the *General Rules of the International*, drafted by Marx in 1864, see Avineri, *The Social and Political Thought*, pp. 61–2; and on Marx's subsequent correlative critique of the bureaucracy as the pseudo-universal class, see *ibid.*, pp. 49–51, and the same author's 'The Hegelian Origins of Marx's Political

But Marx did not see the proletariat simply as the negation of all human values; indeed, he claimed to see in the faces of the French working class, despite its universal deprivation, the positive qualities which would characterize a truly human *Gemeinwesen*. The proletariat manifests genuine human nobility and a desire for the company of other men as a good in itself, not merely a means to other goods; there in the midst of impoverishment, friendship rather than the need to use other men emerges as the social bond. Thus, paradoxically, the positive evidence for the possibility of establishing a society adequate to the demands of man's social species-nature appears in the negative condition of the proletariat, that is, in that universal deprivation which is the basis of Marx's claim that it is the truly universal class.[1] It is the presence of both these negative and positive aspects in the proletariat, as it appeared to Marx in early 1844, that allowed him to substitute it for Hegel's bureaucracy in the interests of achieving what is demanded by Hegel's own notion of an *allgemeine Stand*; because of its universal deprivation *and* its already evident, positive and universally significant qualities, Marx can enthusiastically identify it as the material force which, charged with the lightning of his own thought, will be the medium for achieving the unity and full humanity of social life.[2]

Hegel's identification (in Paragraph 306 of *The Philosophy of Right*) of landed private property governed by primogeniture as a principle of social–political unity provides the occasion for Marx's first systematic examination of the nature and political significance of private property. The fact that Marx had, late in 1842, already witnessed the power of private economic interests to subvert the political pursuit of the common good prepared the way for his criticism of primogeniture in the *Critique*, and, to a certain extent, explains the lengths to which he goes in pursuing his criticism.[3] Private property is examined both in its political and human significance. In both regards, Marx reaches conclusions in the *Critique* which govern subsequent developments in his thought. Once again, his criticism is based on the premise that Hegel's theoretical account accurately depicts factual states of affairs: the peculiarities and contradictions in Hegel's account of primogeniture reflect irrational actualities.

Marx is quick to point out the evident contradictions in Hegel's own

Thought', *The Review of Metaphysics*, vol. XXI, no. 1 (September 1967), esp. p. 39, n. 17.

[1] On these positive qualities in the proletariat, see esp. *MEGA* I, 3, p. 135; his letter to Feuerbach from Paris (11 August 1844), *Werke* XXVII, p. 426; and a remark in *The Holy Family*, *Werke* II, p. 89.

[2] 'Zur Kritik der Hegel'schen Rechts-Philosophie. Einleitung'; p. 142 below.

[3] See translation, below, pp. 97–111.

text: although Hegel wants to identify a necessary basis for the existence of a political spirit in the landed gentry, he is forced to admit that the economic independence provided by entailed landed property implies only the possibility, not the necessity, of such a spirit.[1] More seriously, however, the independence of the landed gentry, based on its independent means of livelihood (entailed property), appears on close examination to imply the opposite of a genuine political sentiment and inclination. For the independence of this property derives from its complete lack of any social or political character. It is a form of property and wealth which is separated from and independent of the state's property and wealth, independent also of the rest of the property system of civil society, and finally, as property that cannot be distributed among the family but only passed on to the first-born son, independent of the volition and laws of the family. It is, in short, private property *par excellence*, that is, property whose social nerves have been severed. It is the epitome of private rights freed from all political, social and ethical bonds.[2] The consciousness proper to such ownership, far from being a genuine political sentiment, or sense of identification with and dependence upon the state, can instead only be a consciousness that one's interests are independent of the interests of society and the state—because one's property is independent.[3]

Nonetheless, Hegel is correct in identifying this private property as a basis of the political state; indeed, it is the dominant force within the modern constitution of the state; it is its basis and guarantee. This fact, however, is hardly to be celebrated; for it means that the state, rather than being the objectification of the political sentiment of the people, and therefore of the political nature of man, is instead the objectification of private property in its most anti-social and anti-political form. At this point Marx turns to an historical elucidation of the way in which the state has become such an objectification. Historical evidence reinforces the conclusion demanded by the analysis of Hegel's text: 'In primogeniture it appears that...the existence of the state is something inhering in, or is an accident of, direct private property, i.e. landed property.'[4]

This critique of the political significance of primogeniture is at once a critique of the political significance of private property in general, and is recognized as such by Marx.[5] What is said here about the place and power of entailed landed property in existing political society holds for private property in general. Rather than being a principle of socio-political unity and a means to the integration of man's social life, as Hegel tries to make it, private property is a principle of social dissolution, a power which disintegrates social life, and which makes the state a sphere of illusory

[1] See below, p. 97.   [2] See below, pp. 98–100.   [3] See below, pp. 103–4.
[4] See below, pp. 109–11.   [5] See for example, pp. 107, 109.

universality masking the egoistic pursuit of private interest, a tool in the competitive struggle for economic advantage.

Marx does not limit his appraisal of primogeniture to the question of its true political implications; he also examines its humanistic implications. In this, he moves the discussion on to a more explicitly philosophical plane. He notes that in primogeniture there is a reversal of the subject–predicate relationship in terms of which Hegel himself understands the nature of property: for Hegel, property is a thing subservient to the will of its owner; the essence of property is its alienability according to the owner's will. Accordingly, the owner is the subject of the will, and his property is the objectification, the predicate, of his will, that is, of himself as willing-subject. But in primogeniture, the property is *inalienable*, not disposable according to the will of the owner. In primogeniture, therefore, the private property appears to be the subject of the will, and the owner's will the predicate of the property. Here, the will of the owner is what is owned.[1] Moreover it passes unchanged and undivided from first-born to first-born, and thus the landed property appears as the substance, the owner as a mere accident: it is the property that inherits the man. Here, the subject is the land, and the predicate is the man. His will becomes the will of his property. He is the serf of his own property; and his political quality is really the political quality inherent in his inherited wealth.[2] This reduction of man to the status of predicate and accident while the property assumes the status of subject and substance is a perversion of the relationship which should obtain between man and his property, that is, between the creative subject of will and those things which objectify his will and creative capacities. Primogeniture epitomizes this perversion. But here, too, the critique of primogeniture merely focuses on the extreme form of private property the criticisms which might apply to all forms of private property in their modern, historically-conditioned existence. In fact, Marx himself subsequently makes this application: this novel use of the categories of transformative criticism specifically directed at the institution of primogeniture is the proto-type for his critique of private property and alienated labor in his *Economic and Philosophic Manuscripts of 1844*,[3] and of his discussion of the fetishism of commodities in *Capital* I.[4]

---

[1] See below, pp. 101, 106.   [2] See below, pp. 106–7.

[3] He moves from an analysis of entailed landed property, which in places repeats verbatim remarks in the *Critique*, in the manuscript entitled 'Grundrente' (*MEGA* I, 3, pp. 67–80; see for example, p. 76), to a general critique of private property as a correlate of alienated labor, in the manuscripts entitled 'Die entfremdete Arbeit' and 'Privateigentum und Arbeit' (*Ibid.*, pp. 81–94, and 107–10).

[4] *Werke* XXIII, pp. 85 ff; English editions, Chicago (1932), pp. 81 ff.; New York

Thus, Marx comes to the conclusion in the *Critique* that private property, instead of being a positive force for social unity is, on the contrary, a power which turns the state into an illusory community and civil society into an agglomeration of atomistic individuals dominated by the products of their own creative activity. This conclusion sets the stage for his own assertion that the abolition of private property is essential to the achievement of the socio-political ideal of the *Gemeinwesen*. Before long he states, in the 'Einleitung' of February 1844, that the proletariat demands the negation of private property as the catalyst of the new world which is coming into being.[1] And in 'Zur Judenfrage', which, like the 'Einleitung', was written immediately after he finished the *Critique*, Marx turns a discussion of the political emancipation of the Jews into a discussion of general, human emancipation which requires the abolition (*Aufhebung*) of private property. Political suppression (*Annulation*) of private property, that is, the abolition of property qualifications for active and passive suffrage, is a first and significant step. Like the political emancipation of the Jews it is the ultimate possible form of human emancipation within the limited framework of the prevailing order. But it does not yet abolish private property any more than political emancipation frees the Jews from the defect of religion, which remains a feature of their private life. In similar fashion, private property continues to function as the dominant power in the non-political sphere of human life, that is, in civil society as distinct from the political state:

All the presuppositions of this egoistic life continue to exist in civil society outside the political sphere, as qualities of civil society. Where the political state has attained to its full development, man leads, not only in thought, in consciousness, but in reality, in life, a double existence—celestial and terrestial. He lives in the political community, where he regards himself as a communal being (*Gemeinwesen*), and in civil society where he acts simply as a private individual, treats other men as means, degrades himself to the role of a mere means, and becomes the plaything of alien powers.

The conflict between the general interest and the private interest, the schism between political state and civil society, the duality of *homme* and *citoyen* remain intact.[2] Genuine human emancipation, on the other hand, is achieved only with the elimination of such conflict and duality, only

(1967), pp. 71 ff. Cf. Avineri, 'The Hegelian Origins of Marx's Political Thought', p. 44; also the same author's lengthy discussion of 'Alienation and Property' (Ch. 4) in his *The Social and Political Thought*, pp. 96–123.

[1] See p. 142 below.
[2] *Werke* I, pp. 354–6; English transl., Bottomore, *Karl Marx: Early Writings*, pp. 11–15.

when the individual man actually lives as a species-being. But this is achieved only in an organization of society which abolishes the preconditions, and thus the very possibility of huckstering and the pursuit of interest and profits; which would abolish, in short, the rule of private property and money.[1]

At this point Marx is within a step of naming the movement which is to be identified with the abolition of private property. He does this in his *Economic and Philosophic Manuscripts of 1844*: it is 'communist' activity which achieves the abolition of private property; and 'communism' itself is identical with the positive abolition of private property and, thereby, of all the alienations institutionalized in the divisions of existing society. This abolition is simultaneously the creation of the *Gemeinwesen*, the community which constitutes a truly human, social life. Thus, the demands of the proletariat, its interests as universal class, coincide with the actuality of communism which, as the positive abolition of private property, is precisely the catalyst of the new world which is coming into being.[2] In this way, Marx's adherence to communism, like his identification of the proletariat as universal class, grows out of his systematic criticism of *The Philosophy of Right*, specifically of Hegel's notion of primogeniture as a principle of socio-political unity.[3]

In criticizing Hegel's doctrine on the Estates, Marx spells out what he only hinted at earlier in the *Rheinische Zeitung* in December 1842, and in his letter to Ruge in March 1843. In the first instance he had characterized an Assembly of Estates as antithetical to genuine popular representation,

[1] *Werke* I, pp. 372–5; *Karl Marx: Early Writings*, pp. 34–7.
[2] *MEGA* I, 3, pp. 112, 114, 115, 134; *Karl Marx: Early Writings*, pp. 153, 155, 156, 176. Cf. his definition of communism in *The German Ideology*, *Werke* III, p. 35. The *1844 Manuscripts* represent, in this regard, the fulfillment of Marx's promise, while still editor of the *RhZ*, to subject communistic ideas to critical scrutiny; see his remark in the manuscript entitled 'Bedürfnis, Produktion und Arbeitsteilung' (*MEGA* I, 3, 134), asserting that communism as critical theory must become communism as practical action (*praxis*), though still governed by theory, or understanding. This notion of communism as a unity of theory and *praxis* is a specific development of Marx's pre-*Critique* notion of philosophy as 'criticism' in its theoretical and practical phase. The place of the proletariat in this development is already established: it is that element within society which is to mediate the transition of critical theory into practical action.
[3] The question of the property system envisaged by Marx as emerging from the 'Aufhebung des Privateigentums', and which he referred to in different places as human, social, and individual property is discussed in some detail, with reference to the relevant passages throughout Marx's writings—including the extremely interesting and generally neglected texts in *Capital*—by Avineri, *The Social and Political Thought*, esp. pp. 114–17, 174–82.

and in the second he characterized the whole institutional structure of the constitutional monarchy as a self-contradictory hybrid.[1]

In *The Philosophy of Right* Hegel describes the Assembly of Estates as a political organ by which the people come to participate in the affairs of the state while, conversely, the aims and concerns of the state become the concerns of the people. The Estates are the mediating organ, the middle term between the crown and the people, the government and the private citizen, the political and civil spheres of modern life; they are the medium *par excellence* for the abolition of the dualism of state and civil society.[2]

But here too, according to Marx, Hegel's own texts betray the truth of the matter, the fact that the Estates are nothing but the formal illusion of popular participation in public affairs, and that the thought and will of the people cannot find realization in the state. All of the inconsistencies and self-contradictions of Hegel's political philosophy are found in his account of the Estates, because all the contradictions of the modern state, of which he is the interpreter, appear most clearly in this political body. Nowhere more than in the Estates is it so evident that the modern state is not an objectification of the political consciousness and sentiment of the people. Instead of enabling the people to participate in public affairs, the Estates render the pursuit of public affairs an illusion and, moreover, an illusion monopolized by bureaucratic officialdom; rather than being the middle term in a rational political order, they are a comic element in a ridiculous mutual reconciliation society which cannot possibly realize the universal aims of social man; instead of mediating the duality between state and civil society they stand between the two spheres like Buridan's Ass.[3] And the reason is that the Estates are an anachronism, a medieval institution offered as the cure for modern ills: the Estate-constitution purports to resolve through a reminiscence of medieval life the specifically modern duality of civil society and the political state.[4]

Moreover, in their modern form the Estates are a hybrid; for while one house, the chamber of peers, relates to its corresponding civil estate (the landed gentry) in almost purely medieval fashion, the other, the chamber of deputies, relates to its civil estate (the commercial and industrial class) in modern fashion, that is, through election though still retaining the medieval feature of issuing from the corporations.[5] Furthermore, they are a contradictory hybrid. On one hand, the relationship of the Estates to

---

[1] See above, pp. x, xxvi–vii.

[2] See esp. Hegel's §§ 301–2, and his remarks to these; for his interpretation of the state on the model of the syllogism, see esp. his remark to § 302; also Knox's note 67 to § 312; p. 372 in his transl. of *The Philosophy of Right*.

[3] See translation, below, pp. 88–9, 93. [4] See p. 83 below.

[5] See below, pp. 112–13, 114, cf. also pp. 83, 96.

civil society makes the state itself a dependent extension of civil society, because in them the legislature's essence—'political sentiment'—is guaranteed by independent private property (the landed property of the gentry who sit in the chamber of peers), and the legislature's existence is guaranteed by the privileges of the corporations (the actual mandators of those sitting in the chamber of deputies).[1] On the other hand, that relationship is intended to guarantee the independence of the state relative to private interests; for the members of the Estates, whether peers or deputies, are to abjure the interests of their civil class in favor of the universal interests of the body politic as a whole. At one and the same time, they are representatives and not representatives of their class interests; at one and the same time, they are members and not members of the state, members and not members of civil society.[2]

Hegel is forced into inconsistency and self-contradiction by his efforts to maintain as rational this irrational situation. He never asks whether the Estates actually meet the requirements of a rational legislative body; he does not, in other words, adopt a truly philosophical standpoint and examine the matter in its own terms.[3] Instead, he accepts the Estates as they are merely in order to satisfy a requirement of his mystical logic, that is, that 'public affairs' have a receptacle in which they achieve explicit existence. And he does this all the more easily, Marx notes with a touch of bitterness, because Hegel is infected with the miserable arrogance of the world of Prussian officialdom which denies the existence of real political consciousness and sentiment in the people.[4]

Marx, of course, assumes the contrary position: the people are the real subjects of political consciousness and sentiment. Accordingly, he demands the establishment of a constitution opposed to the Estates, a constitution adequate to the species-will, the will of all to be actual (active) members of the state, to prove their existence as political and to effect it as such.[5] Moreover, the people are the real subjects of sovereignty. And accordingly, he demands a constitution opposed to the monarchy. These two demands converge in his assertion of democracy as the only constitution adequate to man's true political nature. Only in democracy, he asserts, is man himself really the originator and shaper of the constitution, and the state really an objectification of man's social species-being. Thus, democracy is the generic constitution relative to which monarchy is an aberrant species. At best, monarchy is a constitution in which one man stands as the symbol of the sovereignty inherent in every man; at worst it is a constitution in

---

[1] See p. 114 below. [2] See p. 122–3, 126–7. [3] See p. 115.
[4] See p. 62, 64, 125. [5] See p. 118.

which one man monopolizes the sphere of political existence to the exclusion of everyone else and reduces them, in effect, to a despicable and dehumanized condition.[1]

Moreover, only in democracy do the people fully participate in determining and executing public affairs, the affairs of the state, that is, their own affairs as social beings. The means for this participation is universal suffrage, both active and passive. This alone can achieve what the Estates effect in a purely illusory way, namely, the transcendence of the dualism of political state and civil society. The implementation of universal suffrage elevates civil society to political existence, thereby dissolving civil society as a separate sphere, and simultaneously dissolving the state as a separate and opposed sphere. The genuine abolition (*Aufhebung*) of the historically conditioned, modern dualism of state and civil society—and therefore of the schism within the social being of modern man—is to be effected through democracy in the form of universal suffrage:

> In unrestricted suffrage, both active and passive, civil society has actually raised itself for the first time to an abstraction of itself, to political existence as its true universal and essential existence. But the full achievement of this abstraction is at once also the transcendence (*Aufhebung*) of the abstraction. In actually establishing its political existence as its true existence civil society has simultaneously established its civil existence, in distinction from its political existence, as inessential. And with the one separated, the other, its opposite falls. Within the abstract political state the reform of voting advances the dissolution (*Auflösung*) of this political state, but also the dissolution of civil society.[2]

This doctrinal conclusion, formulated toward the end of the *Critique*, is hinted at earlier in the work when Marx writes that because 'civil society is the non-actuality of political existence, the political existence of civil society is its own dissolution, its separation from itself'; and 'civil society would abandon itself as such if all its members were legislators.' The same notion of universal suffrage as implying the dissolution of the state also clarifies the sense of Marx's endorsement of the anarchist position of certain modern French theorists, in his first discussion of democracy in the *Critique*: 'In true democracy the political state disappears.'[3]

Thus, what is sometimes referred to as Marx's anarchism, his call for the disappearance, dissolution, or abolition of the state, grows out of his systematic critique of *The Philosophy of Right*, and specifically of Hegel's doctrine that the Estates are the principal institutional agency for the integration of man's social and political life; thus his anarchism must be

---

[1] See pp. 20, 29–30; cf. Marx's letter to Ruge (May 1843) cited above (pp. xxvi–vii), and his remarks in the *Critique*, p. 26 below.

[2] See p. 121.   [3] See pp. 31, 90–1, 119.

understood with reference to the theoretical framework within which it is first formulated. Like his doctrine on the proletariat and the abolition of private property, Marx's call for democracy and universal suffrage, which is equivalent to his demand for the abolition of the state, results from his systematic rejection of one of Hegel's institutional conclusions in the interest of establishing the ideal of the *Gemeinwesen*. And again, like his doctrine on the proletariat and the abolition of private property, his advocacy of universal suffrage becomes an integral part of the social and political theory propounded in his subsequent writings, both theoretical and programmatic. There, the establishment of universal suffrage, victory in the 'struggle for democracy', and the 'abolition of the state' are repeatedly equated.[1]

APPENDIX TO INTRODUCTION

Editions of Marx's 'Critique of Hegel's Philosophy of Right' (in chronological order)

1 Aus der Kritik der Hegelschen Rechtsphilosophie. Kritik des Hegelschen Staatsrechts (§§ 261–313)'. Edited by David Rjazanov; in *Karl Marx/Friedrich Engels/ Historisch-kritische Gesamtausgabe* (Marx–Engels-Institut, Moskau), Abteilung 1, Band 1, Halbband 1 (Frankfurt a/M and Berlin, Marx–Engels-Verlag, 1927), pp. 401–553. Based on photocopies of the manuscript prepared by the Marx–Engels-Institut, Moscow, in collaboration with the German Social-Democratic Party, Berlin. An interesting feature is that words and passages crossed out by Marx in the manuscript are given in footnotes. There is a facsimile of part of a manuscript page following p. 550 of this edition.

2 'Kritik der Hegelschen Staatsphilosophe (1841/42)'. Edited by Siegfried Landshut and J. P. Mayer; in *Karl Marx/Der historische Materialismus*, Band 1 (Leipzig, Kröner, 1932), pp. 20–187. Based on the manuscript.

3 Same as 2; in *Karl Marx/Die Frühschriften* (Kröners Taschenausgaben, Band 209). Edited by Siegfried Landshut (Stuttgart, Alfred Kröner Verlag, 1953), pp. 20–149. This is a substantially abridged version of edition 2.

4 'Zur Kritik der Hegelschen Rechtsphilosophie. Kritik des Hegelschen Staatsrechts (§§ 261–313)'. *Karl Marx/Friedrich Engels/Werke* (Institut für Marxismus–Leninismus beim Zentralkomitee der Sozialistischen Einheitspartei Deutschlands), Band 1 (Berlin, Dietz Verlag, 1956 (with subsequent printings)), pp. 203–333. Based on photocopies; p. 219 is same facsimile of manuscript page as in edition 1.

---

1 See, for example, *Werke* III, p. 537; the 'Demands of the Communist Party in Germany' (1848), *Werke* V, p. 3 (English) in *The Communist Manifesto of Karl Marx and Friedrich Engels*, ed. D. Rjazanov (New York, 1963), Appendix H, pp. 345–6; and both the published and unpublished versions of *The Civil War in France* (1871). A detailed account of the place of these notions in Marx's later writings and speeches, with references to their development in the *Critique*, is in Avineri, *The Social and Political Thought*, esp. pp. 202–20.

5 'Kritik des Hegelschen Staatsrechts (§§ 261–313)'. Edited by Hans–Joachim Lieber and Peter Furth; in *Karl Marx Ausgabe/Werke-Schriften-Briefe*, Band I, *Karl Marx/Frühe Schriften* (Stuttgart, Cotta Verlag, 1962), pp. 258–426. Based on a comparison of editions 1 through 4 with the manuscript; variant readings in editions 1 through 4 are given in footnotes (the editors indicate 45 errors in edition 1, 49 in edition 2, 9 in edition 4).

A note on existing translations of the 'Critique'

Bert Andréas lists 18 partial and complete translations in his 'Marx et Engels et la gauche hégélienne', pp. 257–8. The list includes 1 Bulgarian, 2 Chinese, 1 French, 1 Hungarian, 2 Italian, 2 Japanese, 1 Polish, 1 Rumanian, 4 Russian, 1 Serbian, 1 Czech, and 1 Ukrainian. We note here some details of a recent partial English translation which has been published since Andréas compiled his list:

By Loyd Easton and Kurt Guddat, based on a comparison of editions 1 and 4 above, and the manuscript; in *Writings of the Young Marx on Philosophy and Society*. Edited by Easton and Guddat (Garden City (N.Y.), Doubleday and Co., 1967), pp. 152–202. (Includes Marx's commentary on Hegel's Paragraphs 261–9, 279, 287–97, and 308.)

A note on the manuscript

As noted in the Introduction above, the manuscript of the *Critique* is in the form of a 19 × 32 cm. notebook, whose cardboard cover and first *Bogen*, or in-folio sheet of four sides, are missing. Andréas ('Marx et Engels et la gauche hégélienne', p. 356, n. 11) suggests that Marx himself might have removed them when he began his subsequently abandoned revision of the *Critique*. There remain thirty-nine *Bogen* numbered by Marx in Roman numerals II through XL. The individual page sides were numbered by Marx in Arabic numerals to page 87; pages 88–157 were apparently numbered by someone else at a later time. The manuscript begins at the top of page 5, which is the first page side of *Bogen* II.

Pages 7, 12, 47–8, 64, 70, 74, 86, and 134–6 of the manuscript are blank. Other pages, almost always those immediately preceding blank pages, are only partly filled. There is a pattern here which suggests that Marx tried, at times, to relate the material of the *Critique* to the *Bogen* numbers so as to begin a new development in the material at a *Bogen* number. For example, he appears to have left most of manuscript page 46 and all of pp. 47–8 blank in order to begin his examinaton of Hegel's Paragraph 287, which introduces Hegel's doctrine on the Executive Power, on the first page side (49) of *Bogen* XIII. The same appears true at pages 65, 71, 75, 87, and 137. Marx also used the *Bogen* numbers to refer in one part of the *Critique* to the material of another part. Other than in the instances just noted, however, there appears to be no relationship between the *Bogen* numbers and divisions within the material of the *Critique*.

Marx wrote in Gothic script. His handwriting varies from small and tight to large, open and flowing. Here, too, there is a pattern which suggests that as he wrote his script tended to become larger and more open. The change occurs sometimes in the course of several pages, sometimes in the course of a single page, sometimes in as short a space as a paragraph, with the same pattern repeated in successive paragraphs. Looked at overall, the pattern of variation in his handwriting throughout the *Critique* is not such as to suggest that the manuscript was composed over a longer period than the two to four months claimed by Rjazanov, Rubel, Easton and others. One apparent break in composition, which is suggested by a change in Marx's handwriting and occurs in the first half of the manuscript (at his remark on *assemblée constituante* and *assemblée constituée* prior to beginning *Bogen* XIX; below, p. 58) is relatable to his historical research of July–August 1843 (see n. 3 to p. xxxix, above). This would tend to support the claim that the first part of the *Critique* does not predate the summer of that year.

The notebook in which Marx wrote the *Critique* is apparently of Dutch make. To p. 132 of the manuscript, alternate notebook pages bear an elaborate watermark which includes a crowned lion holding a cluster of arrows and a sword (the lion is identical to that on present-day guilder pieces); the lion stands within a double circle containing the words 'concordia resparvae crescunt'; the double circle is surmounted by a crown (also similar to that on guilder pieces). Alternate pages are marked with the name 'Van Gelder'. Pages 133 to the end are approximately 3/8 inch longer, with alternate pages showing a different watermark design which includes the same lion together with a man, both enclosed within a fence; over the lion are the words 'L. Patria'. The pages between these are marked with the initials 'D G & C'. If the notebook is indeed of Dutch make, there is a good probability that Marx obtained it on the occasion of his brief sojourn in Holland following his resignation from the *RhZ* (18 March 1843) and just prior to his retirement to Kreuznach, in which case the existing manuscript could not pre-date the spring of 1843.

The manuscript is permanently housed in the Marx Archives of the Internationaal Instituut voor Sociale Geschiedenis, Amsterdam. The Instituut purchased the archival collection of the German Social-Democratic Party (SPD), including most of Marx's and Engels's literary remains, in 1938. At the time, the SPD was in exile, and the bulk of the Marx-Engels *Nachlass*, including the manuscript of the *Critique*, was hidden in Denmark, having been smuggled out of Germany in the late summer and fall of 1933 to save it from confiscation and probable destruction by the Nazis. It had been transferred piecemeal from London, where both authors died, to the Berlin archives of the SPD beginning in 1895, with most of Marx's manuscripts coming to Berlin following the death of his last surviving daughter, Laura, in 1911. The *Nachlass* was transported back to England in 1938–9 as a precaution against the outbreak of war and the possibility of a German invasion of Holland. After September 1939 it was kept at University College, Oxford. It was returned to Amsterdam and placed in the archives of the Internationaal Instituut voor Sociale Geschiedenis only after the conclusion of hostilities in Europe.[1]

Bibliographical note

This supplements the bibliographical information in the footnotes to the Editor's Introduction. I list here only works that bear directly, in whole or in significant part, on Marx's *Critique of Hegel's Philosophy of Right*, and that have been found most useful to an understanding and appraisal of the work.

---

[1] On the history of the Marx–Engels *Nachlass*, see esp. the excellent study by Paul Mayer, 'Die Geschichte des sozialdemokratischen Parteiarchivs und das Schicksal des Marx-Engels-Nachlasses', *Archiv für Sozialgeschichte* (Herausgegeben von der Friedrich–Ebert–Stiftung), ed. Dr Georg Eckert (Hannover, Verlag für Literatur und Zeitgeschehen GmbH, 1967), VI/VII (1966–7), pp. 5–198. Also Chushichi Tsuzuki, *The Life of Eleanor Marx, 1855–1898: A Socialist Tragedy*, (Oxford, Clarendon Press, 1967), esp. pp. 244–9, 255–66, 335–6.

The sole bibliography of Marx's writings that is scientifically established and approaches completeness is Maximilien Rubel, *Bibliographie des Œuvres de Karl Marx. Avec en appendice un Répertoire des Œuvres de Friedrich Engels* (Paris, Marcel Rivière et Cie 1956; *Supplément*, same publisher, 1960); on the *Critique* and Marx's *Exzerpthefte aus Kreuznach*, see p. 51. A valuable supplement to this for Marx's and Engels's early writings (1843–7), and Engels's 'Ludwig Feuerbach and the End of Classical German Philosophy' (1886), is Bert Andréas's bibliographical study, 'Marx et Engels et la gauche hégélienne', *Annali*, Instituto Giangiacomo Feltrinelli (Milan, 1964/5), vol. 7 (1965), pp. 353–517; the author treats each of the writings individually as to circumstances of composition, manuscript information, editions and translations; his notes are of doctrinal as well as bibliographical interest; on the *Critique*, see pp. 355–8.

The standard biography of Marx, Franz Mehring's *Karl Marx. Geschichte seines Lebens* (Leipzig, 1918), predates the discovery of the *Critique* manuscript; however, an appendix prepared by Eduard Fuchs for the 1933 edition gives an account of the work as well as the other early writings of Marx which came to light in the 1920s; the English version is *Karl Marx. The Story of His Life*, translated by Edward Fitzgerald; in the 1962 edition (Ann Arbor, Univ. of Michigan Press) see pp. 542–4. An additional and very useful source of biographical information is *Karl Marx: Chronik seines Lebens in Einzeldaten*, prepared by the Marx–Engels–Lenin-Institut, Moscow (Moscow, Marx–Engels–Verlag, 1934); on the events surrounding the composition of the *Critique*, see pp. 8–21. A fine biographical study from the point of view of Marx's intellectual development is Maximilien Rubel, *Karl Marx: Essai de biographie intellectuelle* (Paris, Marcel Rivière et Cie, 1957); the author's account of the evolution in Marx's thought through the period of the *Critique*, and a good account of the work itself, is on pp. 55–80.

Of Marx's early theoretical writings, the *Critique* has until recent years received relatively little attention from the commentators. An early study of the work in English is in H. L. Adams, *Karl Marx in his Earlier Writings*, first published in 1940, reissued in 1965 (New York, Russell & Russell); see Ch. IV, 'A Criticism of Hegel', pp. 72–85. More recently, Louis Dupré and especially Shlomo Avineri have emphasized the importance of the work in the development of Marx's thought *vis-à-vis* Hegel; both draw attention to the importance of Marx's criticism of primogeniture; Dupré, however, does not agree that in the *Critique* Marx already calls for the abolition of the state; Dupré's treatment of the work is in *The Philosophical Foundations of Marxism* (New York, Harcourt, Brace & World, 1966), see Ch. IV, 'Marx's Critique of Hegel's Philosophy of the State', pp. 87–108. Avineri uses the *Critique* as the point of departure for his interpretation of Marx's social and political theory overall; see his *The Social and Political Thought of Karl Marx* (Cambridge, The University Press, 1968), esp. Ch. I, 'Hegel's Political Philosophy Reconsidered', pp. 8–40, also 41–64, 202–20. The same author has presented the matter of his Ch. I in two articles, 'Marx's critique of Hegel's "Philosophy of Right" in its systematic setting", *Cahiers de l'Institut de Science Economique Appliquée*, Série Philosophie–Sciences Sociales–Economie (August 1966), pp. 45–81, and 'The Hegelian Origins of Marx's Political Thought', *The Review of Metaphysics*, vol. XXI, no. 1 (September 1967), pp. 35–50, with a valuable appendix, F. Engels's 'Progress of Social Reform on the Continent: Germany and Switzerland' (1843), *ibid.*, 50–6. A brief account of the *Critique*, critical of some of the interpretations of Rubel and Avineri, is in Nicholas Lobkowicz, *Theory and Practice: History of a Concept from Aristotle to Marx* (Notre Dame and London, Notre Dame Univ. Press, 1967), see Ch. 18, 'Civil Society', pp. 259–70.

Among the secondary sources in French we note, in addition to Rubel's *Essai* cited above, the excellent essay of Jean Hyppolite, 'La conception hégélienne de L'Etat et sa critique par Karl Marx', first published in *Cahiers internationaux de Sociologie* vol. II, no. 2 (1947), pp. 142 ff., and reprinted in J. Hyppolite, *Etudes sur Marx et Hegel* (Paris, Marcel Rivière et Cie, 2eme édition, 1965), pp. 120–41. A good account of the content and significance of the *Critique* is also found in Nicolai Lapine, 'La première critique approfondie de la philosophie de Hegel par Marx', *Recherches Internationaux à la lumière du marxisme* (Paris), Cahier 19, pp. 53–71; the article originally appeared in Russian, in *Voprossy filosofii*, the journal of the Institute of Philosophy of the Soviet Academy of Sciences, Moscow, no. 1 (1959), pp. 98–109. A brief treatment of the *Critique* in the context of a general study of Marx's thought is in Charles Wackenheim, *La faillite de la religion d'après Karl Marx* (Paris, Presses Universitaires de France, 1963), pp. 142–52.

Especially good secondary studies in German are Jakob Barion, *Hegel und die marxistische Staatslehre* (Bonn, H. Bouvier Verlag, 1963), Part II, pp. 78–141; and Manfred Friedrich, *Philosophie und Œconomie beim jungen Marx* (Berlin, Duncker und Humblot, 1960), pp. 50–77. Two studies especially useful for their emphasis on the relationship between Feuerbach and Marx, and the former's influence on Marx's critical methodology in the *Critique*, are Klaus Erich Bockmuhl, *Leiblichkeit und Gesellschaft: Studien zur Religionskritik und Anthropologie im Fruhwerk von Ludwig Feuerbach und Karl Marx* (Göttingen, Vandenhoeck und Ruprecht, 1961), esp. pp. 183 ff.; and Werner Schuffenhauer, *Feuerbach und der junge Marx: Zur Enstehungsgeschichte der marxistischen Weltanschauung* (Berlin, VEB Deutscher Verlag der Wissenschaften, 1965), esp. pp. 35–59.

CRITIQUE OF HEGEL'S 'PHILOSOPHY OF RIGHT'

(§§ 261–313)

BY

KARL MARX

Contents

Editorial Note

Marx's ellipses and additions and Knox's additions in the passages from Hegel's *Philosophy of Right* are noted. Additions in Marx's commentary made by the translators for purposes of clarification are within square brackets; so are the additions made by the German editors, which are noted as such. German editors' footnotes are keyed in with asterisks; the footnotes reproduced from the *MEGA* edition, which do not appear in the *Werke* edition, are marked as such. Editorial and translators' footnotes prepared for this English edition are keyed in with arabic numerals.

§ 261. In contrast with the spheres of private rights and private welfare (the family and civil society), the state is from one point of view an external necessity and their higher authority; its nature is such that their laws and interests are subordinate to it and dependent on it. On the other hand, however, it is the end immanent within them, and its strength lies in the unity of its own universal end and aim with the particular interest of individuals, in the fact that individuals have duties to the state in proportion as they have rights against it (see Paragraph 155).

The foregoing paragraph advises us that concrete freedom consists in the identity (as it is supposed to be, two-sided) of the system of particular interest (the family and civil society) with the system of general interest (the state). The relation of these spheres must now be determined more precisely.

From one point of view the state is contrasted with the spheres of family and civil society as an external necessity, an authority, relative to which the laws and interests of family and civil society are subordinate and dependent. That the state, in contrast with the family and civil society, is an external necessity was implied partly in the category of 'transition' (*Übergangs*) and partly in the conscious relationship of the family and civil society to the state. Further, subordination under the state corresponds perfectly with the relation of external necessity. But what Hegel understands by 'dependence' is shown by the following sentence from the Remark to this paragraph:

...It was Montesquieu above all who, in his famous work *L'Esprit des Lois*, kept in sight and tried to work out in detail both the thought of the dependence of laws—in particular, laws concerning the rights of persons—on the specific character of the state, and also the philosophic notion of always treating the part in its relation to the whole.

Thus Hegel is speaking here of internal dependence, or the essential determination of private rights, etc., by the state. At the same time, however, he subsumes this dependence under the relationship of external necessity and opposes it, as another aspect, to that relationship wherein family and civil society relate to the state as to their immanent end.

'External necessity' can only be understood to mean that the laws and interests of the family and civil society must give way in case of collision with the laws and interests of the state, that they are subordinate to it, that their existence is dependent on it, or again that its will and its law appear to their will and their laws as a necessity!

But Hegel is not speaking here about empirical collisions; he is speaking about the relationship of the 'spheres of private rights and private welfare, of the family and civil society,' to the state; it is a question of the *essential relationship* of these spheres themselves. Not only their interests but also their laws and their essential determinations are dependent on the state and subordinate to it. It is related to their laws and interests as higher authority, while their interest and law are related to it as its 'subordinates'. They exist in their dependence on it. Precisely because subordination and dependence are external relations, limiting and contrary to an autonomous being, the relationship of family and civil society to the state is that of external necessity, a necessity which relates by opposition to the inner being of the thing. The very fact that the laws concerning the private rights of persons depend on the specific character of the state and are modified according to it is thereby subsumed under the relationship of 'external necessity', precisely because civil society and family in their true, that is in their independent and complete development, are presupposed by the state as particular spheres. 'Subordination' and 'dependence' are the expressions for an external, artificial, apparent identity, for the logical expression of which Hegel quite rightly uses the phrase 'external necessity'. With the notions of 'subordination' and 'dependence' Hegel has further developed the one aspect of the divided identity, namely that of the alienation within the unity.

On the other hand, however, it is the end immanent within them, and its strength lies in the unity of its own universal end and aim with the particular interest of individuals, in the fact that individuals have duties to the state in proportion as they have rights against it.

Here Hegel sets up an unresolved antinomy: on the one hand external necessity, on the other hand immanent end. The unity of the universal end and aim of the state and the particular interest of individuals must consist in this, that the duties of individuals to the state and their rights against it are identical (thus, for example, the duty to respect property coincides with the right to property).

This identity is explained in this way in the Remark [to § 261]:

Duty is primarily a relation to something which from my point of view is substantive, absolutely universal. A right, on the other hand, is simply the embodiment of this substance and thus is the particular aspect of it and enshrines my particular freedom. Hence at abstract levels, right and duty appear parcelled out on different sides or in different persons. In the state, as something ethical, as the inter-penetration of the substantive and the particular, my obligation to what is substantive is at the same time the embodiment of my particular freedom. This means that in the state duty and right are united in one and the same relation.

§ 262. The actual Idea is mind, which, sundering itself into the two ideal spheres of its concept, family and civil society, enters upon its finite phase, but it does so only in order to rise above its ideality and become explicit as infinite actual mind. It is therefore to these ideal spheres that the actual Idea assigns the material of this its finite actuality, viz., human beings as a mass, in such a way that the function assigned to any given individual is visibly mediated by circumstances, his caprice and his personal choice of his station in life.

Let us translate this into prose as follows:

The manner and means of the state's mediation with the family and civil society are 'circumstance, caprice, and personal choice of station in life'. Accordingly, the rationality of the state [*Staatsvernunft*] has nothing to do with the division of the material of the state into family and civil society. The state results from them in an unconscious and arbitrary way. Family and civil society appear as the dark natural ground from which the light of the state emerges. By material of the state is meant the business of the state, i.e., family and civil society, in so far as they constitute components of the state and, as such, participate in the state.

This development is peculiar in two respects.

1. Family and civil society are conceived of as spheres of the concept of the state, specifically as spheres of its finiteness, as its finite phase. It is the state which sunders itself into the two, which presupposes them, and indeed does this 'only in order to rise above its ideality and become explicit as infinite actual mind'. 'It sunders itself in order to...' It 'therefore assigns to these ideal spheres the material of its finite actuality in such a way that the function assigned to any given individual is visibly mediated, etc'. The so-called 'actual Idea' (mind as infinite and actual) is described as though it acted according to a determined principle and toward a determined end. It sunders itself into finite spheres, and does this 'in order to return to itself, to be for itself'; moreover it does this precisely in such a way that it is just as it actually is.

In this passage the logical, pantheistic mysticism appears very clearly.

The actual situation is that the assignment of the material of the state to the individual is mediated by circumstances, caprice, and personal choice of his station in life. This fact, this actual situation is expressed by speculative philosophy [*der Spekulation*] as appearance, as phenomenon. These circumstances, this caprice, this personal choice of vocation, this actual mediation are merely the appearance of a mediation which the actual Idea undertakes with itself and which goes on behind the scenes. Actuality is not expressed as itself but as another reality. Ordinary empirical existence does not have its own mind [*Geist*] but rather an alien mind as its law, while on the other hand the actual Idea does not have an actuality which is developed out of itself, but rather has ordinary empirical existence as its existence [*Dasein*].

The Idea is given the status of a subject, and the actual relationship of family and civil society to the state is conceived to be its inner imaginary activity. Family and civil society are the presuppositions of the state; they are the really active things; but in speculative philosophy it is reversed. But if the Idea is made subject, then the real subjects—civil society, family, circumstances, caprice, etc.—become unreal, and take on the different meaning of objective moments of the Idea.

[2.] The circumstance, caprice, and personal choice of station in life, through which the material of the state is assigned to the individual, are not said directly to be things which are real, necessary, and justified in and for themselves; *qua* circumstances, caprice, and personal choice they are not declared to be rational. Yet on the other hand they again are, but only so as to be presented for the phenomena of a mediation, to be left as they are while at the same time acquiring the meaning of a determination of the Idea, a result and product of the Idea. The difference lies not in the content, but in the way of considering it, or in the manner of speaking. There is a two-fold history, one esoteric and one exoteric. The content lies in the exoteric part. The interest of the esoteric is always to recover the history of the logical Concept in the state. But the real development proceeds on the exoteric side.

Reasonably, Hegel's sentences mean only the following:

The family and civil society are elements of the state. The material of the state is divided amongst them through circumstances, caprice, and personal choice of vocation. The citizens of the state are members of families and of civil society.

'The actual Idea is mind which, sundering itself into the two ideal spheres of its concept, family and civil society, enters upon its finite phase' —thus the division of the state into the family and civil society is ideal, i.e., necessary, belonging to the essence of the state. Family and civil society are actual components of the state, actual spiritual existences of will; they are the modes of existence of the state; family and civil society make *themselves* into the state. They are the active force. According to

Hegel they are, on the contrary, made by the actual Idea. It is not their own life's course which unites them into the state, but rather the life's course of the Idea, which has distinguished them from itself; and they are precisely the finiteness of this Idea; they owe their existence to a mind [*Geist*] other than their own; they are determinations established by a third [party], not self-determinations; for that very reason they are also determined as finiteness, as the proper finiteness of the 'actual Idea'. The purpose of their existence is not this existence itself, but rather the Idea separates these presuppositions off from itself in order to rise above its ideality and become explicit as infinite actual mind. This is to say that the political state cannot exist without the natural basis of the family and the artificial basis of civil society; they are its *conditio sine qua non*; but the conditions are established as the conditioned, the determining as the determined, the producing as the product of its product. The actual Idea reduces itself into the finiteness of the family and civil society only in order to enjoy and to bring forth its infinity through their transcendence [*Aufhebung*]. It therefore assigns (in order to attain its end) to these ideal spheres the material of this its finite actuality (of this? of what? these spheres are really its finite actuality, its material) to human beings as a mass (the material of the state here is human beings, the mass, the state is composed of them, and this, its composition is expressed here as an action of the Idea, as a parcelling out which it undertakes with its own material. The fact is that the state issues from the mass of men existing as members of families and of civil society; but speculative philosophy expresses this fact as an achievement of the Idea, not the idea of the mass, but rather as the deed of an Idea–Subject which is differentiated from the fact itself) in such a way that the function assigned to the individual (earlier the discussion was only of the assignment of individuals to the spheres of family and civil society) is visibly mediated by circumstances, caprice, etc. Thus empirical actuality is admitted just as it is and is also said to be rational; but not rational because of its own reason, but because the empirical fact in its empirical existence has a significance which is other than it itself. The fact, which is the starting point, is not conceived to be such but rather to be the mystical result. The actual becomes phenomenon, but the Idea has no other content than this phenomenon. Moreover, the Idea has no other than the logical aim, namely, 'to become explicit as infinite actual mind'. The entire mystery of the *Philosophy of Right* and of Hegelian philosophy in general is contained in these paragraphs.

§ 263. In these spheres in which its moments, particularity and individuality, have their immediate and reflected reality, mind is present as their objective universality glimmering in them as the power of reason in necessity (see Paragraph 184), i.e., as the institutions considered above.

§ **264.** Mind is the nature of human beings *en masse* and their nature is therefore twofold: (i) at one extreme, explicit individuality of consciousness and will, and (ii) at the other extreme, universality which knows and wills what is substantive. Hence they attain their right in both these respects only in so far as both their private personality and its substantive basis are actualized. Now in the family and civil society they acquire their right in the first of these respects directly and in the second indirectly, in that (i) they find their substantive self-consciousness in social institutions which are the universal implicit in their particular interests, and (ii) the Corporation supplies them with an occupation and an activity directed on a universal end.

§ **265.** These institutions are the components of the constitution (i.e., of rationality developed and actualized) in the sphere of particularity. They are, therefore, the firm foundation not only of the state but also of the citizen's trust in it and sentiment towards it. They are the pillars of public freedom since in them particular freedom is realized and rational, and therefore there is *implicitly* present even in them the union of freedom and necessity.

§ **266.** But mind is objective and actual to itself not merely as this (which?)[1] necessity...,[2] but also as the ideality and the heart of this necessity. Only in this way is this substantive universality *aware* of itself as its own object and end, with the result that the necessity appears to itself in the shape of freedom as well.

Thus the transition of the family and civil society into the political state is this: the mind of those spheres, which is the mind of the state in its implicit moment, is now also related to itself as such, and is actual to itself as their inner reality. Accordingly, the transition is not derived from the specific essence of the family, etc., and the specific essence of the state, but rather from the universal relation of necessity and freedom. Exactly the same transition is effected in the *Logic* from the sphere of Essence to the sphere of Concept, and in the Philosophy of Nature from Inorganic Nature to Life. It is always the same categories offered as the animating principle now of one sphere, now of another, and the only thing of importance is to discover, for the particular concrete determinations, the corresponding abstract ones.

§ **267.** This necessity in ideality is the inner self-development of the Idea. As the substance of the individual subject, it is his political sentiment [patriotism];[3] in distinction therefrom, as the substance of the objective world, it is the organism of the state, i.e., it is the strictly political state and its constitution.

Here the subject is 'the necessity in ideality', the 'Idea within itself', and the predicate is political sentiment and the political constitution.

---

[1] Marx's insertion.   [2] Marx's ellipsis.   [3] Knox's addition.

Said in common language, political sentiment is the subjective, and the political constitution the objective substance of the state. The logical development from the family and civil society to the state is thus pure appearance, for what is not clarified is the way in which familial and civil sentiment, the institution of the family and those of society, as such, stand related to the political sentiment and political institutions and cohere with them.

The transition involved in mind existing 'not merely as necessity and realm of appearance' but as actual for itself and particular as 'the ideality of this necessity' and the soul of this realm is no transition whatever, because the soul of the family exists for itself as love, etc.[1] The pure ideality of an actual sphere, however, could exist only as knowledge [*Wissenschaft*].

The important thing is that Hegel at all times makes the Idea the subject and makes the proper and actual subject, like 'political sentiment', the predicate. But the development proceeds at all times on the side of the predicate.

§ 268 contains a nice exposition concerning political sentiment, or patriotism, which has nothing to do with the logical development except that Hegel defines it as 'simply a product of the institutions subsisting in the *state* since rationality is actually present in the state', while on the other hand these institutions are equally an objectification of the political sentiment. Cf. the Remark to this paragraph.

§ 269. The patriotic sentiment acquires its specifically determined content from the various members of the organism of the state. This organism is the development of the Idea to its differences and their objective actuality. Hence these different members are the various powers of the state with their functions and spheres of action, by means of which the universal continually engenders itself, and engenders itself in a necessary way because their specific character is fixed by the nature of the concept. Throughout this process the universal maintains its identity, since it is itself the presupposition of its own production. This organism is the constitution of the state.

The constitution of the state is the organism of the state, or the organism of the state is the constitution of the state. To say that the different parts of an organism stand in a necessary relation which arises out of the nature of the organism is pure tautology. To say that when the political constitution is determined as an organism the different parts of the constitution, the different powers, are related as organic determinations and have a rational relationship to one another is likewise tautology. It is a great advance to consider the political state as an organism, and hence no longer

[1] Marx here refers to Hegel's doctrine on the Family, contained in §§ 161 ff. in *The Philosophy of Right*; see especially § 163.

to consider the diversity of powers as organic,* but rather as living and rational differences. But how does Hegel present this discovery?

1. 'This organism is the development of the Idea to its differences and their objective actuality.' It is not said that this organism of the state is its development to differences and their objective actuality. The proper conception is that the development of the state or of the political constitution to differences and their actuality is an organic development. The actual differences, or the different parts of the political constitution are the presupposition, the subject. The predicate is their determination as organic. Instead of that, the Idea is made subject, and the differences and their actuality are conceived to be its development and its result, while on the other hand the Idea must be developed out of the actual difference. What is organic is precisely the idea of the differences, their ideal determination.

[2.] But here the Idea is spoken of as a subject which is developed to *its* differences. From this reversal of subject and predicate comes the appearance that an idea other than the organism is under discussion. The point of departure is the abstract Idea whose development in the state is the political constitution. Thus it is a question not of the political idea, but rather of the abstract Idea in the political element. When Hegel says, 'this organism (namely, the state, or the constitution of the state) is the development of the Idea to its differences, etc.', he tells us absolutely nothing about the specific idea of the political constitution. The same thing can be said with equal truth about the animal organism as about the political organism. By what means then is the animal organism distinguished from the political? No difference results from this general determination; and an explanation which does not give the *differentia specifica* is no explanation. The sole interest here is that of recovering the Idea simply, the logical Idea in each element, be it that of the state or of nature; and the real subjects, as in this case the political constitution, become their mere names. Consequently, there is only the appearance of a real understanding, while in fact these determinate things are and remain uncomprehended because they are not understood in their specific essence.

'Hence these different members are the various powers of the state with their functions and spheres of action.' By reason of this small word 'hence' ['*so*'] this statement assumes the appearance of a consequence, a deduction and development. Rather, one must ask 'How is it' ['*Wie so?*'] that when the empirical fact is that the various members of the organism of the state

* An obvious writing error; the word should probably read 'mechanical' or 'inorganic'.

are the various powers (and) their functions and spheres of action, the philosophical predicate is that they are members of an organism [?]

Here we draw attention to a stylistic peculiarity of Hegel, one which recurs often and is a product of mysticism. The entire paragraph reads:

The patriotic sentiment acquires its specifically determined content from the various members of the organism of the state. This organism is the development of the Idea to its differences and their objective actuality. Hence these different members are the various powers of the state with their functions and spheres of action, by means of which the universal continually engenders itself, and engenders itself in a necessary way because their specific character is fixed by the nature of the concept. Throughout this process the universal maintains its identity, since it is itself the presupposition of its own production. This organism is the constitution of the state.

1. The patriotic sentiment acquires its specifically determined content from the various members of the organism of the state... These different members are the various powers of the state with their functions and spheres of action.

2. The patriotic sentiment acquires its specifically determined content from the various members of the organism of the state. This organism is the development of the Idea to its differences and their objective actuality... by means of which the universal continually engenders itself, and engenders itself in a necessary way because their specific character is fixed by the nature of the concept. Throughout this process the universal maintains its identity, since it is itself the presupposition of its own production. This organism is the constitution of the state.

As can be seen, Hegel links the two subjects, namely, the 'various members of the organism' and the 'organism', to further determinations. In the third sentence the various members are defined as the various powers. By inserting the word '*hence*' it is made to appear as if these various powers were deduced from the interposed statement concerning the organism as the development of the Idea.

He then goes on to discuss the various powers. The statement that the universal continually engenders itself while maintaining its identity throughout the process, is nothing new, having been implied in the definition of the various powers as members of the organism, as organic members; or rather, this definition of the various powers is nothing but a paraphrase of the statement about the organism being 'the development of the Idea to its differences, etc.'

These two sentences are identical: [1] This organism is 'the development of the Idea to its differences and their objective actuality' or to differences by means of which the universal (the universal here is the same as the Idea) continually engenders itself, and engenders itself in a necessary way because their specific character is fixed by the nature of the concept;

and [2] 'Throughout this process the universal maintains its identity, since it is itself the presupposition of its own production.' The second is merely a more concise explication of 'the development of the Idea to its differences'. Thereby, Hegel has advanced not a single step beyond the universal concept of the Idea or at most of the organism in general (for strictly speaking it is a question only of this specific idea). Why then is he entitled to conclude that 'this organism is the constitution of the state'? Why not 'this organism is the solar system'? The reason is that he later defined the various members of the state as the various powers. Now the statement that 'the various members of the state are the various powers' is an empirical truth and cannot be presented as a philosophical discovery, nor has it in any way emerged as a result of an earlier development. But by defining the organism as the development of the Idea, by speaking of the differences of the Idea, then by interpolating the concrete data of the various powers the development assumes the appearance of having arrived at a determinate content. Following the statement that 'the patriotic sentiment acquires its specifically determined content from the various members of the organism of the state' Hegel was not justified in continuing with the expression, '*This* organism...,' but rather with '*the* organism is the development of the Idea, etc.' At least what he says applies to every organism, and there is no predicate which justifies the subject, '*this* organism'. What Hegel really wants to achieve is the determination of the organism as the constitution of the state. But there is no bridge by which one can pass from the universal idea of the organism to the particular idea of the organism of the state or the constitution of the state, nor will there ever be. The opening statement speaks of the various members of the organism of the state which are later defined as the various powers. Thus the only thing said is that the various powers of the organism of the state, or the state organism of the various powers, is the political constitution of the state. Accordingly, the bridge to the political constitution does not go from the organism of the Idea and its differences, etc., but from the presupposed concept of the various powers or the organism of the state.

In truth, Hegel has done nothing but resolve the constitution of the state into the universal, abstract idea of the organism; but in appearance and in his own opinion he has developed the determinate reality out of the universal Idea. He has made the subject of the idea into a product and predicate of the Idea. He does not develop his thought out of what is objective [*aus dem Gegenstand*], but what is objective in accordance with a ready-made thought which has its origin in the abstract sphere of logic. It is not a question of developing the determinate idea of the political constitution, but of giving the political constitution a relation to the abstract Idea, of classifying it as a member of its (the Idea's) life history. This is an obvious mystification.

Another determination is that the specific character of the various powers is fixed by the nature of the concept, and for that reason the universal engenders them in a necessary way. Therefore the various powers do not have their specific character by reason of their own nature, but by reason of an alien one. And just as the necessity is not derived from their own nature still less is it critically demonstrated. On the contrary, their realization is predestined by the nature of the concept, sealed in the holy register of the Santa Casa (the *Logic*). The soul of objects, in this case that of the state, is complete and predestined before its body, which is, properly speaking, mere appearance. The 'concept' is the Son within the 'Idea', within God the Father, the *agens*, the determining, differentiating principle. Here 'Idea' and 'Concept' are abstractions rendered independent.

§ 270. (1) The abstract actuality or the substantiality of the state consists in the fact that its end is the universal interest as such and the conservation therein of particular interests since the universal interest is the substance of these. (2) But this substantiality of the state is also its *necessity*, since its substantiality is divided into the distinct spheres of its activity which correspond to the moments of its concept, and these spheres, owing to this substantiality, are thus actually fixed determinate characteristics of the state, i.e., its *powers*. (3) But this very substantiality of the state is mind knowing and willing itself after passing through the forming process of education. The state, therefore, knows what it wills and knows it in its universality, i.e., as something thought. Hence it works and acts by reference to consciously adopted ends, known principles, and laws which are not merely implicit but are actually present to consciousness; and further, it acts with precise knowledge of existing conditions and circumstances, inasmuch as its actions have a bearing on these.

(We will look at the Remark to this paragraph, which treats the relationship of state and church, later.)

The employment of these logical categories deserves altogether special attention.

(1) The abstract actuality or the substantiality of the state consists in the fact that its end is the universal interest as such and the conservation therein of particular interests since the universal interest is the substance of these.

That the universal interest as such and as the subsistence of particular interests is the end of the state is precisely the abstractly defined actuality and subsistence of the state. The state is not actual without this end. This is the essential object of its will, but at the same time it is merely a very general definition of this object. This end *qua* Being is the principle of subsistence for the state.

(2) But this (abstract actuality or)[1] substantiality of the state is its *necessity*, since its substantiality is divided into the distinct spheres of its activity which correspond to the moments of its concept, and these spheres, owing to their substantiality, are thus actually fixed determinate characteristics of the state, i.e., its *powers*.

This abstract actuality or substantiality is its (the state's) necessity, since its actuality is divided into distinct spheres of activity, spheres whose distinction is rationally determined and which are, for that reason, fixed determinate characteristics. The abstract actuality of the state, its substantiality, is necessity inasmuch as the genuine end of the state and the genuine subsistence of the whole is realized only in the subsistence of the distinct spheres of the state's activity.

Obviously the first definition of the state's actuality was abstract; it cannot be regarded as a simple actuality; it must be regarded as activity, and as a differentiated activity.

The abstract actuality or the substantiality of the state...is...[2] its necessity, since its substantiality is divided into the distinct spheres of its activity which correspond to the moments of its concept, and these spheres, owing to this substantiality, are thus actually fixed determinate characteristics of the state, i.e., its powers.

The condition of substantiality is the condition of necessity; i.e., the substance appears to be divided into independent but essentially determined actualities or activities. These abstractions can be applied to any actual thing. In so far as the state is first considered according to the model of the abstract it will subsequently have to be considered according to the model of concrete actuality, necessity, and realized difference.

(3) But this very substantiality of the state is mind knowing and willing itself after passing through the forming process of education. The state, therefore, knows what it wills and knows it in its universality, i.e., as something thought. Hence it works and acts by reference to consciously adopted ends, known principles, and laws which are not merely implicit but are actually present to consciousness; and further, it acts with precise knowledge of existing conditions and circumstances, inasmuch as its actions have a bearing on these.

Now let's translate this entire paragraph into common language as follows:

1. The self-knowing and self-willing mind is the substance of the state; (the educated self-assured mind is the subject and the foundation, the autonomy of the state).

2. The universal interest, and within it the conservation of the particular interests, is the universal end and content of this mind, the existing substance of the state, the nature *qua* state of the self-knowing and willing mind.

---

[1] Marx's insertion.   [2] Marx's ellipses.

3. The self-knowing and willing mind, the self-assured, educated mind attains the actualization of this abstract content only as a differentiated activity, as the existence of various powers, as an organically structured power.

Certain things should be noted concerning Hegel's presentation.

a) Abstract actuality, necessity (or substantial difference), substantiality, thus the categories of abstract logic, are made subjects. Indeed, abstract actuality and necessity are called 'its', the state's, actuality and necessity; however (1) 'it'—i.e., abstract actuality or substantiality—is its [, the state's,] necessity. (2) It [, abstract actuality or substantiality,] is what is divided into the distinct spheres of its activity which correspond to the moments of its concept. The moments of its concept are, 'owing to this substantiality...thus actually fixed' determinations, powers. (3) Substantiality is no longer taken to be an abstract characteristic of the state, as *its* substantiality; rather, as such it is made subject, and then in conclusion it is said, 'but this very substantiality of the state is mind knowing and willing itself after passing through the forming process of education'.

b) Also it is not said in conclusion that the educated, etc., mind is substantiality, but on the contrary that substantiality is the educated, etc., mind. Thus mind becomes the predicate of its predicate.

c) Substantiality, after having been defined (1) as the universal end of the state, then (2) as the various powers, is defined (3) as the educated, self-knowing and willing, actual mind. The real point of departure, the self-knowing and willing mind, without which the end of the state and the powers of the state would be illusions devoid of principle or support, inessential and even impossible existents, appears to be only the final predicate of substantiality, which had itself previously been defined as the universal end and as the various powers of the state. Had the actual mind been taken as the starting point, with the universal end its content, then the various powers would be its modes of self-actualization, its real or material existence, whose determinate character would have had to develop out of the nature of its end. But because the point of departure is the Idea, or Substance as subject and real being, the actual subject appears to be only the final predicate of the abstract predicate.

The end of the state and the powers of the state are mystified in that they take the appearance of modes of existence of the substance, drawn out of and divorced from their real existence, the self-knowing and willing mind, the educated mind.

d) The concrete content, the actual determination appears to be formal, and the wholly abstract formal determination appears to be the concrete

content. What is essential to determinate political realities is not that they can be considered as such but rather that they can be considered, in their most abstract configuration, as logical-metaphysical determinations. Hegel's true interest is not the philosophy of right but logic. The philosophical task is not the embodiment of thought in determinate political realities, but the evaporation of these realities in abstract thought. The philosophical moment is not the logic of fact but the fact of logic. Logic is not used to prove the nature of the state, but the state is used to prove the logic.

[There are three concrete determinations:]

1. the universal interest and the conservation therein of the particular interests as the end of the state;

2. the various powers as the actualization of this end of the state;

3. the educated, self-assured, willing and acting mind as the subject of this end and its actualization.

These concrete determinations are considered to be extrinsic, to be *hors d'oeuvres*. Their importance to philosophy is that in them the state takes on the following logical significance:

1. abstract actuality or substantiality;

2. the condition of substantiality passes over into the condition of necesity or substantial actuality;

3. substantial actuality is in fact concept, or subjectivity.

With the exclusion of these concrete determinations, which can just as well be exchanged for those of another sphere such as physics which has other concrete determinations, and which are accordingly unessential, we have before us a chapter of the *Logic*.

The substance must be 'divided into the distinct spheres of its activity which correspond to the moments of its concept, and these spheres, owing to this substantiality, are thus actually fixed determinate characteristics of the state'. The gist of this sentence belongs to logic and is ready-made prior to the philosophy of right. That these moments of the concept are, in the present instance, distinct spheres of its (the state's) activity and the fixed determinate characteristics of the state, or powers of the state, is a parenthesis belonging to the philosophy of right, to the order of political fact. In this way the entire philosophy of right is only a parenthesis to logic. It goes without saying that the parenthesis is only an *hors d'oeuvre* of the real development. Cf. for example the Addition to § 270:

Necessity consists in this, that the whole is sundered into the differences of the concept and that this divided whole yields a fixed and permanent determinacy, though one which is not fossilized but perpetually recreates itself in its dissolution. Cf. also the *Logic*.

§ **271.** The constitution of the state is, in the first place, the organization of the state and the self-related process of its organic life, a process whereby it differentiates its moments within itself and develops them to self-subsistence.

Secondly, the state is an individual, unique and exclusive, and therefore related to others. Thus it turns its differentiating activity outward and accordingly establishes within itself the ideality of its subsisting inward differentiations.

Addition: The inner side of the state as such is the civil power while its outward tendency is the military power, although this has a fixed place inside the state itself.

I. THE CONSTITUTION (on its internal side only)

§ **272.** The constitution is rational in so far as the state inwardly differentiates and determines its activity in accordance with the nature of the concept. The result of this is that each of these powers is in itself the totality of the constitution, because each contains the other moments and has them effective in itself, and because the moments, being expressions of the differentiation of the concept, simply abide in their ideality and constitute nothing but a single individual whole.

Thus the constitution is rational in so far as its moments can be reduced to abstract logical moments. The state has to differentiate and determine its activity not in accordance with its specific nature, but in accordance with the nature of the Concept, which is the mystified mobile of abstract thought. The reason of the constitution is thus abstract logic and not the concept of the state. In place of the concept of the constitution we get the constitution of the Concept. Thought is not conformed to the nature of the state, but the state to a ready made system of thought.

§ **273.** The state as a political entity is thus (how 'thus'?)[1] cleft into three substantive divisions:
  (a) the power to determine and establish the universal—the Legislature;
  (b) the power to subsume single cases and the spheres of particularity under the universal—the Executive;
  (c) the power of subjectivity, as the will with the power of ultimate decision—the Crown. In the crown, the different powers are bound into an individual unity which is thus at once the apex and basis of the whole, i.e., of constitutional monarchy.

We will return to this division after examining the particulars of its explanation.

§ **274.** Mind is actual only as that which it knows itself to be, and the state, as the mind of a nation, is both the law permeating all relationships within the state and also, at the same time the manners and consciousness of its citizens. It follows, therefore,

---

[1] Marx's insertion.

that the constitution of any given nation depends in general on the character and development of its self-consciousness. In its self-consciousness its subjective freedom is rooted and so, therefore, is the actuality of its constitution...Hence every nation has the constitution appropriate to it and suitable for it.

The only thing that follows from Hegel's reasoning is that a state in which the character and development of self-consciousness and the constitution contradict one another is no real state. That the constitution which was the product of a bygone self-consciousness can become an oppressive fetter for an advanced self-consciousness, etc., etc., are certainly trivialities. However, what would follow is only the demand for a constitution having within itself the characteristic and principle of advancing in step with consciousness, with actual man, which is possible only when man has become the principle of the constitution. Here Hegel is a *sophist*.

(a) The Crown

§ 275. The power of the crown contains in itself the three moments of the whole (see § 272) viz. (α) the *universality* of the constitution and the laws; (β) counsel, which refers the *particular* to the universal; and (γ) the moment of ultimate decision, as the *self-determination* to which everything else reverts and from which everything else derives the beginning of its actuality. This absolute self-determination constitutes the distinctive principle of the power of the crown as such, and with this principle our exposition is to begin.

All the first part of this paragraph says is that both the universality of the constitution and the laws and counsel, or the reference of the particular to the universal, are the crown. The crown does not stand outside the universality of the constitution and the laws once the crown is understood to be the crown of the (constitutional) monarch.

What Hegel really wants, however, is nothing other than that the universality of the constitution and the laws is the crown, the sovereignty of the state. So it is wrong to make the crown the subject and, inasmuch as the power of the sovereign can also be understood by the crown, to make it appear as if he [, the sovereign,] were the master and subject of this moment. Let us first turn to what Hegel declares to be the distinctive principle of the power of the crown as such, and we find that it is 'the moment of ultimate decision, as the self-determination to which everything else reverts and from which everything else derives the beginning of its actuality', in other words this 'absolute self-determination'.

Here Hegel is really saying that the actual, i.e., individual will is the power of the crown. § 12 says it this way:

When...the will gives itself the form of individuality..., this constitutes the resolution of the will, and it is only in so far as it resolves that the will is an actual will at all.

In so far as this moment of ultimate decision or absolute self-determination is divorced from the universality of content [i.e., the constitution and laws,] and the particularity of counsel it is actual will as arbitrary choice [*Willkür*]. In other words: arbitrary choice is the power of the crown, or the power of the crown is arbitrary choice.

§ 276. The fundamental characteristic of the state as a political entity is the substantial unity, i.e., the ideality, of its moments. (α) In this unity, the particular powers and their activities are dissolved and yet retained. They are retained, however, only in the sense that their authority is no independent one but only one of the order and breadth determined by the Idea of the whole; from its might they originate, and they are its flexible limbs while it is their single self.

Addition: Much the same thing as this ideality of the moments in the state occurs with life in the physical organism.

It is evident that Hegel speaks only of the idea of the particular powers and their activities. They are to have authority only of the order and breadth determined by the idea of the whole; they are to originate from its might. That it should be so lies in the idea of the organism. But it would have to be shown how this is to be achieved. For in the state conscious reason must prevail; [and] substantial, bare internal and therefore bare external necessity, the accidental [. . .]* of the powers and activities cannot be presented as something rational.

§ 277. (β) The particular activities and agencies of the state are its essential moments and therefore are proper to *it*. The individual functionaries and agents are attached to their office not on the strength of their immediate personality, but only on the strength of their universal and objective qualities. Hence it is in an external and contingent way that these offices are linked with particular persons, and therefore the functions and powers of the state cannot be private property.

It is self-evident that if particular activities and agencies are designated as activities and agencies of the state, as state functions and state powers, then they are not private but state property. That is a tautology.

The activities and agencies of the state are attached to individuals (the state is only active through individuals), but not to the individual as physical but political; they are attached to the political quality of the individual. Hence it is ridiculous to say, as Hegel does, that 'it is in an external and contingent way that these offices are linked with particular persons'. On the contrary, they are linked with them by a *vinculum substantiale*, by reason of an essential quality of particular persons. These offices are the natural action of this essential quality. Hence the absurdity of Hegel's conceiving the activities and agencies of the state in the abstract,

---

* The word is unclear; perhaps 'entwining' [*Verschränkung*] or 'entangling' [*Verschlingung*].

and particular individuality in opposition to it. He forgets that particular individuality is a human individual, and that the activities and agencies of the state are human activities. He forgets that the nature of the particular person is not his beard, his blood, his abstract *Physis*, but rather his social quality, and that the activities of the state, etc., are nothing but the modes of existence and operation of the social qualities of men. Thus it is evident that individuals, in so far as they are the bearers of the state's activities and powers, are to be considered according to their social and not their private quality.

§ 278. These two points (α) and (β) constitute the sovereignty of the state. That is to say, sovereignty depends on the fact that the particular functions and powers of the state are not self-subsistent or firmly grounded either on their own account or in the particular will of the individual functionaries, but have their roots ultimately in the unity of the state as their single self.

[Remark:] Despotism means any state of affairs where law has disappeared and where the particular will as such, whether of a monarch or a mob...[1] counts as law, or rather takes the place of law; while it is precisely in legal, constitutional government that sovereignty is to be found as the moment of ideality—the ideality of the particular spheres and functions. That is to say, sovereignty brings it about that each of these spheres is not something independent, self-subsistent in its aims and modes of working, something immersed solely in itself, but that instead, even in these aims and modes of working, each is determined by and dependent on the aim of the whole (the aim which has been denominated in general terms by the rather vague expression 'welfare of the state').

This ideality manifests itself in a twofold way:

(i) In times of peace, the particular spheres and functions pursue the path of satisfying their particular aims and minding their own business, and it is in part only by way of the unconscious necessity of the thing that their self-seeking is turned into a contribution to reciprocal support and to the support of the whole...[1] In part, however, it is by the direct influence of higher authority that they are not only continually brought back to the aims of the whole and restricted accordingly...,[1] but are also constrained to perform direct services for the support of the whole.

(ii) In a situation of exigency, however, whether in home or foreign affairs, the organism of which these particular spheres are members fuses into the single concept of sovereignty. The sovereign is entrusted with the salvation of the state at the sacrifice of these particular authorities whose powers are valid at other times, and it is then that that ideality comes into its proper actuality.

Thus this ideality is not developed into a comprehended, rational system. In times of peace it appears either as merely an external constraint effected by the ruling power on private life through direct influence of higher authority, or a blind uncomprehended result of self-seeking. This ideality has its proper actuality only in the state's situation of war or exigency, such that here its essence is expressed as the actual, existent state's

---

[1] Marx's ellipsis.

situation of war and exigency, while its 'peaceful' situation is precisely the war and exigency of self-seeking.

Accordingly, sovereignty, the ideality of the state, exists merely as internal necessity, as idea. And Hegel is satisfied with that because it is a question merely of the idea. Sovereignty thus exists on the one hand only as unconscious, blind substance. We will become equally well acquainted with its other actuality.

§ 279. Sovereignty, at first simply the universal *thought* of this ideality, comes into *existence* only as subjectivity sure of itself, as the will's abstract and to that extent ungrounded self-determination in which finality of decision is rooted. This is the strictly individual aspect of the state, and in virtue of this alone is the state *one*. The truth of subjectivity, however, is attained only in a subject, and the truth of personality only in a person; and in a constitution which has become mature as a realization of rationality, each of the three moments of the concept has its explicitly actual and separate formation. Hence this absolutely decisive moment of the whole is not individuality in general, but a single individual, the monarch.

1. Sovereignty, at first simply the universal thought of this ideality, comes into existence only as subjectivity sure of itself...The truth of subjectivity is attained only in a subject, and the truth of personality only in a person. In a constitution which has become mature as a realization of rationality, each of the three moments of the concept has...explicitly actual and separate formation.

2. Sovereignty comes into existence only...as the will's abstract and to that extent ungrounded self-determination in which finality of decision is rooted. This is the strictly individual aspect of the state, and in virtue of this alone is the state one...(and in a constitution which has become mature as a realization of rationality, each of the three moments of the concept has its explicitly actual and separate formation). Hence this absolutely decisive moment of the whole is not individuality in general, but a single individual, the monarch.

The first sentence says only that the universal thought of this ideality, whose sorry existence we have just seen, would have to be the self-conscious work of subjects and, as such, exist for and in them.

Had Hegel started with the real subjects as the bases of the state it would not have been necessary for him to let the state become subjectified in a mystical way. 'However, the truth of subjectivity', says Hegel, 'is attained only in a subject, and the truth of personality only in a person.' This too is a mystification. Subjectivity is a characteristic of subjects and personality a characteristic of the person. Instead of considering them to be predicates of their subjects Hegel makes the predicates independent and then lets them be subsequently and mysteriously converted into their subjects.

The existence of the predicate is the subject; thus the subject is the existence of subjectivity, etc. Hegel makes the predicates, the object, independent, but independent as separated from their real independence, their subject. Subsequently, and because of this, the real subject appears to be the result; whereas one has to start from the real subject and examine its objectification. The mystical substance becomes the real subject and the real subject appears to be something else, namely a moment of the mystical substance. Precisely because Hegel starts from the predicates of universal determination instead of from the real *Ens* (ὑποκείμενον, subject), and because there must be a bearer of this determination, the mystical Idea becomes this bearer. This is the dualism: Hegel does not consider the universal to be the actual essence of the actual, finite thing, i.e., of the existing determinate thing, nor the real *Ens* to be the true subject of the infinite.

Accordingly, sovereignty, the essence of the state, is here first conceived to be an independent being; it is objectified. Then, of course, this object must again become subject. However the subject then appears to be a self-incarnation of sovereignty, which is nothing but the objectified spirit of the state's subjects.

This basic defect of the development aside, let us consider the first sentence of the paragraph. As it stands it says nothing more than that sovereignty, the ideality of the state as person, as subject, exists evidently as many persons, many subjects, since no single person absorbs in himself the sphere of personality, nor any single subject the sphere of subjectivity. What kind of ideality of the state would it have to be which, instead of being the actual self-consciousness of the citizens and the communal soul of the state, were *one* person, *one* subject [?] Nor has Hegel developed any more with this sentence. But consider now the second sentence which is joined with this one. What is important to Hegel is representing the monarch as the actual 'God-man', the actual incarnation of the Idea.

Sovereignty...[1] comes into existence only...[1] as the will's abstract and to that extent ungrounded self-determination in which finality of decision is rooted. This is the strictly individual aspect of the state, and in virtue of this alone is the state one... In a constitution which has become mature as a realization of rationality, each of the three moments of the concept has its explicitly actual and separate formation. Hence this absolutely decisive moment of the whole is not individuality in general, but a single individual, the monarch.

We previously called attention to this sentence. The moment of deciding, of arbitrary yet determinate decision is the sovereign power of will in general. The idea of sovereign power, as Hegel develops it, is nothing other than the idea of the arbitrary, of the will's decision.

[1] Marx's ellipses.

But even while conceiving of sovereignty as the ideality of the state, the actual determination of the part through the idea of the whole, Hegel now makes it 'the will's abstract and to that extent ungrounded self-determination in which finality of decision is rooted. This is the strictly individual aspect of the state'. Before, the discussion was about subjectivity, now it's about individuality. The state as sovereign must be one, one individual, it must possess individuality. The state is one not only in this individuality; individuality is only the natural moment of its oneness, the state's determination as nature [*Naturbestimmung*]. 'Hence this absolutely decisive moment of the whole is not individuality in general, but a single individual, the *monarch*.' How so? Because 'each of the three moments of the concept has its explicitly actual and separate formation'. One moment of the concept is oneness, or unity; alone this is not yet one individual. And what kind of constitution would it have to be in which universality, particularity, and unity each had its explicitly actual and separate formation? Because it is altogether a question of no abstraction but of the state, of society, Hegel's classification can be accepted. What follows from that? The citizen as determining the universal is lawgiver, and as the one deciding, as actually willing, is sovereign. Is that supposed to mean that the individuality of the state's will is one individual, a particular individual distinct from all others? Universality too, legislation, has an explicitly actual and separate formation. Could one conclude from that that legislation is these particular individuals[?]

The Common Man:	Hegel:
2. The monarch has the sovereign power, or sovereignty.	2. The sovereignty of the state is the monarch.
3. Sovereignty does what it wills.	3. Sovereignty is 'the will's abstract and to that extent ungrounded self-determination in which finality of decision is rooted'.

Hegel makes all the attributes of the contemporary European constitutional monarch into absolute self-determinations of the will. He does not say the will of the monarch is the final decision, but rather the final decision of the will is the monarch. The first statement is empirical, the second twists the empirical fact into a metaphysical axiom. Hegel joins together the two subjects, sovereignty as subjectivity sure of itself and sovereignty as ungrounded self-determination of the will, as the individual will, in order to construct out of that the Idea as 'one individual'.

It is evident that self-assured subjectivity also must actually will, must will as unity, as an individual. But who ever doubted that the state acts through individuals? If Hegel wanted to develop the idea that the state must have one individual as representative of its individual oneness, then he did not establish the monarch as this individual. The only positive result of this paragraph is that in the state the monarch is the moment of individual will, of ungrounded self-determination, of caprice or arbitrariness.

Hegel's Remark to this paragraph is so peculiar that we must examine it closely:

> The immanent development of a science, the derivation of its entire content from the concept in its simplicity...[1] exhibits this peculiarity, that one and the same concept—the will in this instance—which begins by being abstract (because it is at the beginning), maintains its identity even while it consolidates its specific determinations, and that too solely by its own activity, and in this way gains a concrete content. Hence it is the basic moment of personality, abstract at the start in immediate rights, which has matured itself through its various forms of subjectivity, and now—at the stage of absolute rights, of the state, of the completely concrete objectivity of the will —has become the personality of the state, its certainty of itself. This last reabsorbs all particularity into its single self, cuts short the weighing of pros and cons between which it lets itself oscillate perpetually now this way and now that, and by saying 'I will', makes its decision and so inaugurates all activity and actuality.

To begin with it is not a peculiarity of science that the fundamental concept of the thing always reappears.

But also no advance has then taken place. Abstract personality was the subject of abstract right; there has been no progress, because as personality of the state it remains abstract personality. Hegel should not have been surprised at the real person—and persons make the state—reappearing everywhere as his essence. He should have been surprised at the reverse, and yet still more at the person as personality of the state reappearing in the same impoverished abstraction as does the person of private right.

Hegel here defines the monarch as the personality of the state, its certainty of itself. The monarch is personified sovereignty, sovereignty become man, incarnate state- [or political-] consciousness, whereby all other persons are thus excluded from this sovereignty, from personality, and from state- [or political-] consciousness. At the same time however Hegel can give this '*Souveraineté-Personne*' no more content than 'I will', the moment of arbitrariness in the will. The state-reason and state-consciousness is a unique empirical person to the exclusion of all others, but this personified Reason has no content except the abstraction, 'I will'. *L'Etat c'est moi.*

Further, however, personality like subjectivity in general, as infinitely self-related, has its truth (to be precise, its most elementary, immediate truth) only in

---

[1] Marx's ellipsis.

a person, in a subject existing 'for' himself, and what exists 'for' itself is just simply a unit.

It is obvious that personality and subjectivity, being only predicates of the person and the subject, exist only as person and subject; and indeed that the person is one. But Hegel needed to go further, for clearly the one has truth only as many one's. The predicate, the essence, never exhausts the spheres of its existence in a single one but in many one's.

Instead of this Hegel concludes: 'The personality of the state is actual only as one person, the monarch.'

Thus, because subjectivity is actual only as subject, and the subject actual only as one, the personality of the state is actual only as one person. A beautiful conclusion. Hegel could just as well conclude that because the individual man is one the human species is only a single man.

Personality expresses the concept as such; but at the same time the person enshrines the actuality of the concept, and only when the concept is determined as a person is it the Idea or truth.

To be sure, personality is merely an abstraction without the person, but only in its species-existence as persons is person the actual idea of personality.

A so-called 'artificial [*moralische*] person', be it a society, a community, or a family, however inherently concrete it may be, contains personality only abstractly, as one moment of itself. In an 'artificial person', personality has not yet achieved its true mode of existence. The state, however, is precisely this totality in which the moments of the concept have attained the actuality correspondent to their degree of truth.

A great confusion prevails here. The artificial person, society, etc., is called abstract, precisely those species-forms [*Gattungsgestaltungen*] in which the actual person brings his actual content to existence, objectifies himself, and leaves behind the abstraction of 'person *quand même*'. Instead of recognizing this actualization of the person as the most concrete thing, the state is to have the priority in order that the moments of the concept, individuality, attain a mystical existence. Rationality does not consist in the reason of the actual person achieving actuality, but in the moments of the abstract concept achieving it.

The concept of the monarch is therefore of all concepts the hardest for ratiocination, i.e., for the method of reflection employed by the Understanding. This method refuses to move beyond isolated categories and hence here again knows only *raisonne-ment*, finite points of view, and deductive argumentation. Consequently it exhibits the dignity of the monarch as something deduced, not only in its form but in its essence. The truth is, however, that to be something not deduced but purely self-originating is precisely the concept of monarchy. Akin then to this reasoning (to be sure!)[1] is the idea of treating the monarch's right as grounded in the authority of God, since it is in its divinity that its unconditional character is contained.

In a certain sense every inevitable existent is purely self-originating; in this respect the monarch's louse as well as the monarch. Hegel, in saying that, has not said something special about the monarch. But should something specifically distinct from all other objects of science and of the philosophy of right be said about the monarch, then this would be real foolishness, correct only in so far as the '*one* Person-idea' is something derived only from the imagination and not the intellect.

We may speak of the 'sovereignty of the people' in the sense that any people whatever is self-subsistent *vis-à-vis* other peoples, and constitutes a state of its own, etc.

That is a triviliality. If the sovereign is the actual sovereignty of the state then the sovereign could necessarily be considered *vis-à-vis* others as a self-subsistent state, even without the people. But he is sovereign in so far as he represents the unity of the people, and thus he is himself merely a representative, a symbol of the sovereignty of the people. The sovereignty of the people is not due to him but on the contrary he is due to it.

We may also speak of sovereignty in home affairs residing in the people, provided that we are speaking generally about the whole state and meaning only what was shown above (see Paragraphs 277, 278), namely that it is to the state that sovereignty belongs.

As though the people [*das Volk*] were not the real state. The state is an abstraction; the people alone is the concrete. And it is noteworthy that Hegel, who without hesitation ascribes living qualities to the abstraction, ascribes a living quality like that of sovereignty to the concrete [—i.e. to the people—] only with hesitation and conditions.

The usual sense, however, in which men have recently begun to speak of the 'sovereignty of the people' is that it is something opposed to the sovereignty existent in the monarch. So opposed to the sovereignty of the monarch, the sovereignty of the people is one of the confused notions based on the wild idea of the 'people'.

The confused notions and the wild idea are only here on Hegel's pages. Certainly if sovereignty exists in the monarch then it is foolishness to speak of an opposed sovereignty in the people, for it lies in the concept of sovereignty that it can have no double and absolutely opposed existence. But:

1. the question is exactly: Is not the sovereignty existent in the monarch an illusion? Sovereignty of the monarch or sovereignty of the people, that is the question;

[1] Marx's insertion.

2. a sovereignty of the people in opposition to that existent in the monarch can also be spoken of. But then it is not a question of one and the same sovereignty taking form on two sides but rather of two completely opposed concepts of sovereignty, one such that it can come to existence in a monarch, the other such that it can come to existence only in a people. This is like asking, is God the sovereign or is man? One of the two is a fiction [*eine Unwarheit*] even though an existing fiction.

Taken without its monarch and the articulation of the whole which is the indispensable and direct concomitant of monarchy, the people is a formless mass and no longer a state. It lacks every one of those determinate characteristics—sovereignty, government, judges, magistrates, class-divisions [*Stände*], etc.,—which are to be found only in a whole which is inwardly organized. By the very emergence into a people's life of moments of this kind which have a bearing on an organization, on political life, a people ceases to be that indeterminate abstraction which, when represented in a quite general way, is called the 'people'.

This whole thing is a tautology. If a people has a monarch and an articulation which is its indispensable and direct concomitant, i.e., if it is articulated as a monarchy, then extracted from this articulation it is certainly a formless mass and a quite general notion.

If by 'sovereignty of the people' is understood a republican form of government, or to speak more specifically... [1] a democratic form, then... [1] such a notion cannot be further discussed in face of the Idea of the state in its full development.

That is certainly correct if one has only such a notion and no developed idea of democracy.

Democracy is the truth of monarchy, monarchy is not the truth of democracy. Monarchy is necessarily democracy in contradiction with itself, whereas the monarchial moment is no contradiction within democracy. Monarchy cannot, while democracy can be understood in terms of itself. In democracy none of the moments obtains a significance other than what befits it. Each is really only a moment of the whole *Demos*. In monarchy one part determines the character of the whole; the entire constitution must be modified according to the immutable head. Democracy is the generic constitution; monarchy is a species, and indeed a poor one. Democracy is content and form; monarchy *should* be only form, but it adulterates the content.

In monarchy the whole, the people, is subsumed under one of its modes of existence, the political constitution; in democracy the constitution itself appears only as one determination, and indeed as the self-determination of the people. In monarchy we have the people of the constitution, in democracy the constitution of the people. Democracy is the

---

[1] Marx's ellipses.

resolved mystery of all constitutions. Here the constitution not only in itself, according to essence, but according to existence and actuality is returned to its real ground, actual man, the actual people, and established as its own work. The constitution appears as what it is, the free product of men. One could say that this also applies in a certain respect to constitutional monarchy; only the specific difference of democracy is that here the constitution is in general only one moment of the people's existence, that is to say the political constitution does not form the state for itself.

Hegel proceeds from the state and makes man into the subjectified state; democracy starts with man and makes the state objectified man. Just as it is not religion that creates man but man who creates religion, so it is not the constitution that creates the people but the people which creates the constitution. In a certain respect democracy is to all other forms of the state what Christianity is to all other religions. Christianity is the religion κατ' ἐξοχήν, the essence of religion, deified man under the form of a particular religion. In the same way democracy is the essence of every political constitution, socialized man under the form of a particular constitution of the state. It stands related to other constitutions as the genus to its species; only here the genus itself appears as an existent, and therefore opposed as a particular species to those existents which do not conform to the essence. Democracy relates to all other forms of the state as their Old Testament. Man does not exist because of the law but rather the law exists for the good of man. Democracy is *human existence*, while in the other political forms man has only *legal* existence. That is the fundamental difference of democracy.

All remaining forms of the state are certain, determined, particular forms of the state. In democracy the formal principle is simultaneously the material principle. For that reason it is the first true unity of the universal and the particular. In monarchy for example, [or] in the republic as merely a particular form of the state, political man has his particular and separate existence beside the unpolitical, private man. Property, contract, marriage, civil society appear here (just as Hegel quite rightly develops them for abstract forms of the state, except that he means to develop the Idea of the state) as particular modes of existence alongside the political state; that is, they appear as the content to which the political state relates as organizing form, or really only as the determining, limiting intelligence which says now 'yes' now 'no' without any content of its own. In democracy the political state, as placed alongside this content and differentiated from it, is itself merely a particular content, like a particular form of existence of the people. In monarchy, for example, this particular entity, the political constitution, has the meaning of the universal which governs and determines all the particulars. In democracy the state as particular is only particular, and as universal it is the real universal, i.e., it is nothing definite in distinction from the other content. The modern French have conceived it thus: In true democracy the *political state disappears* [*der politische Staat untergehe*]. This is correct inasmuch as *qua* political state, *qua* constitution it is no longer equivalent to the whole.

In all states distinct from democracy the state, the law, the constitution is dominant without really governing, that is, materially permeating the content of the remaining non-political spheres. In democracy the constitution, the law, the state, so far as it is political constitution, is itself only a self-determination of the people, and a determinate content of the people.

Furthermore it is evident that all forms of the state have democracy for their truth, and for that reason are false to the extent that they are not democracy.

In the ancient state the political state shaped the content of the state, with the other spheres being excluded; the modern state is an accomodation between the political and the non-political state.

In democracy the abstract state has ceased to be the governing moment. The struggle between monarchy and republic is itself still a struggle within the abstract form of the state. The political republic [—that is, the republic merely as political constitution—] is democracy within the abstract form of the state. Hence the abstract state-form of democracy is the republic; but here [in true democracy] it ceases to be mere political constitution.

Property, etc., in brief the entire content of law and the state is, with small modification, the same in North America as in Prussia. There, accordingly, the republic is a mere state form just as the monarchy is here. The content of the state lies outside these constitutions. Hence Hegel is right when he says that the political state is the constitution, i.e., that the material state is not political. Merely an external identity, a mutual determination, obtains here. It was most difficult to form the political state, the constitution, out of the various moments of the life of the people. It was developed as the universal reason in opposition to the other spheres i.e., as something opposed to them. The historical task then consisted in their revindication. But the particular spheres, in doing that, are not conscious of the fact that their private essence declines in relation to the opposite essence of the constitution, or political state, and that its opposite existence is nothing but the affirmation of their own alienation. The political constitution was until now the religious sphere, the religion of popular life, the heaven of its universality in opposition to the earthly existence of its actuality. The political sphere was the sole sphere of the state within the state, the sole sphere in which the content, like the form, was species-content, the true universal, but at the same time in such a way that, because this sphere opposed the others, its content also became formal and particular. Political life in the modern sense is the Scholasticism of popular life. Monarchy is the fullest expression of this alienation. The republic is the negation of this alienation within its own sphere. It is obvious that the political constitution as such is perfected for the first time when the private spheres have attained independent existence. Where commerce and property in land are not free, not yet autonomous, there is also not yet the political constitution. The Middle Ages was the democracy of non-freedom.

The abstraction of the state as such belongs only to modern times because the abstraction of private life belongs only to modern times. The abstraction of the political state is a modern product.

In the Middle Ages there was serf, feudal property, trade corporation, corporation of scholars, etc., that is, in the Middle Ages property, trade, society, man was political; the material content of the state was fixed by reason of its form; every private sphere had a political character or was a political sphere, or again, politics was also the character of the private spheres. In the Middle Ages the political constitution was the constitution of private property, but only because the constitution of private property was a political one. In the Middle Ages popular life and state [i.e., political] life were identical. Man was the actual principle of the state, but he was unfree man. It was therefore the democracy of unfreedom, accomplished alienation. The abstract, reflected opposition [between popular life and state-, or political-life] belong only to modern times. The Middle Ages was the real dualism; modern times is the abstract dualism.

At the stage at which constitutions are divided, as above mentioned, into democracy, aristocracy, and monarchy, the point of view taken is that of a still substantial unity, abiding in itself, without having yet embarked on its infinite differentiation and the plumbing of its own depths. At that stage, the moment of the final, self-determining decision of the will does not come on the scene explicitly in its own proper actuality as an organic moment immanent in the state.

In immediate monarchy, democracy, aristocracy there is yet no political constitution in distinction from the actual material state or from the remaining content of popular life. The political state does not yet appear as the form of the material state. Either, as in Greece, the *res publica* was the real private concern, the real content of the citizen, and the private man was slave, that is, the political state as political was the true and sole content of the citizen's life and will; or, as in Asiatic despotism, the political state was nothing but the private will of a single individual, and the political state, like the material state, was slave. What distinguishes the modern state from these states in which a substantial unity between people and state obtained is not that the various moments of the constitution are formed into particular actuality, as Hegel would have it, but rather that the constitution itself has been formed into a particular actuality alongside the real life of the people, the political state has become the constitution of the rest of the state.

§ 280. This ultimate self in which the will of the state is concentrated is, when thus taken in abstraction, a single self and therefore is *immediate* individuality. Hence its natural character is implied in its very conception. The monarch, therefore, is essentially characterized as *this* individual, in abstraction from all his other characteristics, and *this* individual is raised to the dignity of monarchy in an immediate, natural fashion, i.e., through his birth in the course of nature.

We have already heard that subjectivity is subject and that the subject is necessarily an empirical individual, a *one*. Now we are told that the concept of naturality, of corporeality, is implied in the concept of immediate individuality. Hegel has proven nothing but what is self-evident, namely, that subjectivity exists only as a corporeal individual, and what is obvious, namely, that natural birth appertains to the corporeal individual.

Hegel thinks he has proven that the subjectivity of the state, sovereignty, the monarch, is 'essentially characterized as *this* individual, in abstraction from all his other characteristics, and this individual is raised to the dignity of monarch in an immediate, natural fashion, i.e., through his birth in the course of nature'. Sovereignty, monarchial dignity, would thus be born. The *body* of the monarch determines his dignity. Thus at the highest point of the state bare *Physis* rather than reason would be the determining factor. Birth would determine the quality of the monarch as it determines the quality of cattle.

Hegel has demonstrated that the monarch must be born, which no one questions, but not that birth makes one a monarch.

That man becomes monarch by birth can as little be made into a metaphysical truth as can the Immaculate Conception of Mary. The latter notion, a fact of consciousness, just as well as the empirical fact of the birth of man to the monarchy, can be understood as rooted in human illusion and conditions.

In the Remark, which we examine more closely, Hegel takes pleasure in having demonstrated the irrational to be absolutely rational.

This transition of the concept of pure self-determination into the immediacy of being and so into the realm of nature is of a purely speculative character, and apprehension of it therefore belongs to logic.

Indeed it is purely speculative. But what is purely speculative is not the transition from pure self-determination, from an abstraction, to pure naturality (to the contingency of birth), to the other extreme, *car les extrêmes se touchent*. What is speculative is that this is called a 'transition of the concept', and that absolute contradiction is presented as identity, and ultimate inconsistency presented as consistency.

This can be considered as Hegel's positive acknowledgment: with the hereditary monarch in the place of self-determining reason, abstract natural determinacy appears not as what it is, not as natural determinacy, but as the highest determination of the state; this is the positive point at which the monarchy can no longer preserve the appearance of being the organization of the rational will.

Moreover, this transition is on the whole the same(?)[1] as that familiar to us in the nature of willing in general, and there the process is to translate something from subjectivity (i.e., some purpose held before the mind) into existence...[2] But the proper form of the Idea and of the transition here under consideration is the immediate conversion of the pure self-determination of the will (i.e., of the simple concept itself) into a single and natural existent without the mediation of a particular content (like a purpose in the case of action).

Hegel says that the conversion of the sovereignty of the state (of a self-determination of the will) into the body of the born monarch (into existence) is *on the whole* the transition of the content in general, which the will makes in order to actualize an end which is thought of, that is, to translate it into an existent. But Hegel says 'on the whole'. And the proper difference which he specifies [—namely, immediate conversion of the pure self-determination of the will into a single and natural existent without the mediation of a particular content—] is so proper that it eliminates all analogy and puts *magic* in the place of the 'nature of willing in general'.

First of all, the conversion of the purpose held before the mind into the existent is here immediate, magical. Second, the subject here is the pure self-determination of the will, the simple concept itself; it is the essence of will which, as a mystical subject, decides. It is no real, individual, conscious will; it is the abstraction of the will which changes into a natural existent; it is the pure Idea which embodies itself as one individual.

Third, since the actualization of the volition in a natural existent takes place immediately, i.e., without a medium—which the will requires as a rule in order to objectify itself—then even a particular, determinate end is lacking; no mediation of a particular content, like a purpose in the case of action, takes place, which is evident because no acting subject is present,

---

[1] Marx's insertion.   [2] Marx's ellipsis.

and the abstraction, the pure idea of will, in order to act must act mystically. Now an end which is not particular is no end, and an act without an end is an endless, senseless act. Thus this whole parallel with the teleological act of the will shows itself finally to be a mystification, an empty action of the Idea. [In fact,] the medium here is the absolute will and the word of the philosopher; the particular end is the end of the philosophizing subject, namely, constructing the hereditary monarch out of the pure Idea; and the actualization of the end is Hegel's simple affirmation.

In the so-called 'ontological' proof of the existence of God, we have the same conversion of the absolute concept into existence (the same mystification),[1] which conversion has constituted the depth of the Idea in the modern world, although recently (and rightly)[1] it has been declared *inconceivable*.

But since the idea of the monarch is regarded as being quite familiar to ordinary (i.e., understanding)[1] consciousness, the Understanding clings here all the more tenaciously to its separation and the conclusions which its astute ratiocination deduces therefrom. As a result, it denies that the moment of ultimate decision in the state is linked *implicitly and actually* (i.e. in the rational concept) with the immediate birthright of the monarch.

It is denied that ultimate decision is a birthright, and Hegel asserts that the monarch is the ultimate decision through birth. But who has ever doubted that the ultimate decision in the state is joined to a real bodily individual and is linked with the immediate birthright?

§ 281. Both moments in their undivided unity—(a) the will's ultimate ungrounded self, and (b) therefore its similarly ungrounded objective existence (existence being the category which is at home in nature)—constitute the Idea of something against which caprice is powerless, the 'majesty' of the monarch. In this unity lies the actual unity of the state, and it is only through this, its inward and outward immediacy, that the unity of the state is saved from the risk of being drawn down into the sphere of particularity and its caprices, ends and opinions, and saved too from the war of factions round the throne and from the enfeeblement and overthrow of the power of the state.

The two moments are [a] the contingency of the will, caprice, and [b] the contingency of nature, birth; thus, His Majesty: Contingency. Contingency is thus the actual unity of the state.

The way in which, according to Hegel, an inward and outward immediacy [of the state] is to be saved from collision, [due to caprice, factions,] etc., is incredible, since collision is precisely what it makes possible.

What Hegel asserts of the elective monarch applies even more to the hereditary monarchy:

---

[1] Marx's insertions.

In an elective monarchy...the nature of the relation between king and people implies that the ultimate decision is left with the particular will, and hence the constitution becomes a Compact of Election, i.e., a surrender of the power of the state at the discretion of the particular will. The result of this is that the particular offices of state turn into private property, etc.

§ 282. The right to pardon criminals arises from the sovereignty of the monarch, since it is this alone which is empowered to actualize mind's power of making undone what has been done and wiping out a crime by forgiving and forgetting it.

The right to pardon is the right to exercise clemency, the ultimate expression of contingent and arbitrary choice. Significantly this is what Hegel makes the essential attribute of the monarch. In the Addition to this very paragraph he defines the source of pardon as 'self-determined [or groundless] decision' [*die grundlose Entscheidung*].

§ 283. The second moment in the power of the crown is the moment of particularity, or the moment of a determinate content and its subsumption under the universal. When this acquires a special objective existence, it becomes the supreme council and the individuals who compose it. They bring before the monarch for his decision the content of current affairs of state or the legal provision required to meet existing needs, together with their objective aspects, i.e., the grounds on which decision is to be based, the relative laws, circumstances, etc. The individuals who discharge these duties are in direct contact with the person of the monarch and therefore the choice and dismissal alike of these individuals rest with his unrestricted caprice.

§ 284. It is only for the *objective* side of decision, i.e., for knowledge of the problem and the attendant circumstances, and for the legal and other reasons which determine its solution, that men are answerable; in other words, it is these alone which are capable of objective proof. It is for this reason that these may fall within the province of a council which is distinct from the personal will of the monarch as such. Hence it is only councils or their individual members that are made answerable. The personal majesty of the monarch, on the other hand, as the final *subjectivity* of decision, is above all answerability for acts of government.

Here Hegel describes in a wholly empirical way the ministerial power as it is usually defined in constitutional states. The only thing philosophy does with this empirical fact is to make it the existence and the predicate of the moment of particularity in the power of the crown.

(The ministers represent the rational objective side of the sovereign will. Hence also the *honor* of being answerable falls to them, while the monarch is compensated with the imaginary coin of 'Majesty'.) Thus the speculative moment is quite poor. But then the development is based particularly on wholly empirical grounds, and indeed very abstract and bad empirical grounds.

Thus, for example, the choice of ministers is placed in the unrestricted caprice of the monarch because they are in direct contact with the person of the monarch, i.e., because they are ministers. In the same way the unrestricted choice of the monarch's personal servants can be developed out of the absolute Idea.

The basis for the answerability of the ministers is certainly better: 'It is only for the objective side of decision, i.e., for knowledge of the problem and the attendant circumstances, and for the legal and other reasons which determine its solution, that men are answerable: in other words, it is these alone which are capable of objective proof.' Evidently 'the final subjectivity of decision', pure subjectivity, pure caprice, is not objective, hence also capable of no objective proof nor therefore of responsibility, once an individual is the blessed, sanctioned existence of caprice. Hegel's proof is conclusive if the constitutional provisions are taken as the point of departure; but these provisions themselves are not proven simply by analyzing them, and this is all Hegel has done.

The whole uncritical character of Hegel's philosophy of right is rooted in this confusion.

§ 285. The third moment in the power of the crown concerns the absolute universality which subsists subjectively in the conscience of the monarch and objectively in the whole of the constitution and the laws. Hence the power of the crown presupposes the other moments in the state just as it is presupposed by each of them.

§ 286. The *objective* guarantee of the power of the crown, of the hereditary right of succession to the throne, and so forth, consists in the fact that just as monarchy has its own actuality in distinction from that of the other rationally determined moments in the state, so these others explicitly possess the rights and duties appropriate to their own character. In the rational organism of the state, each member, by maintaining itself in its own position, *eo ipso* maintains the others in theirs.

Hegel does not see that with this third moment, the 'absolute universality', he obliterates the first two, or vice versa. 'The power of the crown presupposes the other moments in the state just as it is presupposed by each of them.' If this supposition is taken as real and not mystical, then the crown is established not through birth but through the other moments, and accordingly is not hereditary but fluid, i.e., determined by the state and assigned by turns to individuals of the state in accordance with the organization of the other moments. In a rational organism the head cannot be iron and the body flesh. In order to preserve themselves the members must be equally of one flesh and blood. But the hereditary monarch is not equal, he is of other stuff. Here the prosaic character of the rationalistic will of the other members of the state faces the magic of nature. Moreover, members can mutually maintain themselves only in so far as the whole organism is fluid and each of them is taken up [*aufgehoben*] in this fluidity, in so far as no one of them, as in this case the head of the state, is unmoved and inalterable. Thus by means of this determination Hegel abolishes sovereignty by birth.

A second point has to do with the question of irresponsibility. If the prince violates the whole of the constitution, and the laws, his irresponsibility ceases because his constitutional existence ceases. But precisely these laws and this constitution make him irresponsible. Thus they contradict themselves, and this *one* stipulation abolishes law and constitution. The constitution of constitutional monarchy is *irresponsibility*.

Hegel, however, is content with saying that just as monarchy has its own actuality in distinction from that of the other rationally determined moments in the state, so these others explicitly possess the rights and duties appropriate to their own character. Therefore he must call the constitution of the Middle Ages an organization. Thus Hegel has only a mass of particular spheres united in a relation of external necessity, and indeed an individual monarch belongs only to this situation. In a state wherein each determination exists explicitly, the sovereignty of the state must also be established as a particular individual.

Résumé of Hegel's development of the Crown or the Idea of State Sovereignty

The Remark to § 279 says:

We may speak of the 'sovereignty of the people' in the sense that any people whatever is self-subsistent *vis-à-vis* other peoples, and constitutes a state of its own, like the British people for instance. But the peoples of England, Scotland, or Ireland, or the peoples of Venice, Genoa, Ceylon, etc. are not sovereign peoples at all now that they have ceased to have rulers or supreme governments of their own.

Thus here sovereignty of the people is nationality, and the sovereignty of the prince is nationality; or in other words the principle of principality is nationality, which explicitly and exclusively forms the sovereignty of a people. A people whose sovereignty consists *only* in nationality has a monarch. The different nationality of peoples cannot be better established and expressed than by means of different monarchs. The cleft between one absolute individual and another is the cleft between these nationalities.

The Greeks (and Romans) were national because and in so far as they were the sovereign people. The Germans are sovereign because and in so far as they are national. (*Vid. pag.* XXXIV.)[1]

---

[1] Here Marx refers to material found on pp. 130–2 of *Bogen* XXXIV in the manuscript. All of the German language editions insert at this point the material from the indicated manuscript pages which begins with the indented text from Hegel's Remark to § 279, given immediately below, and concludes (on our p. 40) with, 'He is the lone private person in whom the relation of the private person in general to the state is actualized.'

(ad xii) A so-called 'artificial person', the same Remark says further, be it a society, a community, or a family, however inherently concrete it may be, contains personality only abstractly, as one moment of itself. In an 'artificial person', personality has not achieved its true mode of existence. The state, however, is precisely this totality in which the moments of the concept have attained the actuality correspondent to their degree of truth.

This artificial person, society, family, etc., has personality within it only abstractly; against that, in the monarch, the person has the state in him.

In fact, the abstract person brings his personality to its real existence only in the artificial person, society, family, etc. But Hegel conceives of society, family, etc., the artificial person in general, not as the realization of the actual, empirical person but as the *real* person which, however, has the moment of personality in it only abstractly. Whence also comes his notion that it is not actual persons who come to be a state but the state which must first come to be an actual person. Instead of the state being brought forth, therefore, as the ultimate reality of the person, as the ultimate social reality of man, a single empirical man, an empirical person, is brought forth as the ultimate actuality of the state. This inversion of subject into object and object into subject is a consequence of Hegel's wanting to write the biography of the abstract Substance, of the Idea, with human activity, etc., having consequently to appear as the activity and result of something other than man; it is a consequence of Hegel's wanting to allow the essence of man to act for itself as an imaginary individual instead of acting in its actual, human existence, and it necessarily has as its result that an empirical existent is taken in an uncritical manner to be the real truth of the Idea, because it is not a question of bringing empirical existence to its truth but of bringing the truth to empirical existence, and thereupon the obvious is developed as a real moment of the Idea. (More later concerning this inevitable change of the empirical into speculation and of speculation into the empirical.)

In this way the impression of something mystical and profound is also created. That man has been born is quite vulgar, so too that this existence established through physical birth comes to be social man, etc., and citizen; man becomes everything that he becomes through his birth. But it is very profound and striking that the idea of the state is directly born, that it has brought itself forth into empirical existence in the birth of the sovereign. In this way no content is gained, only the form of the old content altered. It has received a philosophical form, a philosophical certification.

Another consequence of this mystical speculation is that a particular empirical existent, a single empirical existent in distinction from the others is conceived to be the existence of the Idea. It makes once again a deep mystical impression to see a particular empirical existent established by the Idea, and hence to encounter at all levels an incarnation of God.

If the modes of man's social existence, as found for example in the development of family, civil society, state, etc., are regarded as the actualization and objectification of man's essence, then family, civil society, etc., appear as qualities inhering in subjects. Man then remains what is essential within these realities, while these then appear as his actualized universality, and hence also as something common to all men. But if, on the contrary, family, civil society, state, etc., are determinations of the Idea, of Substance as subject, then they must receive an empirical actuality, and the mass of men in which the idea of civil society is developed takes on the identity of citizen of civil society, and that in which the idea of the state is developed takes on that of citizen of the state. In this case the sole concern is with allegory, i.e., with ascribing to any empirical existent the meaning of actualized Idea; and thus it is evident that these receptacles have fulfilled their destiny once they have become a determinate incarnation of a life-moment of the Idea. Consequently the universal appears everywhere as a determinate particular thing, while the individual nowhere arrives at his true universality.

At the most profound and speculative level it therefore appears necessary when the most abstract determinations which in no way really ripen to true social actuality, the natural bases of the state like birth (in the case of the prince) or private property (as in primogeniture), appear to be the highest, immediate Idea-become-man.

It is evident that the true method is turned upside down. What is most simple is made most complex and vice versa. What should be the point of departure becomes the mystical result, and what should be the rational result becomes the mystical point of departure.

If however the prince is the abstract person who has the state in him, then this can only mean that the essence of the state is the abstract private person. It utters its secret only when at the peak of its development. He is the lone private person in whom the relation of the private person in general to the state is actualized.

The prince's hereditary character results from his concept. He is to be the person who is specified from the entire race of men, who is distinguished from all other persons. But then what is the ultimate fixed difference of one person from all others? The body. And the highest function of the body is sexual activity. Hence the highest constitutional act of the king is his sexual activity, because through this he makes a king and carries on his body. The body of his son is the reproduction of his own body, the creation of a royal body.

(b) *The Executive*

§ **287.** There is a distinction between the monarch's decisions and their execution and application, or in general between his decisions and the continued execution or maintenance of past decisions, existing laws, regulations, organizations for the securing of common ends, and so forth. This task of...[1] subsuming the particular under the universal is comprised in the executive power, which also includes the powers of the judiciary and the police. The latter have a more immediate bearing on the particular concerns of civil society and they make the universal interest authoritative over its particular aims.

This is the usual interpretation of the executive. The only thing which can be mentioned as original with Hegel is that he coordinates executive, police, and judiciary, where as a rule the administrative and judiciary powers are treated as opposed.

§ **288.** Particular interests which are common to everyone fall within civil society and lie outside the absolutely universal interest of the state proper (see Paragraph 256). The administration of these is in the hands of Corporations (see Paragraph 251), commercial and professional as well as municipal, and their officials, directors, managers, and the like. It is the business of these officials to manage the private property and interests of these particular spheres and, from that point of view, their authority rests on the confidence of their commonalties and professional equals. On the other hand, however, these circles of particular interests must be subordinated to the higher interests of the state, and hence the filling of positions of responsibilty in Corporations, etc., will generally be effected by a mixture of popular election by those interested with appointment and ratification by higher authority.

This is a simple description of the empirical situation in some countries.

§ **289.** The maintenance of the state's universal interest, and of legality, in this sphere of particular rights, and the work of bringing these rights back to the universal, require to be superintended by holders of the executive power, by (a) the executive civil servants and (b) the higher advisory officials (who are organized into committees). These converge in their supreme heads who are in direct contact with the monarch.

Hegel has not developed the executive. But given this, he has not demonstrated that it is anything more than a function, a determination of the citizen in general. By viewing the particular interests of civil society as such, as interests which lie outside the absolutely universal interest of the state, he has only deduced the executive as a particular, separate power.

[Remark to 289:] Just as civil society is the battlefield where everyone's individual private interest meets everyone else's, so here we have the struggle (a) of private interests against particular matters of common concern and (b) of both of these together against the organization of the state and its higher outlook. At the same time the corporation mind, engendered when the particular spheres gain their title to

---

[1] Marx's ellipsis.

rights, is now inwardly converted into the mind of the state, since it finds in the state the means of maintaining its particular ends. This is the secret of the patriotism of the citizens in the sense that they know the state as their substance, because it is the state that maintains their particular spheres of interest together with the title, authority, and welfare of these. In the corporation mind the rooting of the particular in the universal is directly entailed, and for this reason it is in that mind that the depth and strength which the state possesses in sentiment is seated.

This is especially worth noting:

(1) because of the definition of civil society as the *bellum omnium contra omnes*;

(2) because private egoism is revealed to be the secret of the patriotism of the citizens and the depth and strength which the state possesses in sentiment;

(3) because the 'burgher', the man of particular interest as opposed to the universal, the member of civil society, is considered to be a fixed individual whereas the state likewise in fixed individuals opposes the 'burghers'.

One would suppose that Hegel would have to define 'civil society' as well as the 'family' as a determination of each political individual, and so too the later state qualities as equally a determination of the political individual. But with Hegel it is not one and the same individual who develops a new determination of his social essence. It is the essence of the will, which allegedly develops its determinations out of itself. The subsisting, distinct and separated, empirical existences of the state are conceived to be immediate incarnations of one of these determinations.

Just as the universal as such is rendered independent it is immediately mixed in with what empirically exists, and then this limited existent is immediately and uncritically taken for the expression of the Idea.

Here Hegel comes into contradiction with himself only in so far as he does not conceive of the 'family' man in the same way he conceived of the member of civil society, i.e., as a fixed breed excluded from other qualities.

§ **290.** Division of labor...[1] occurs in the business of the executive also. For this reason, the organization of officials has the abstract though difficult task of so arranging that (a) civil life shall be governed in a concrete manner from below where it is concrete, but that (b) none the less the business of government shall be divided into its abstract branches manned by special officials as different centers of administration, and further that (c) the operations of these various departments shall converge again when they are directed on civil life from above, in the same way as they converge into a general supervision in the supreme executive.

The Addition to this paragraph is to be considered later.

[1] Marx's ellipsis.

§ 291. The nature of the executive functions is that they are objective and that in their substance they have been explicitly fixed by previous decisions (see Paragraph 287); these functions have to be fulfilled and carried out by individuals. Between an individual and his office there is no immediate natural link. Hence individuals are not appointed to office on account of their birth or native personal gifts. The *objective* factor in their appointment is knowledge and proof of ability. Such proof guarantees that the state will get what it requires; and since it is the sole condition of appointment, it also guarantees to every citizen the chance of joining the class of civil servants [*dem allgemeinen Stande*].

§ 292. Since the objective qualification for the civil service is not genius (as it is for work as an artist, for example), there is of necessity an indefinite plurality of eligible candidates whose relative excellence is not determinable with absolute precision. The selection of one of the candidates, his nomination to office, and the grant to him of full authority to transact public business—all this, as the linking of two things, a man and his office, which in relation to each other must always be fortuitous, is the *subjective* aspect of election to office, and it must lie with the crown as the power in the state which is sovereign and has the last word.

§ 293. The particular public functions which the monarch entrusts to officials constitute one part of the objective aspect of the sovereignty residing in the crown. Their specific discrimination is therefore given in the nature of the thing. And while the actions of the officials are the fulfillment of their duty, their office is also a right exempt from contingency.

Note only the objective aspect of the sovereignty residing in the crown.

§ 294. Once an individual has been appointed to his official position by the sovereign's act (see Paragraph 292), the tenure of his post is conditional on his fulfilling his duties. Such fulfillment is the very essence of his appointment, and it is only consequential that he finds in his office his livelihood and the assured satisfaction of his particular interests (see Paragraph 264), and further that his external circumstances and his official work are freed from other kinds of subjective dependence and influence.

What the service of the state...[1] requires, it says in the Remark, is that men shall forgo the selfish and capricious satisfaction of their subjective ends; by this very sacrifice, they acquire the right to find their satisfaction in, but only in, the dutiful discharge of their public functions. In this fact, so far as public business is concerned, there lies the link between universal and particular interests which constitutes both the concept of the state and its inner stability (see Paragraph 260)...[1] The assured satisfaction of particular needs removes the external compulsion which may tempt a man to seek ways and means of satisfying them at the expense of his official duties. Those who are entrusted with affairs of state find in its universal power the protection they need against another subjective phenomenon, namely the personal passions of the governed, whose primitive interests, etc., suffer injury as the universal interest of the state is made to prevail against them.

§ 295. The security of the state and its subjects against the misuse of power by ministers and their officials lies directly in their hierarchical organization and their

---

[1] Marx's ellipsis.

answerability; but it lies too in the authority given to societies and Corporations, because in itself this is a barrier against the intrusion of subjective caprice into the power entrusted to a civil servant, and it completes from below the state control which does not reach down as far as the conduct of individuals.

§ **296.** But the fact that a dispassionate, upright, and polite demeanor becomes customary [in civil servants][1] is (i) partly a result of direct education in thought and ethical conduct. Such an education is a mental counterpoise to the mechanical and semi-mechanical activity involved in acquiring the so-called 'sciences' of matters connected with administration, in the requisite business training, in the actual work done, etc. (ii) The size of the state, however, is an important factor in producing this result, since it diminishes the stress of family and other personal ties, and also makes less potent and so less keen such passions as hatred, revenge, etc. In those who are busy with the important questions arising in a great state, these subjective interests automatically disappear, and the habit is generated of adopting universal interests, points of view, and activities.

§ **297.** Civil servants and the members of the executive constitute the greater part of the middle class, the class in which the consciousness of right and the developed intelligence of the mass of the people is found. The sovereign working on the middle class at the top, and Corporation-rights working on it at the bottom, are the institutions which effectively prevent it from acquiring the isolated position of an aristocracy and using its education and skill as means to an arbitrary tyranny.

Addition [to § 297.] The middle class, to which civil servants belong, is politically conscious and the one in which education is most prominent. . .[2] It is a prime concern of the state that a middle class should be developed, but this can be done only if the state is an organic unity like the one described here, i.e., it can be done only by giving authority to spheres of particular interests, which are relatively independent, and by appointing an army of officials whose personal arbitrariness is broken against such authorized bodies. Action in accordance with everyone's rights, and the habit of such action, is a consequence of the counterpoise to officialdom which independent and self-subsistent bodies create.

What Hegel says about 'the Executive' does not merit the name of a philosophical development. Most of the paragraphs could be found verbatim in the Prussian *Landrecht*. Yet the administration proper is the most difficult point of the development.

Because Hegel has already claimed the police and the judiciary to be spheres of civil society, the executive is nothing but the administration, which he develops as the bureaucracy.

First of all, the 'Corporations', as the self-government of civil society, presuppose the bureaucracy. The sole determination arrived at is that the choice of the administrators and their officials, etc., is a mixed choice originating from the members of civil society and ratified by the proper authority (or as Hegel says, 'higher authority').

Over this sphere, for the maintenance of the state's universal interest

---

[1] Knox's addition.　[2] Marx's ellipsis.

and of legality, stand holders of the executive power, the executive civil servants and the advisory officials, which converge into the monarch.

A division of labor occurs in the business of the executive. Individuals must prove their capability for executive functions, i.e., they must sit for examinations. The choice of the determinate individual for civil service appointment is the prerogative of the royal authority. The distribution of these functions is given in the nature of the thing. The official function is the duty and the life's work of the civil servants. Accordingly they must be paid by the state. The guarantee against malpractice by the bureaucracy is partly its hierarchy and answerability, and on the other hand the authority of the societies and Corporations; its humaneness is a result partly of direct education in thought and ethical conduct and partly of the size of the state. The civil servants form the greater part of the middle class. The safeguard against its becoming like an aristocracy and tyranny is partly the sovereign at the top and partly Corporation-rights at the bottom. The middle class is the class of education. *Voila tout!* Hegel gives us an empirical description of the bureaucracy, partly as it actually is, and partly according to the opinion which it has of itself. And with that the difficult chapter on 'the Executive' is brought to a close.

Hegel proceeds from the separation of the state and civil society, the separation of the particular interests and the absolutely universal; and indeed the bureaucracy is founded on this separation. Hegel proceeds from the presuppositon of the Corporations; and indeed the bureaucracy presupposes the Corporations, in any event the 'corporation mind'. Hegel develops no content of the bureaucracy, but merely some general indications of its formal organization; and indeed the bureaucracy is merely the formalism of a content which lies outside the bureaucracy itself.

The Corporations are the materialism of the bureaucracy, and the bureaucracy is the spiritualism of the Corporations. The Corporation is the bureaucracy of civil society, and the bureaucracy is the Corporation of the state. In actuality, the bureaucracy as civil society of the state is opposed to the state of civil society, the Corporations. Where the bureaucracy is to become a new principle, where the universal interest of the state begins to become explicitly a singular and thereby a real interest, it struggles against the Corporations as every consequence struggles against the existence of its premises. On the other hand once the real life of the state awakens and civil society frees itself from the Corporations out of its inherent rational impulse, the bureaucracy seeks to restore them; for as soon as the state of civil society falls so too does the civil society of the state. The spiritualism vanishes with its opposite materialism. The consequence struggles for the existence of its premises as soon as a new principle struggles not against the existence of the premises but against the principle of their existence. The same mind that creates the Corporation in society creates the bureaucracy in the state. Thus as soon as the corporation mind is attacked so too is the mind of the bureaucracy; and whereas the bureaucracy earlier fought the existence of the Corporations in order to create room for its own existence, now it seeks vigorously to sustain the existence of the Corporations in order to save the Corporation mind, which is its own mind.

The bureaucracy is the state formalism of civil society. It is the state's consciousness, the state's will, the state's power, as a Corporation. (The universal interest can behave *vis-à-vis* the particular only as a particular so long as the particular behaves *vis-à-vis* the universal as a universal. The bureaucracy must thus defend the imaginary universality of particular interest, i.e., the Corporation mind, in order to defend the imaginary particularity of the universal interests, i.e., its own mind. The state must be Corporation so long as the Corporation wishes to be state.) Being the state's consciousness, will, and power as a Corporation, the bureaucracy is thus a particular, closed society within the state. The bureaucracy wills the Corporation as an imaginary power. To be sure, the individual Corporation also has this will for its particular interest in opposition to the bureaucracy, but it wills the bureaucracy against the other Corporation, against the other particular interest. The bureaucracy as the completed Corporation therefore wins the day over the Corporation which is like incomplete bureaucracy. It reduces the Corporation to an appearance, or wishes to do so, but wishes this appearance to exist and to believe in its own existence. The Corporation is civil society's attempt to become state; but the bureaucracy is the state which has really made itself into civil society.

The state formalism, which the bureaucracy is, is the state as formalism, and Hegel has described it precisely as such a formalism. Because this state formalism constitutes itself as a real power and becomes itself its own material content, it is evident that the bureaucracy is a tissue of practical illusion, or the illusion of the state. The bureaucratic mind is through and through a Jesuitical, theological mind. The bureaucrats are the Jesuits and theologians of the state. The bureaucracy is *la république prêtre*.

Since the bureaucracy according to its essence is the state as formalism, so too it is according to its end. The real end of the state thus appears to the bureaucracy as an end opposed to the state. The mind of the bureaucracy is the formal mind of the state. It therefore makes the formal mind of the state, or the real mindlessness of the state, a categorical imperative. The bureaucracy asserts itself to be the final end of the state. Because the bureaucracy makes its formal aims its content, it comes into conflict everywhere with the real aims. Hence it is obliged to present what is formal for the content and the content for what is formal. The aims of the state are transformed into aims of bureaus, or the aims of bureaus into the aims of the state. The bureaucracy is a circle from which no one can escape. Its hierarchy is a hierarchy of knowledge. The highest point entrusts the understanding of particulars to the lower echelons, whereas these, on the other hand, credit the highest with an understanding in regard to the universal; and thus they deceive one another.

The bureaucracy is the imaginary state alongside the real state; it is the spiritualism of the state. As a result everything has a double meaning, one real and one bureaucratic, just as knowledge is double, one real and one bureaucratic (and the same with the will). A real thing, however, is treated according to its bureaucratic essence, according to its otherwordly, spiritual essence. The bureaucracy has the being of the state, the spiritual being of society, in its possession; it is its private property. The general spirit of the bureaucracy is the secret, the mystery, preserved inwardly by means of the hierarchy and externally as a closed corporation. To make public the mind and the disposition of the state appears therefore to the bureaucracy as a betrayal of its mystery. Accordingly authority is the principle of its knowledge and being, and the deification of authority is its mentality. But at the very heart of the bureaucracy this spiritualism turns into a crass materialism, the materialism of passive obedience, of trust in authority, the mechanism of an ossified and formalistic behavior, of fixed principles, conceptions, and traditions. As far as the individual bureaucrat is concerned, the end of the state becomes his private end: a pursuit of higher posts, the building of a career. In the first place, he considers real life to be purely material, for the spirit of this life has its separate existence in the bureaucracy. Thus the bureaucrat must make life as materialistic as possible. Secondly, real life is material for the bureaucrat, i.e., in so far as it becomes an object of bureaucratic action, because his spirit is prescribed for him, his end lies outside of him, his existence is the existence of the bureau. The state, then, exists only as various bureau-minds whose connexion consists of subordination and dumb obedience. Real knowledge appears to be devoid of content just as real life appears to be dead, for this imaginary knowledge and life pass for what is real and essential. Thus the bureaucrat must use the real state Jesuitically, no matter whether this Jesuitism be conscious or unconscious. But given that his antithesis is knowledge, it is inevitable that he likewise attain to self-consciousness and, at that moment, deliberate Jesuitism.

While the bureaucracy is on one hand this crass materialism, it manifests its crass spiritualism in its will to do everything, i.e., in its making the will the *causa prima*, for it is pure active existence which receives its content from without; thus it can manifest its existence only through forming and restricting this content. The bureaucrat has the world as a mere object of his action.

When Hegel calls the Executive power the objective aspect of the sovereignty residing in the crown, it is precisely in the same sense that the Catholic Church was the real existence of the sovereignty, content, and spirit of the Blessed Trinity. In the bureaucracy the identity of the state's interest and the particular private aim is established such that the state's interest becomes a particular private aim opposed to the other private aims.

The abolition [*Aufhebung*] of the bureaucracy can consist only in the universal interest becoming really—and not, as with Hegel, becoming purely in thought, in abstraction—a particular interest; and this is possible only through the particular interest really becoming universal. Hegel starts from an unreal opposition and thereby brings it to a merely imaginary identity which, in fact, is itself all the more contradictory. Such an identity is the bureaucracy.

Now let's follow his development in its particulars.

The sole philosophical statement which Hegel makes concerning the Executive is that of the 'subsuming' of the individual and particular under the universal, etc.

Hegel is satisfied with that. On one hand, the category of 'subsumption' of the particular, etc. This category must be actualized. Now, he picks anyone of the empirical existences of the Prussian or Modern state (just as it is), which among other things actualizes this category even though this category does not express its specific nature. Applied mathematics is also a subsuming of the particular, etc. Hegel doesn't enquire whether this is the rational, the adequate mode of subsumption. He holds fast only to the one category and is satisfied with finding a corresponding existence for it. Hegel gives his logic a political body; he does not give the logic of the political body (§ 287).

On the relationship of the Corporations and societies to the executive we are told first of all that it is required that their administration (the nomination of their magistracy) generally be effected by a mixture of popular election by those interested with appointment and ratification by higher authority. The mixed choice of administrators of the societies and Corporations would thus be the first relationship between civil society and state or executive, their first identity (§ 288). This identity, according to Hegel himself, is quite superficial, a *mixtum compositum*, a mixture. To the degree that this identity is superficial, opposition is sharp. It is the business of these officials (namely the officials of the Corporations, societies, etc.) to manage the private property and interests of these particular spheres and, from that point of view, their authority rests on the confidence of their commonalties and professional equals. On the other hand, however, these circles of particular interests must be subordinated to the higher interests of the state. From this results the so-called 'mixed choice'.

The administration of the Corporation thus has within it the opposition of private property and interest of the particular spheres against the higher interest of the state: opposition between private property and state.

We need not emphasize that the resolution of this opposition in the mixed choice is a simple accommodation, a treaty, an avowal of the unresolved dualism which is itself a dualism, a mixture. The particular interests of the Corporations and societies have a dualism within their own sphere, which likewise shapes the character of their administration.

However, the crucial opposition stands out first in the relationship of these 'particular interests which are common to everyone', etc., which 'lie outside the absolutely universal interest of the state proper', and this 'absolutely universal interest of the state proper'. But in the first instance once again, it is within this sphere.

The maintenance of the state's universal interest, and of legality, in this sphere of particular rights, and the work of bringing these rights back to the universal, require to be superintended by holders of the executive power, by (a) the executive civil servants, and (b) the higher advisory officials (who are organized into committees). These converge in their supreme heads who are in direct contact with the monarch. (§ 289)

Incidentally, let us draw attention to the construction of the executive committees, which are unknown, for example, in France. To the same extent that Hegel adduces these officials as advisory it is certainly obvious that they are organized into committees.

Hegel has the state proper, the executive, move into the management of the state's universal interest and of legality, etc. within civil society via holders [of the executive power]; and according to him these executive office holders, the executive civil servants are in reality the true representation of the state, not 'of' but 'against' civil society. The opposition between state and civil society is thus fixed; the state does not reside within but outside of civil society; it affects civil society merely through office holders to whom is entrusted the management of the state within this sphere. The opposition is not overcome by means of these office holders but has become a legal and fixed opposition. The state becomes something alien to the nature of civil society; it becomes this nature's otherworldly realm of deputies which makes claims against civil society. The police, the judiciary, and the administration are not deputies of civil society itself, which manages its own general interest in and through them. Rather, they are office holders of the state whose purpose is to manage the state in opposition to civil society. Hegel clarifies this opposition further in the candid Remark [to § 289] which we examined earlier.[1]

The nature of the executive functions is that they are objective and... [2] have been explicitly fixed by previous decisions. (§ 291)

Does Hegel conclude from this that [the executive functions] all the more easily require no hierarchy of knowledge, that they could be executed perfectly by civil society itself? On the contrary.

He makes the profound observation that they are to be executed by individuals, and that between them and these individuals there is no immediate natural link. This is an allusion to the crown, which is nothing but the natural power of arbitrary choice, and thus can be born. The crown is nothing but the representative of the natural moment in the will, the dominion of physical nature in the state.

The executive civil servants are distinguished by the fact that they earn their appointments; hence they are distinguished essentially from the sovereign.

The objective factor in their appointment (namely, to the State's business)[3] is knowledge (subjective caprice lacks this factor)[3] and proof of ability. Such proof guarantees that the state will get what it requires; and since it is the sole condition of appointment, it also guarantees to every citizen the chance of joining the class of civil servants [dem allgemeinen Stande].

The chance which every citizen has to become a civil servant is thus the second affirmative relationship between civil society and state, the second identity. Like the first it is also of a quite superficial and dualistic nature. Every Catholic has the chance to become a priest (i.e., to separate himself from the laity as well as the world). Does the clergy on that account face the Catholic any less as an opposite power? That each has the possibility of gaining the privilege of another sphere proves only that his own sphere is not the actuality of this privilege.

In a true state it is not a question of the possibility of every citizen to dedicate himself to the universal in the form of a particular class, but of the capability of the universal class to be really universal, i.e., to be the class of every citizen. But Hegel proceeds from the postulate of the pseudo-

[1] See above, pp. 41–2. [2] Marx's ellipsis. [3] Marx's insertions.

50

universal, the illusory universal class, universality fixed in the form of a particular class.

The identity which he has constructed between civil society and the state is the identity of two hostile armies in which each soldier has the 'chance' to become through desertion a member of the other hostile army; and in this Hegel indeed correctly describes the present empirical state of affairs.

It is the same with his construction of the examinations. In a rational state, taking an examination belongs more properly to becoming a shoemaker than an executive civil servant, because shoemaking is a skill without which one can be a good citizen of the state, a social man; but the necessary state knowledge is a condition without which a person in the state lives outside the state, is cut off from himself, deprived of air. The examination is nothing other than a masonic rite, the legal recognition of the privileged knowledge of state citizenship.

The link of state office and individual, this objective bond between the knowledge of civil society and the knowledge of the state, in other words the examination, is nothing but the bureaucratic baptism of knowledge, the official recognition of the transubstantiation of profane into holy knowledge (it goes without saying that in the case of every examination the examiner knows all). No one ever heard of the Greek or Roman statesmen taking an examination. But then what is a Roman statesman even as against a Prussian official!

In addition to the objective bond of the individual with the state office, in addition, that is, to the examination, there is another bond—royal caprice:

Since the objective qualification for the civil service is not genius (as it is for work as an artist, for example), there is of necessity an indefinite plurality of eligible candidates whose relative excellence is not determinable with absolute precision. The selection of one of the candidates, his nomination to office, and the grant to him of full authority to transact public business—all this, as the linking of two things, a man and his office, which in relation to each other must always be fortuitous, is the subjective aspect of election to office, and it must lie with the crown as the power in the state which is sovereign and has the last word. [§ 292]

The prince is at all times the representative of chance or contingency. Besides the objective moment of the bureaucratic confession of faith (the examination) there belongs in addition the subjective [moment] of the royal favor, in order that the faith yield fruit.

'The particular public functions which the monarch entrusts to officials constitute one part of the objective aspect of the sovereignty residing in the crown.' (The monarch distributes and entrusts the particular state activities as functions to the officials, i.e., he distributes the state among the bureaucrats, entrusts it like the holy Roman Church entrusts consecrations. Monarchy is a system of emanation; the monarch leases out the functions of the state.) Here Hegel distinguishes for the first time the objective aspect from the subjective aspect of the sovereignty residing in the cown. Prior to this he mixed the two together. The sovereignty residing in the crown is taken here in a clearly mystical way, just as theologians find the personal God in nature. [Earlier[1]] it still meant that the crown is the subjective aspect of the sovereignty residing in the state (§ 293).

In § 294 Hegel develops the salary of the civil servants out of the Idea. Here the real identity of civil society and the state is established in the salary of the civil servants, or in the fact that civil service also guarantees security in empirical existence. The wage of the civil servant is the highest identity which Hegel constructs out of all this. The transformation of the activities of the state into ministries presupposes the separation of the state from society.

When Hegel says [in the Remark to § 294]:

> What the service of the state...[2] requires is that men shall forgo the selfish and capricious satisfaction of their subjective ends, (this is required in the case of every post of service)[3] and by this very sacrifice they acquire the right to find their satisfaction in, but only in, the dutiful discharge of their public functions. In this fact, so far as public business is concerned, there lies the link between universal and particular interests which constitutes both the concept of the state and its inner stability,

this holds good (1.) of every servant, and (2.) it is correct that the salary of the civil servants constitutes the inner stability of the most modern monarchies. In contrast to the member of civil society only the civil servants' existence is guaranteed.*

At this point Hegel cannot fail to see that he has constructed the executive as an antithesis to civil society, and indeed as a dominant extreme. How does he now establish a condition of identity?

According to § 295 the security of the state and its subjects against the misuse [den Missbrauch] of power by ministers and their officials lies partly in their hierarchical organization (as if the hierarchy itself were not the principal abuse [der Hauptmissbrauch], and the matching personal sins of the civil servants were not at all to be compared with their inevitable hierarchical sins; the hierarchy punishes the civil servant to the extent that he sins against the hierarchy or commits a sin in excess of the hierarchy; but it takes him under its protection when the heirarchy sins through him;

---

[1] German editors' addition.   [2] Marx's ellipsis.   [3] Marx's insertion.
* (*MEGA* editors) Marx struck out the rest of the unfinished sentence: 'for they are a holy...'

moreover the hierarchy is only with great difficulty convinced of the sins of its member) and in the authority given to societies and Corporations, because in itself this is a barrier against the intrusion of subjective caprice into the power entrusted to a civil servant, and it completes from below the state control (as if this control were not exercised with the outlook of the bureaucratic hierarchy) which does not reach down as far as the conduct of individuals.

Thus the second guarantee against the caprice of the bureaucracy lies in the privileges of the Corporations.

Thus if we ask Hegel what is civil society's protection against the bureaucracy, he answers:

(1) The hierarchial organization of the bureaucracy. *Control.* This, that the adversary is himself bound hand and foot, and if he is like a hammer *vis-à-vis* those below he is like an anvil in relation to those above. Now, where is the protection against the hierarchy? The lesser evil will surely be abolished through the greater inasmuch as it vanishes in comparison with it.

(2) *Conflict*, the unresolved conflict between bureaucracy and Corporation. *Struggle*, the possibility of struggle, is the guarantee against being overcome. Later (§ 297) in addition to this Hegel adds as guarantee the 'institutions [of] the sovereign working...at the top', by which is to be understood, once again, the hierarchy.

However Hegel further adduces two moments (§ 296):

In the civil servant himself, something which is supposed to humanize him and make dispassionate, upright, and polite demeanor customary, namely, direct education in thought and ethical conduct, which is said to hold 'the mental counterpoise' to the mechanical character of his knowledge and actual work. As if the mechanical character of his bureaucratic knowledge and his actual work did not hold the 'counterpoise' to his education in thought and ethical conduct. And will not his actual mind and his actual work as substance triumph over the accident of his prior endowment? His office is indeed his substantial situation and his bread and butter. Fine, except that Hegel sets direct education in thought and ethical conduct against the mechanism of bureaucratic knowledge and work! The man within the civil servant is supposed to secure the civil servant against himself. What a unity! Mental counterpoise. What a dualistic category!

Hegel further adduces the size of the state, which in Russia certainly doesn't guarantee against the caprice of the executive civil servants, and in any case is a circumstance which lies outside the 'essence' of the bureaucracy.

Hegel has developed the 'Executive' as bureaucratic officialdom [*Staatsbediententum*].

Here in the sphere of the 'absolutely universal interest of the state proper' we find nothing but unresolved conflict. The civil servants' examination and livelihood constitute the final synthesis.

Hegel adduces the impotency of the bureaucracy, its conflict with the Corporation, as its final consecration.

In § 297 an identity is established in so far as 'civil servants and the members of the executive constitute the greater part of the middle class'. Hegel praises this 'middle class' as the pillar of the state so far as honesty and intelligence are concerned (in the Addition to this paragraph).

It is a prime concern of the state that a middle class should be developed, but this can be done only if the state is an organic unity like the one described here, i.e., it can be done only by giving authority to spheres of particular interests, which are relatively independent, and by appointing an army of officials whose personal arbitrariness is broken against such authorized bodies.

To be sure the people can appear as one class, the middle class, only in such an organic unity; but is something that keeps itself going by means of the counterbalancing of privileges an organic unity? The executive power is the one most difficult to develop; it, much more than the legislature, belongs to the entire people.

Later (in the Remark to § 308) Hegel expresses the proper spirit of the bureaucracy when he characterizes it as 'business routine' and the 'horizon of a restricted sphere'.

(c) *The Legislature*

§ 298. The legislature is concerned (a) with the laws as such in so far as they require fresh and extended determination; and (b) with the content of home affairs affecting the entire state (a very general expression).[1] The legislature is itself a part of the constitution which is presupposed by it and to that extent lies absolutely outside the sphere directly determined by it; nonetheless, the constitution becomes progressively more mature in the course of the further elaboration of the laws and the advancing character of the universal business of government.

Above all it is noteworthy that Hegel emphasizes the way in which the legislature is itself a part of the constitution which is presupposed by it and lies absolutely outside the sphere directly determined by it, since he had made this statement neither of the Crown nor of the Executive, for both

---

[1] Marx's insertion. Actually a pun which is lost in translation.

of which it is equally true. But only with the Legislature does Hegel construct the constitution in its entirety, and thus he is unable to presuppose it. However, we recognize his profundity precisely in the way he always begins with and accentuates the antithetical character of the determinate elements (as they exist in our states).

The legislature is itself a part of the constitution which lies absolutely outside the sphere directly determined by it. But the constitution is certainly not self-generating. The laws which 'require fresh and extended determination' must have received formulation. A legislature must exist or have existed before and outside of the constitution. There must exist a legislature outside of the actual empirical, established legislature. But, Hegel will answer, we presuppose an existing state. Hegel, however, is a philosopher of right, and develops the generic idea of the state [die Staatsgattung]. He is not allowed to measure the idea by what exists; he must measure what exists by the idea.

The collision is simple. The legislature is the power which is to organize the universal. It is the power of the constitution. It extends beyond the constitution.

On the other hand, however, the legislature is a constitutional power. Thus it is subsumed under the constitution. The constitution is law for the legislature. It has given laws to the legislature and continues to do so. The legislature is only legislature within the constitution, and the constitution would stand *hors de loi* if it stood outside the legislature. *Voilà la collision*! In recent French history much nibbling away [at the constitution] has occurred.[1]

How does Hegel resolve this antinomy?

First of all it is said that the constitution is presupposed by the legislature and to that extent it lies absolutely outside the sphere directly determined by it. *'Nonetheless'*—nonetheless in the course of the further elaboration

---

[1] Marx's sentence is: 'Innerhalb der jüngsten französischen Geschichte ist mancherlei herumgeknuspert worden.' We take him to be alluding here to the events of post-1789 French political history, specifically to the fact that none of the French constitutions within that period were changed in a way provided for in the constitution itself, but were either violently overthrown or changed by extra-constitutional, and therefore extra-legal measures. 'Recent French history' would thus provide concrete examples of the collision between constitution and legislature which Marx wishes to point up. His remarks in the pages immediately following also suggest this interpretation. Here, too, Marx appears to be drawing on the research in political history which he was pursuing in the summer of 1843 simultaneously with his writing of the *Critique*, and which is recorded in his Kreuznach *Exzerpthefte*. For his sources in French history, see *MEGA* I, 1/2, pp. xxiv–xxvi, 118 ff.

of the laws and the advancing character of the universal business of government it becomes progressively more mature.

That is to say, then: directly, the constitution lies outside the sphere of the legislature; indirectly, however, the legislature modifies the constitution. The legislature does in an indirect way what it neither can nor may do in a direct way. It picks the constitution apart *en détail*, since it cannot alter it *en gros*. It does by virtue of the nature of things and circumstances what according to the constitution it was not supposed to do. It does materially and in fact what it does not do formally, legally, or constitutionally.

With that, Hegel has not resolved the antinomy; he has simply transformed it into another antinomy. He has placed the real effect of the legislature, its constitutional effect, in contradiction with its constitutionally determined character. The opposition between constitution and legislature remains. Hegel has defined the factual and the legal action of the legislature as a contradiction—the contradiction between what the legislature should be and what it really is, between what it believes itself to be doing and what it really does.

How can Hegel present this contradiction as the truth? 'The advancing character of the universal business of government' enlightens us just as little, for it is precisely this advancing character which needs explanation.

In the Addition [to this paragraph] Hegel contributes hardly anything to the solution of these problems. He does, however, bring them more into focus:

> The constitution must in and by itself be the fixed and recognized ground on which the legislature stands, and for this reason it must not first be constructed. Thus the constitution is, but just as essentially it becomes, i.e., it advances and matures. This advance is an alteration which is imperceptible and which lacks the form of alteration.

That is to say, according to the law (illusion) the constitution *is*, but according to reality (truth) it *becomes*. According to its determinate character the constitution is unalterable; but it really is changed, only this change is unconscious and lacks the form of alteration. The appearance contradicts the essence. The appearance is the conscious law of the constitution, and the essence is its unconscious law, which contradicts the other. What is in the nature of the thing is not found in the law. Rather, the opposite is in the law.

Is it the fact, then, that in the state—which, according to Hegel, is the highest existence of freedom, the existence of self-conscious reason—not law, the existence of freedom, but rather blind natural necessity governs? And if the law of the thing is recognized as contradicting the legal definition, why not acknowledge the law of the thing, in this case reason, as the law of the state? And how then consciously retain this dualism? Hegel wants always to present the state as the actualization of free mind; however, *re vera* he resolves all difficult conflicts through a natural necessity which is the antithesis of freedom. Thus, the transition of particular interest into universal interest is not a conscious law of the state, but is mediated through chance and ratified *contrary* to consciousness. And in the state Hegel wants everywhere the realization of free will! (Here we see Hegel's substantial viewpoint.)

Hegel uses as examples to illustrate the gradual alteration of the constitution the conversion of the private wealth of the German princes and their families into state property, and the conversion of the German emperors' personal administration of justice into an administration through delegates. His choice of examples is unfortunate. In the first case, for instance, the transition happened only in such a way that all state property was transformed into royal private property.

Moreover, these changes are particular. Certainly, entire state constitutions have changed such that as new requirements gradually arose the old broke down; but for the new constitution a real revolution was always necessary.

Hence the advance from one state of affairs to another, Hegel concluded [in the Addition], is tranquil in appearance and unnoticed. In this way a constitution changes over a long period of time into something quite different from what it was originally.

The category of gradual transition is, first of all, historically false; and secondly, it explains nothing.

In order not only that the constitution be altered, thus that this illusory appearance not be in the end forcefully shattered, but also that man do consciously what he is otherwise forced to do unconsciously by the nature of the thing, it is necessary that the movement of the constitution, that progress, be made the principle of the constitution, thus that the real corner stone of the constitution, the people, be made the principle of the constitution. Progress itself is then the constitution.

Should the constitution itself, therefore, belong within the domain of the legislature? This question can be posed only (1) if the political state exists as the pure formalism of the actual state, if the political state is a domain apart, if the political state exists as constitution; (2) if the legislature is of a source different than the executive etc.

The legislature produced the French Revolution. In general, when it has appeared in its special capacity as the ruling element, the legislature has produced the great organic, universal revolutions. It has not attacked the constitution, but a particular antiquated constitution, precisely because the legislature was the representative of the people, i.e., of the species-will [*des Gattungswillens*]. The executive, on the other hand, produced the small, retrograde revolutions, the reactions. It revolted not against an old constitution in favor of a new one, but against the constitution as such, precisely because the executive was the representative of the particular will, subjective caprice, the magical part of the will.

Posed correctly, the question is simply this: Does a people have the right to give itself a new constitution? The answer must be an unqualified yes, because the constitution becomes a practical illusion the moment it ceases to be a true expression of the people's will.

The collision between the constitution and the legislature is nothing more than a conflict of the constitution with itself, a contradiction in the concept of the constitution.

The constitution is nothing more than an accommodation between the political and non-political state; hence it is necessarily in itself a treaty between essentially heterogeneous powers. Here, then, it is impossible for the law to declare that one of these powers, which is a part of the constitution, is to have the right to modify the constitution itself, which is the whole.

In so far as we speak of the constitution as a particular thing, however, it must be considered a part of the whole.

In so far as the constitution is understood to be the universal and fundamental determinations of the rational will, then clearly every people (state) presupposes this and must form it to its political credo. Actually, this is a matter of knowledge rather than of will. The will of a people can no more exceed the laws of reason than can the will of an individual. In the case of an irrational people one cannot speak at all of a rational organization of the state. In any case, here in the philosophy of right we are concerned with the species-will.

The legislature does not make the law, it merely discovers and formulates it.*

The resolution of this conflict has been attempted by differentiating between *assemblée constituante* and *assemblée constituée*.

§ 299. Legislative business (the concerns of the legislature)[1] is more precisely determined in relation to private individuals, under these two heads: (α) provision by

---

* (*MEGA* editors) The remainder of the sentence, as follows, was struck out by Marx: '...so that in democracy, accordingly, the legislature does not decide the organization of the whole...'
[1] Marx's insertion.

the state for their well being and happiness, and (β) the exaction of services from them. The former comprises the laws dealing with all sorts of private rights, the rights of communities, Corporations, and organizations affecting the entire state, and further it indirectly (see Paragraph 298) comprises the whole of the constitution. As for the services to be exacted, it is only if these are reduced to terms of money, the really existent and universal value of both things and services, that they can be fixed justly and at the same time in such a way that any particular tasks and services which an individual may perform come to be mediated through his own arbitrary will.

Concerning this determination of the legislature's business, Hegel himself notes, in the Remark to this paragraph:

The proper object of universal legislation may be distinguished in a general way from the proper function of administrative officials or of some kind of state regulation, in that the content of the former is wholly universal, i.e., determinate laws, while it is what is particular in content which falls to the latter, together with ways and means of enforcing the law. This distinction, however, is not a hard and fast one, because a law, by being a law, is *ab initio* something more than a mere command in general terms (such as 'Thou shalt not kill'. . . ¹). A law must in itself be something determinate, but the more determinate it is, the more readily are its terms capable of being carried out as they stand. At the same time, however, to give to laws such a fully detailed determinacy would give them empirical features subject inevitably to alteration in the course of their being actually carried out, and this would contravene their character as laws. The organic unity of the powers of the state itself implies that it is one single mind which both firmly establishes the universal and also brings it into its determinate actuality and carries it out.

But it is precisely this organic unity which Hegel has failed to construct. The various powers each have a different principle, although at the same time they are all equally real. To take refuge from their real conflict in an imaginary organic unity, instead of developing the various powers as moments of an organic unity, is therefore an empty, mystical evasion.

The first unresolved collision was that between the constitution as a whole and the legislature. The second is that between the legislature and the executive, i.e., between the law and its execution.

The second determination found in this paragraph [299] is that the only service the state exacts from individuals is money.

The reasons Hegel gives for this are:

(1) money is the really existent and universal value of both things and services;

(2) the services to be exacted can be fixed justly only by means of this reduction;

(3) only in this way can the services be fixed in such a way that the

¹ Marx's ellipsis.

particular tasks and services which an individual may perform come to be mediated through his own arbitrary will. Hegel notes in the Remark [to this paragraph]:

ad. 1. In the state it may happen, to begin with, that the numerous aptitudes, possessions, pursuits, and talents of its members, together with the infinitely varied richness of life intrinsic to these—all of which are at the same time linked with their owner's mentality—are not subject to direct levy by the state. It lays claim only to a single form of riches, namely money. (Services requisitioned for the defense of the state in war arise for the first time in connection with the duty considered in the next sub-division of this book.) We shall consider personal duty with regard to the military only later—not because of the following sub-division, but for other reasons.[1] In fact, however, money is not one particular type of wealth amongst others, but the universal form of all types so far as they are expressed in an external embodiment and so can be taken as 'things'.

In our day, it continues in the Addition, the state purchases what it requires.

ad 2. Only by being translated into terms of this extreme culmination of externality (sc. wherein riches are transformed into the externality of existence, in which they can be grasped as an object)[2] can services exacted by the state be fixed quantitatively and so justly and equitably.

The Addition reads: By means of money, however, the justice of equality can be achieved much more efficiently. Otherwise, if assessment depended on concrete ability, a talented man would be more heavily taxed than an untalented one.

ad 3. In Plato's *Republic*, the Guardians are left to allot individuals to their particular classes and impose on them their particular tasks...[3] Under the feudal monarchies the services required from vassals were equally indeterminate, but they had also to serve in their particular capacity, e.g. as judges. The same particular character pertains to tasks imposed in the East and in Egypt in connection with colossal architectural undertakings, and so forth. In these circumstances the principle of subjective freedom is lacking, i.e., the principle that the individual's substantive activity—which in any case becomes something particular in content in services like those mentioned—shall be mediated through his particular volition. This is a right which can be secured only when the demand for service takes the form of a demand for something of universal value, and it is this right which has brought with it this conversion of the state's demands into demands for cash.

The Addition reads: In our day, the state purchases what it requires. This may at first sight seem an abstract, heartless, and dead state of affairs, and for the state to be satisfied with indirect services may also look like decadence in the state. But the principle of the modern state requires that the whole of an individual's activity shall be mediated through his will...[3] But nowadays respect for subjective freedom is publicly recognized precisely in the fact that the state lays hold of a man only by that which is capable of being held.

Do what you want, pay what you must.

[1] This sentence is Marx's insertion.   [2] Parenthetic sentence is Marx's insertion.
[3] Marx's ellipsis.

The beginning of the Addition reads:

The two sides of the constitution bear respectively on the rights and the services of individuals. Services are now almost entirely reduced to money payments, and military service is now almost the only personal one exacted.

§ 300. In the legislature as a whole the other powers are the first two moments which are effective, (i) the monarchy as that to which ultimate decisions belong: (ii) the executive as the advisory body since it is the moment possessed of (α) a concrete knowledge and oversight of the whole state in its numerous facets and the actual principles firmly established within it, and (β) a knowledge in particular of what the state's power needs. The last moment in the legislature is the Estates.

The monarchy and the executive are—the legislature. If, however, the legislature is the whole, then the monarchy and the executive must accordingly be moments of the legislature. The supervening Estates are the legislature merely, or the legislature in distinction from the monarchy and the executive.

§ 301. The Estates have the function of bringing public affairs into existence not only implicitly, but also actually, i.e., of bringing into existence the moment of subjective formal freedom, the public consciousness as an empirical universal, of which the thoughts and opinions of the Many are particulars.

The Estates are civil society's deputation to the state, to which it [i.e., civil society] is opposed as the 'Many'. The Many must for a moment deal consciously with universal affairs as if they were their own, as objects of public consciousness, which, according to Hegel, is nothing other than the empirical universal, of which the thoughts and opinions of the Many are particulars. (And in fact, it is no different in modern or constitutional monarchies.) It is significant that Hegel, who shows such great respect for the state-mind [*dem Staatsgeist*]—the ethical spirit, state-consciousness —absolutely disdains it when it faces him in actual empirical form.

This is the enigma of mysticism. The same fantastic abstraction that rediscovers state-consciousness in the degenerate form of bureaucracy, a hierarchy of knowledge, and that uncritically accepts this incomplete existence as the actual and full-valued existence—the same mystical abstraction admits with equanimity that the actual empirical state-mind, public consciousness, is a mere potpourri of the 'thoughts and opinions of the Many'. As it imputes to the bureaucracy an essence which is foreign to it, so it grants to the actuality of that essence only the inferior form of appearance. Hegel idealizes the bureaucracy and empiricizes public consciousness. He can treat actual public consciousness very much *à part* precisely because he has treated the *à part* consciousness as the public consciousness. He need concern himself all the less with the actual existence of the state-mind in that he believes he has sufficiently realized it in its *soi-disant* existences. So long as the state-mind mystically haunted the fore-court it received many plaudits. Now that we have caught it *in persona* it is barely respected.

'The Estates have the function of bringing public affairs into existence not only implicitly [*an sich*], but also actually [*für sich*].' And indeed it comes into existence actually as the public consciousness, as 'an empirical universal, of which the thoughts and opinions of the Many are particulars'.

The process in which 'public affairs' becomes subject, and thus gains autonomy, is here presented as a moment of the life-process of public affairs. Instead of having subjects objectifying themselves in public affairs Hegel has public affairs becoming the subject. Subjects do not need public affairs as their true affairs, but public affairs needs subjects for its formal existence. It is an affair of public affairs that it exist also as subject.

Here the difference between the 'being-in-itself' [*Ansichsein*] and the 'being-for-itself' [*Fürsichsein*] of public affairs must be especially considered.

Public affairs already exists 'in-itself' [i.e., implicitly] as the business of the executive etc. Thus, public affairs exists without actually being *public* affairs; nothing less, for it is not the affair of civil society. It has already found its essential existence, its being-in-itself. The fact that public affairs now actually becomes public consciousness, or empirical universal, is purely formal and, as it were, only a symbolic coming to actuality. The formal or empirical existence of public affairs is separated from its substantial existence. The truth of the matter is that public affairs as being-in-itself is not actually public, and actual empirical public affairs is only formal.

Hegel separates content and form, being-in-itself and being-for-itself, and allows the latter the superficial status of formal moment. The content is complete and exists in many forms which are not the forms of this content; while, clearly, the form which is supposed to be the actual form of the content doesn't have the actual content for its content.

Public affairs is complete without being the actual affairs of the people. The actual affairs of the people have been established without the activity of the people. The Estates are the illusory existence of the affairs of the state as being an affair of the people. The illusion is that public affairs are public affairs, or that truly public affairs are the affair of the people. It has come to the point in our states as well as in the Hegelian philosophy of right where the tautological sentence, 'The public affairs are the public affairs', can appear only as an illusion of practical consciousness. The Estates are the political illusion of civil society. Subjective freedom appears in Hegel as formal freedom (it is important, however, that what is free be done freely, that freedom doesn't prevail as an unconscious natural instinct of society), precisely because Hegel has not presented objective freedom as the actualization, the activity, of subjective freedom. Because he has given the presumed or actual content of freedom a mystical bearer, the actual subject of freedom takes on a formal meaning. The separation of the in-itself and the for-itself, of substance and subject, is abstract mysticism.

Hegel, in his Remark [to § 301] presents the Estates quite rightly as something 'formal' and 'illusory'.

Both the knowledge and the will of the Estates are treated partly as unimportant and partly as suspect; that is to say, the Estates make no significant contribution.

1. The idea uppermost in men's minds when they speak about the necessity or the expediency of 'summoning the Estates' is generally something of this sort: (i) The deputies of the people, or even the people themselves, must know best what is in their best interest, and (ii) their will for its promotion is undoubtedly the most disinterested. So far as the first of these points is concerned, however, the truth is that if 'people' means a particular section of the citizens, then it means precisely that section which does not know what it wills. To know what one wills, and still more to know what the absolute will, Reason, wills, is the fruit of profound apprehension (which is found, no doubt, in the bureaus)[1] and insight, precisely the things which are not popular.

Further along in the paragraph we read the following about the Estates themselves:

The highest civil servants necessarily have a deeper and more comprehensive insight into the nature of the state's organization and requirements. They are also more habituated to the business of government and have greater skill in it, so that even without the Estates they are able to do what is best, just as they also continually have to do while the Estates are in session.

And it goes without saying that this is perfectly true in the organization described by Hegel.

2. As for the conspicuously good will for the general welfare which the Estates are supposed to possess, it has been pointed out already...[2] that to regard the will of the executive as bad, or as less good [than that of the ruled][3] is a presupposition characteristic of the rabble or of the negative outlook generally. This presupposition might at once be answered on its own ground by the counter-charge that the Estates start from isolated individuals, from a private point of view, from particular interests, and so are inclined to devote their activities to these at the expense of the general interests, while *per contra* the other moments in the power of the state explicitly take up the standpoint of the state from the start and devote themselves to the universal end.

Therefore the knowledge and will of the Estates are partly superfluous

---

[1] Marx's insertion.   [2] Marx's ellipsis.   [3] Knox's insertion.

and partly suspect. The people do not know what they want. In the possession of political knowledge [*Staatswissenschaft*] the Estates are not equal to the officials, who have a monopoly on it. The Estates are superfluous for the execution of public affairs. The officials can carry out this execution without the Estates; moreover they must, in spite of the Estates, do what is best. Thus the Estates, with regard to their content, are pure superfluity. Their existence, therefore, is a pure formality in the most literal sense.

Furthermore, the sentiment of the Estates, their will, is suspect, for they start from the private point of view and private interests. In truth, private interest is their public affairs, not public affairs their private interest. But what a way for public affairs to obtain form as public affairs—i.e., through a will which doesn't know what it wills, or at least lacks any special knowledge of the universal, a will, furthermore, whose actual content is an opposing interest!

In modern states, as in Hegel's *Philosophy of Right*, the conscious, true actuality of public affairs is merely formal, or only what is formal constitutes actual public affairs.

Hegel is not to be blamed for depicting the nature of the modern state as it is, but rather for presenting what is as the essence of the state. The claim that the rational is actual is contradicted precisely by an irrational actuality, which everywhere is the contrary of what it asserts and asserts the contrary of what it is.

Instead of showing how public affairs exists for-itself, 'subjectively, and thus actually as such', and that it also has the form of public affairs, Hegel merely shows that formlessness is its subjectivity; and a form without content must be formless. The form which public affairs obtains in a state which is not the state of public affairs can be nothing but a non-form, a self-deceiving, self-contradicting form, a form which is pure appearance [*eine Scheinform*] and which will betray itself as this appearance.

Only for the sake of logic does Hegel want the luxury of the Estates. The being-for-itself of public affairs as empirical universal must have an existence [*ein Dasein*]. Hegel does not search for an adequate actualization of the being-for-itself of public affairs, but contents himself with finding an empirical existent which can be dissolved into this logical category. This is the Estates. And Hegel himself does not fail to note how pitiful and full of contradiction this existent is. Yet he still reproaches ordinary consciousness for being discontent with this satisfaction of logic, for being unwilling to see actuality dissolved into logic by this arbitrary abstraction, for wanting logic, rather, to be transformed into concrete objectivity.

I say arbitrary abstraction, for since the executive power wills, knows, and actualizes public affairs, arises from the people, and is an empirical plurality (Hegel himself tells us that it is not a totality), why should we not be able to characterize the executive as the 'being-for-itself of public affairs'? Or, again, why not the Estates as their being-in-itself, since it is only in the executive that [public affairs] receives illumination, determinacy, execution, and independence?

The true antithesis, however, is this: public affairs must somewhere be represented in the state as actual, and thus as empirical public affairs; it must appear somewhere in the crown and robes of the universal, whereby the universal automatically becomes a fiction, an illusion.

Here it is a question of the opposition of the universal as 'form', in the form of universality, and the universal as 'content'.

In science, for example, an individual can fully perform public affairs, and it is always individuals who do so. But public affairs become actually public only when they are no longer the affair of an individual but of society. This changes not only the form but also the content. In this case, however, it is a question of the state in which the people itself constitutes the public affairs, a question of the will which has its true existence as species-will only in the self-conscious will of the people, and, moreover, a question of the idea of the state.

The modern state, in which public affairs and their pursuit is a monopoly while monopolies are the actual public affairs, has effected the peculiar device of appropriating public affairs as a pure form. (In fact, only the form is public affairs.) With that, the modern state has found the appropriate form for its content, which only appears to be actual public affairs.

The constitutional state is the state in which the state-interest is only formally the actual interest of the people, but is nevertheless present as a distinct form alongside of the actual state. Here the state-interest has again received formal actuality as the people's interest; but it is to have only this formal actuality. It has become a formality, the *haut goût* of the life of the people—a ceremony. The Estates are the sanctioned, legal lie of constitutional states, the lie that the state is the people's interest or the people the interest of the state. This lie will betray itself in its content. The lie has established itself as the legislature precisely because the legislature has the universal as its content and, being more an affair of knowledge than of will, is the metaphysical power of the state; whereas had the same lie established itself as the executive etc., it would have had either immediately to dissolve itself or be transformed into a truth. The metaphysical power of the state was the most likely seat for the metaphysical, universal illusion of the state.

[Remark to § 301.] The Estates are a guarantee of the general welfare and public freedom. A little reflection will show that this guarantee does not lie in their particular power of insight...[1] the guarantee lies on the contrary (α) in the additional (!!)[2] insight of the deputies, insight in the first place into the activity of such officials as are not immediately under the eye of the higher functionaries of state, and in particular into the more pressing and more specialized needs and deficiencies which are directly in their view; (β) in the fact that the anticipation of criticism from the Many, particularly of public criticism, has the effect of inducing officials to devote their best attention beforehand to their duties and the schemes under consideration, and to deal with these only in accordance with the purest motives. This same compulsion is effective also on the members of the Estates themselves.

As for the general guarantee which is supposed to lie peculiarly in the Estates, each of the other political institutions shares with the Estates in being a guarantee of public welfare and rational freedom, and some of these institutions, as for instance the sovereignty of the monarch, hereditary succession to the throne, the judicial system etc., guarantee these things far more effectively than the Estates can. Hence the specific function which the concept assigns to the Estates is to be sought in the fact that in them the subjective moment in universal freedom—the private judgment and private will of the sphere called 'civil society' in this book—comes into existence integrally related to the state. This moment is a determination of the Idea once the Idea has developed to totality, a moment arising as a result of an inner necessity not to be confused with external necessities and expediences. The proof of this follows, like all the rest of our account of the state, from adopting the philosophical point of view.

Public, universal freedom is allegedly guaranteed in the other institutions of the state, while the Estates constitute its alleged self-guarantee. [But the fact is] that the people rely more heavily on the Estates, in which the self-assurance of their freedom is thought to be, than on the institutions which are supposed to assure their freedom independent of their own participation, institutions which are supposed to be verifications of their freedom without being manifestations of it. The coordinating function Hegel assigns to the Estates, alongside the other institutions, contradicts the essence of the Estates.

Hegel solves the problem by finding the 'specific function which the concept assigns to the Estates' in the fact that in them 'the private judgment and private will...of civil society...comes into existence integrally related to the state'. It is the reflection of civil society on the state. Just as the bureaucrats are delegates of the state to civil society, so the Estates are delegates of civil society to the state. Consequently, it is always a case of transactions of two opposing wills.

What is said in the Addition to this paragraph, namely:

The attitude of the executive to the Estates should not be essentially hostile, and a belief in the necessity of such hostility is a sad mistake.

is a sad truth.

---

[1] Marx's ellipsis.   [2] Marx's insertion.

'The executive is not a party standing over against another party.' Just the contrary.

The taxes voted by the Estates, moreover, are not to be regarded as a present given to the state. On the contrary they are voted in the best interests of the voters themselves.

Voting for taxes in a constitutional state is, by the very idea of it, necessarily a present.

The real significance of the Estates lies in the fact that it is through them that the state enters the subjective consciousness of the people and that the people begins to participate in the state.

This last statement is quite correct. In the Estates the people begins to participate in the state, just as the state enters the people's subjective consciousness as something opposed. But how can Hegel possibly pass off this *beginning* as the full reality!

§ 302. Regarded as a mediating organ, the Estates stand between the government in general on the one hand and the nation broken up into particulars (people and associations) on the other. Their function requires them to possess a political and administrative sense and temper, no less than a sense for the interests of individuals and particular groups. At the same time the significance of their position is that, in common with the organized executive, they are a middle term preventing both the extreme isolation of the power of the crown, which otherwise might seem a mere arbitrary tyranny, and also the isolation of particular interests of persons, societies, and Corporations. Further, and more important, they prevent individuals from having the appearance of a mass or an aggregate and so from acquiring an unorganized opinion and volition and from crystallizing into a powerful bloc in opposition to the organized state.

On the one hand we have the state and the executive, always taken as identical, and on the other the nation broken up into particulars (people and associations). The Estates stand as a mediating organ between the two. The Estates are the middle term wherein political and administrative sense and temper meet and are to be united with the sense and temper of individuals and particular groups. The identity of these two opposed senses and tempers, in which identity the state was supposed to actually lie, acquires a symbolic appearance in the Estates. The transaction between state and civil society appears as a particular sphere. The Estates are the synthesis between state and civil society. But how the Estates are to begin to unite in themselves two contradictory tempers is not indicated. The Estates are the established contradiction of the state and civil society within the state. At the same time they are the demand for the dissolution of this contradiction.

At the same time the significance of their position is that, in common with the organized executive they are the middle term etc.

The Estates not only mediate between the people and the executive, but they also prevent the extreme isolation of the power of the crown, whereby it would appear as mere arbitrary tyranny, and also the isolation of the particular interests etc. Furthermore they prevent individuals from having the appearance of a mass or an aggregate. This mediating function is what the Estates have in common with the organized executive power. In a state in which the position of the Estates prevents individuals from having the appearance of a mass or an aggregate, and so from acquiring an unorganized opinion and volition and from crystallizing into a powerful bloc in opposition to the organized state, the organized state exists outside the mass and the aggregate; or, in other words, the mass and aggregate belong to the organization of the state. But its unorganized opinion and volition is to be prevented from crystallizing into an opinion and volition in opposition to the state, through which determinate orientation it would become an organized opinion and volition. At the same time this powerful bloc is to remain powerful only in such a way that understanding remains foreign to it, so that the mass is unable to make a move on its own and can only be moved by the monopolists of the organized state and be exploited as a powerful bloc. Where it is not a matter of the particular interests of persons, societies and Corporations isolating themselves from the state, but rather of the individuals being prevented from having the appearance of a mass or an aggregate and from acquiring an unorganized opinion and volition and from crystallizing into a powerful bloc in opposition to the state, precisely then it becomes evident not that a particular interest contradicts the state, but rather that the actual organized universal thought of the mass and aggregate is not the thought of the organized state and cannot find its realization in the state. What is it then that makes the Estates appear to be the mediation against this extreme? It is merely the isolation of the particular interests of persons, societies and Corporations; or the fact that their isolated interests balance their account with the state through the Estates while, at the same time, the unorganized opinion and volition of a mass or aggregate employed its volition (its activity) in creating the Estates and its opinion in judging their activity, and enjoyed the illusion of its own objectification. The Estates preserve the state from the unorganized aggregate only through the disorganization of this very aggregate.

At the same time, however, the mediation of the Estates is to prevent the isolation of the particular interests of persons, societies and Corporations. This they achieve, first, by coming to an understanding with the interest of the state and, second, by being themselves the political isolation of these particular interests, this isolation as political act, in that through them these isolated interests achieve the rank of the universal.

Finally, the Estates are to mediate against the isolation of the power of the crown as an extreme (which otherwise might seem a mere arbitrary tyranny). This is correct in so far as the principle of the power of the crown (arbitrary will) is limited by means of the Estates, at least can operate only in fetters, and in so far as the Estates themselves become a partaker and accessory of the power of the crown.

In this way, either the power of the crown ceases to be actually the extreme of the power of the crown (and the power of the crown exists only as an extreme, a onesidedness, because it is not an organic principle) and becomes a mere appearance of power [*eine Scheingewalt*], a symbol, or else it loses only the *appearance* of arbitrary tyranny. The Estates mediate against the isolation of particular interests by presenting this isolation as a political act. They mediate against the isolation of the power of the crown as an extreme partly by becoming themselves a part of that power, partly by making the executive power an extreme.

All the contradictions of modern state-organizations converge in the Estates. They mediate in every direction because they are, from every direction, the middle term.

It should be noted that Hegel develops the content of the Estates' essential political activity, viz., the legislature, less than he does their position, or political rank.

It should be further noted that, while the Estates, according to Hegel, stand between the government in general on the one hand and the nation broken up into particulars (people and associations) on the other, the significance of their position as developed above is that, in common with the organized executive, they are a middle term.

Regarding the first position, the Estates represent the nation over against the executive, but the nation *en miniature*. This is their oppositional position.

Regarding the second, they represent the executive over against the nation, but the amplified executive. This is their conservative position. They are themselves a part of the executive over against the people, but in such a way that they simultaneously have the significance of representing the people over against the executive.

Above, Hegel called the legislature a 'totality' (§ 300). In fact, however, the Estates are this totality, the state within the state; but it is precisely in them that it becomes apparent that the state is not a totality but a duality. The Estates represent the state in a society that is no state. The state is a *mere representation* [*eine blosse Vorstellung*].[1]

[1] Here Marx appears to be playing on the word 'representation' (*Vorstellung*) in

In the Remark Hegel says:

It is one of the most important discoveries of logic that a specific moment, which, by standing in an opposition, has the position of an extreme, ceases to be such and is a moment in an organic whole by being at the same time a mean.

(Thus the Estates are at one and the same time (1) the extreme of the nation over against the executive, but (2) the mean between nation and executive; or, in other words, the opposition within the nation itself. The opposition between the executive and the nation is mediated through the opposition between the Estates and the nation. From the point of view of the executive the Estates have the position of the nation, but from the point of view of the nation they have the position of the executive. The nation in its occurrence as image, phantasy, illusion, representation— i.e., the imagined nation, or the Estates, which are immediately situated as a particular power in dissociation from the actual nation—abolishes [*hebt auf*] the actual opposition between the nation and the executive. Here the nation is already dressed out, exactly as required in this particular organism, so as to have no determinate character.)

[The Remark continues:]

In connection with our present topic it is all the more important to emphasize this aspect of the matter because of the popular, but most dangerous, prejudice which regards the Estates principally from the point of view of their opposition to the executive, as if that were their essential attitude. If the Estates become an organ in the whole by being taken up into the state, they evince themselves solely through their mediating function. In this way their opposition to the executive is reduced to a show. There may indeed be an appearance of opposition between them, but if they were opposed, not merely superficially, but actually and in substance, then the state would be in the throes of destruction. That the clash is not of this kind is evident in the nature of the thing, because the Estates have to deal, not with the essential elements in the organism of the state, but only with rather specialized and trifling matters, while the passion which even these arouse spends itself in party cravings in connection with purely subjective interests such as appointments to higher offices of state.

In the Addition it says: 'The constitution is essentially a system of mediation.'

§ 303. The universal class, or, more precisely, the class of civil servants, must, purely in virtue of its character as universal, have the universal as the end of its essential activity. In the Estates, as an element in the legislative power, the unofficial class acquires its political significance and efficacy; it appears, therefore, in the Estates neither as a mere indiscriminate multitude nor as an aggregate dispersed into its atoms, but as what it already is, namely a class subdivided into two, one subclass

---

order to turn Hegel's own notion of 'representation' as a function of imagination back on him in criticizing his doctrine of the state.

[the agricultural class]¹ being based on a tie of substance between its members, and the other [the business class]¹ on particular needs and the work whereby these are met . . .² It is only in this way that there is a genuine link between the particular which is effective in the state and the universal.

Here we have the solution of the riddle. 'In the Estates, as an element in the legislative power, the unofficial class acquires its political significance.' It is understood that the unofficial, or private class [der Privatstand] acquires this significance in accordance with what it is, with its articulation within civil society; (Hegel has already designated the universal class as the class dedicated to the executive; the universal class, therefore, is represented in the legislature by the executive.)

The Estates are the political significance of the unofficial class, i.e., of the unpolitical class, which is a contradictio in adjecto; or to put it another way, in class as described by Hegel the unofficial class (or, more correctly, unofficial class difference) has a political significance. The unofficial class belongs to the essence, to the very political reality [zur Politik] of this state, which thus gives it also a political significance, that is, one that differs from its actual significance.

In the Remark it says:

This runs counter to another prevalent idea, the idea that since it is in the legislature that the unofficial class rises to the level of participating in matters of state, it must appear there in the form of individuals, whether individuals are to choose representatives for this purpose, or whether every single individual is to have a vote in the legislature himself. This atomistic and abstract point of view vanishes at the stage of the family, as well as that of civil society where the individual is in evidence only as a member of a general group. The state, however, is essentially an organization each of whose members is in itself a group of this kind, and hence no one of its moments should appear as an unorganized aggregate. The Many, as units—a congenial interpretation of 'people', are of course something connected, but they are connected only as an aggregate, a formless mass whose commotion and activity could therefore only be elementary, irrational, barbarous, and frightful.

The circles of association in civil society are already communities. To picture these communities as once more breaking up into a mere conglomeration of individuals as soon as they enter the field of politics, i.e., the field of the highest concrete universality, is eo ipso to hold civil and political life apart from one another and as it were to hang the latter in the air, because its basis could then only be the abstract individuality of caprice and opinion, and hence it would be grounded on chance and not on what is absolutely stable and justified.

So-called 'theories' of this kind involve the idea that the classes [Stände] of civil society and the Estates [Stände], which are the 'classes' given a political significance, stand wide apart from each other. But the German language, by calling them both Stände has still maintained the unity which in any case they actually possessed in former times.

---

¹ Knox's additions.　　² Marx's ellipsis.

'The universal class, or, more precisely, the class of civil servants. Hegel proceeds from the hypothesis that the universal class is the class of civil servants. For him, universal intelligence is attached permanently to a class.

'In the Estates as an element etc.' Here, the political significance and efficacy of the unofficial class is precisely its particular significance and efficacy. The unofficial class is not changed into a political class, but appears as the unofficial class in its political significance and efficacy. It does not have political significance and efficacy simply; its political efficacy and significance are those of the unofficial class as unofficial or private. Accordingly, the unofficial class can appear in the political sphere only in keeping with the class difference found in civil society. The class difference within civil society becomes a political difference.

Even the German language, says Hegel, expresses the identity of the classes of civil society with the classes given a political significance; it expresses a unity which in any case they actually possessed in former times —a unity, one should thus conclude, which no longer exists.

Hegel finds that, in this way there is a genuine link between the particular which is effective in the state and the universal. In this way the separation of civil and political life is to be abolished and their identity established.

Hegel finds support in the following: 'The circles of association (family and civil society) are already communities.' How can one want these to break up into a mere conglomeration of individuals as soon as they enter the field of politics, i.e., the field of the highest concrete universality?

It is important to follow this development very carefully.

The peak of Hegelian identity, as Hegel himself admits, was the Middle Ages. There, the classes of civil society in general and the Estates, or classes given political significance, were identical. The spirit of the Middle Ages can be expressed thus: the classes of civil society and the political classes were identical because civil society was political society, because the organic principle of civil society was the principle of the state.

But Hegel proceeds from the separation of civil society and the political state as two actually different spheres, firmly opposed to one another. And indeed this separation does actually exist in the modern state. The identity of the civil and political classes in the Middle Ages was the expression of the identity of civil and political society. This identity has disappeared; and Hegel presupposes it as having disappeared. The identity of the civil and political classes, if it expressed the truth, could be now only an expression of the separation of civil and political society! Or rather, only the separation of the civil and political classes expresses the true relationship of modern civil and political society.

Secondly: the political classes Hegel deals with here have a wholly different meaning than those political classes of the Middle Ages, which are said to be identical with the classes of civil society.

The whole existence of the medieval classes was political; their existence was the existence of the state. Their legislative activity, their grant of taxes for the realm was merely a particular issue of their universal political significance and efficacy. Their class was their state. The relationship to the realm was merely one of transaction between these various states and the nationality, because the political state in distinction from civil society was nothing but the representation of nationality. Nationality was the *point d'honneur*, the κατ᾽ ἐξοχὴν political sense of these various Corporations etc., and taxes etc., pertained only to them. That was the relationship of the legislative classes to the realm. The classes were related in a similar way within the particular principalities. There, the principality, the sovereignty was a particular class which enjoyed certain privileges but was equally inconvenienced by the privileges of the other classes. (With the Greeks, civil society was a slave to political society.) The universal legislative efficacy of the classes of civil society was in no way the acquisition of political significance and efficacy by the unofficial, or private class, but was rather a simple issue of its actual and universal political significance and efficacy. The appearance of the private class as legislative power was simply a complement of its sovereign and governing (executive) power; or rather it was its appropriation of wholly public affairs as a private affair, its acquisition, *qua* private class, of sovereignty. In the Middle Ages, the classes of civil society were as such simultaneously legislative because they were not private classes, or because private classes were political classes. The medieval classes did not, as political Estates, acquire a new character. They did not become political classes because they participated in legislation; rather they participated in legislation because they were political classes. But what does that have in common with Hegel's unofficial class which, as a legislative element, acquires political bravura, an ecstatic condition, a remarkable, stunning, extraordinary political significance and efficacy?

All the contradictions of the hegelian presentation are found together in this development.

1. He has presupposed the separation of civil society and the political state (which is a modern situation), and developed it as a necessary moment of the Idea, as an absolute truth of Reason. He has presented the political state in its modern form of the separation of the various powers. For its

body he has given the actual acting state the bureaucracy, which he ordains to be the knowing spirit over and above the materialism of civil society. He has opposed the state, as the actual universal, to the particular interest and need of civil society. In short, he presents everywhere the conflict between civil society and the state.

2. He opposes civil society as unofficial, or private class to the political state.

3. He calls the Estates, as element of the legislative power, the pure political formalism of civil society. He calls them a relationship of civil society to the state which is a reflection of the former on the latter, a reflection which does not alter the essence of the state. A relationship of reflection is also the highest identity between essentially different things.

On the other hand:

1. Hegel wants civil society, in its self-establishment as legislative element, to appear neither as a mere indiscriminate multitude nor as an aggregate dispersed into its atoms. He wants no separation of civil and political life.

2. He forgets that he is dealing with a relationship of reflection, and makes the civil classes as such political classes; but again only with reference to the legislative power, so that their efficacy itself is proof of the separation.

He makes the Estates the expression of the separation [of civil and political life]; but at the same time they are supposed to be the representative of an identity—an identity which does not exist. Hegel is aware of the separation of civil society and the political state, but he wants the unity of the state expressed within the state; and this is to be achieved by having the classes of civil society, while remaining such, form the Estates as an element of legislative society. (cf. xiv, x)[1]

§ 304. The Estates, as an element in political life, still retain in their own function the class distinctions already present in the lower spheres of civil life. The position of the classes is abstract to begin with, i.e., in contrast with the whole principle of monarchy or the crown, their position is that of an extreme—empirical universality. This extreme opposition implies the possibility, though no more, of harmonization, and the equally likely possibility of set hostility. This abstract position changes into a rational relation (into a syllogism, see Remark to Paragraph 302) only if the middle term between the opposites comes into existence. From the point of view of the crown, the executive already has this character (see Paragraph 300). So, from the point of

---

[1] Marx refers here to the material in *Bögen* xiv and x of the manuscript. In our translation, see pp. 44–8, and 31–4.

view of the classes, one moment in them must be adapted to the task of existing as in essence the moment of mediation.

§ 305. The principle of one of the classes of civil society is in itself capable of adaptation to this political position. The class in question is the one whose ethical life is natural, whose basis is family life, and, so far as its livelihood is concerned, the possession of land. Its particular members attain their position by birth, just as the monarch does, and, in common with him, they possess a will which rests on itself alone.

§ 306. This class is more particularly fitted for political position and significance in that its capital is independent alike of the state's capital, the uncertainty of business, the quest for profit, and any sort of fluctuation in possessions. It is likewise independent of favour, whether from the executive or the mob. It is even fortified against its own willfulness, because those members of this class who are called to political life are not entitled, as other citizens are, either to dispose of their entire property at will, or to the assurance that it will pass to their children, whom they love equally, in similarly equal divisions. Hence their wealth becomes inalienable, entailed, and burdened by primogeniture.

Addition: This class has a volition of a more independent character. On the whole, the class of landed-property owners is divided into an educated section and a section of farmers. But over against both of these sorts of people there stands the business class, which is dependent on needs and concentrated on their satisfaction, and the civil servant class, which is essentially dependent on the state. The security and stability of the agricultural class may be still further increased by the institution of primogeniture, though this institution is desirable only from the point of view of politics, since it entails a sacrifice for the political end of giving the eldest son a life of independence. Primogeniture is grounded on the fact that the state should be able to reckon not on the bare possibility of political inclinations, but on something necessary. Now an inclination for politics is of course not bound up with wealth, but there is a relatively necessary connection between the two, because a man with independent means is not hemmed in by external circumstances and so there is nothing to prevent him from entering politics and working for the state. Where political institutions are lacking, however, the foundation and encouragement of primogeniture is nothing but a chain on the freedom of private rights, and either political meaning must be given to it, or else it will in due course disappear.

§ 307. The right of this section of the agriculture class is thus based in a way on the natural principle of the family. But this principle is at the same time reversed owing to hard sacrifices made for political ends, and thereby the activity of this class is essentially directed to those ends. As a consequence of this, this class is summoned and entitled to its political vocation by birth without the hazards of election. It therefore has the fixed substantive position between the subjective willfulness or contingency of both extremes; and while it mirrors in itself. . .[1] the moment of the monarchical power, it also shares in other respects the needs and rights of the other extreme [i.e., civil society][2] and hence it becomes a support at once of the throne and society.

Hegel has accomplished the masterpiece: he has developed peerage by birthright, wealth by inheritance, etc. etc., this support of the throne and society, out of the absolute Idea.

[1] Marx's ellipsis.   [2] Knox's addition.

Hegel's keenest insight lies in his sensing the separation of civil and political society to be a contradiction. But his error is that he contents himself with the appearance of its dissolution, and passes it off as the real thing; while the 'so-called theories' which he despises demand the separation of the civil and political classes, and rightly, for they express a consequence of modern society, in that here the political Estates are precisely nothing but the factual expression of the actual relationship of state and civil society—their separation.

Hegel has failed to identitfy the issue in question here. It is the issue of representative versus Estate constitution. The representative constitution is a great advance, for it is the open, genuine, consistent expression of the condition of the modern state. It is the unconcealed contradiction.

Before we take up this matter itself, let's take another look at this Hegelian presentation.

In the Estates as an element in the legislative power, the unofficial class acquires its political significance.

Earlier (in the Remark to § 301) it was said:

Hence the specific function which the concept assigns to the Estates is to be sought in the fact that in them...the private judgment and private will of the sphere called 'civil society' in this book come into existence integrally related to the state.

The meaning of these two, taken in combination, is as follows: Civil society is the unofficial class, or, the unofficial class is the immediate, essential, concrete class of civil society. Only within the Estates as an element of the legislative power does it acquire political significance and efficacy. This is a new endowment, a particular function, for precisely its character as unofficial class expresses its opposition to political significance and efficacy, the privation of political character, and the fact that civil society actually lacks political significance and efficacy. The unofficial class is the class of civil society, or civil society is the unofficial class. Thus, in consequence, Hegel also excludes the universal class from the Estates as an element of the legislative power:

The universal class, or, more precisely, the class of civil servants, must purely in virtue of its character as universal, have the universal as the end of its essential activity.

In virtue of its character, civil society, or the unofficial class, does not have the universal as the end of its essential activity. Its essential activity is not a determination of the universal; it has no universal character. The unofficial class is the class of civil society as opposed to the [political (?)] class.[1] The class of civil society is not a political class.

[1] Following Lieber and Furth: 'Der Privatstand ist der Stand der bürgerlichen Gesellschaft gegen den Stand.' (*Werke* has: ...gegen den Staat.)

In declaring civil society to be the unofficial class, Hegel has declared the class differences of civil society to be non-political differences and civil and political life to be heterogeneous in character, even antitheses. How then does he proceed?

[The unofficial class][1] appears, therefore, in the Estates neither as a mere indiscriminate multitude nor as an aggregate dispersed into its atoms, but as what it already is, namely a class subdivided into two, one sub-class [the agricultural class][2] being based on a tie of substance between its members, and the other [the business class][2] on particular needs and the work whereby these are met (see Paragraph 201 ff.). It is only in this way that there is a genuine link between the particular which is effective in the state and the universal.

To be sure, civil society (the unofficial class), in its legislative activity in the Estates, cannot appear as a mere indiscriminate multitude because the mere indiscriminate multitude exists only in imagination or fantasy, but not in actuality. What actually exists is only accidental multitudes of various sizes (cities, villages, etc.). These multitudes, or this aggregate not only *appears* but everywhere really *is* an aggregate dispersed into its atoms; and when it appears in its political-class activity it *must* appear as this atomistic thing. The unofficial class, civil society, cannot appear here as what it already is. For what is it already? Unofficial class, i.e., opposition to and separation from the state. In order to achieve political significance and efficacy it must rather renounce itself as what it already is, as unofficial class. Only through this does it acquire its political significance and efficacy. This political act is a complete transubstantiation. In this political act civil society must completely renounce itself as such, as unofficial class, and assert a part of its essence which not only has nothing in common with the actual civil existence of its essence, but directly opposes it.

What the universal law is appears here in the individual. Civil society and the state are separated. Consequently the citizen of the state and the member of civil society are also separated. The individual must thus undertake an essential schism within himself. As actual citizen he finds himself in a two-fold organization: (α) the bureaucratic, which is an external formal determination of the otherworldly state, of the executive power, which does not touch him and his independent actuality; (β) the social, the organization of civil society, within which he stands outside the state as a private man, for civil society does not touch upon the political state as such. The former [the bureaucratic] is an organization of the state to which he continually contributes the material. The latter [the social] is a civil organization whose material is not the state. In the

---

[1] Translators' addition.   [2] Knox's additions.

former the state relates to him as formal opposition; in the latter he himself relates to the state as material opposition. Thus, in order to behave as actual citizen of the state, to acquire political significance and efficacy, he must abandon his civil actuality, abstract from it, and retire from this entire organization into his individuality. He must do this because the only existence that he finds for his state-citizenship is his pure, bare individuality, for the existence of the state as executive is complete without him, and his existence in civil society is complete without the state. Only in opposition to these exclusively existing communities, only as an individual, can he be a citizen of the state. His existence as citizen is an existence lying outside the realm of his communal existences, and is hence purely individual. The legislature as a power is precisely the organization, the communal embodiment, which his political existence is supposed to receive. Prior to the legislature, civil society, or the unofficial class, does not exist as political-organization. In order that it come to existence as such, its actual organization, actual civil life, must be established as non-existing, for the Estates as an element of the legislative power have precisely the character of rendering the unofficial class, civil society, non-existent. The separation of civil society and the political state appears necessarily to be a separation of the political citizen, the citizen of the state, from civil society, i.e., from his own actual, empirical reality; for as a state-idealist he is a being who is completely other, distinct, different from and opposed to his own actuality. Here civil society effects within itself the relationship of the state and civil society, a relationship which already exists on the other side [i.e., within the state] as the bureaucracy. In the Estates the universal becomes actually, explicitly [*für sich*] what it is implicitly [*an sich*], namely, opposition to the particular. The citizen must renounce his class, civil society, the unofficial class, in order to achieve political significance and efficacy; for it is precisely this class which stands between the individual and the political state.

If Hegel already contrasts the whole of civil society as unofficial class to the political state, then it is self-evident that the distinctions within the unofficial class, i.e., the various civil classes, have only an unofficial significance with regard to the state; in other words, they have no political significance. For the various civil classes are simply the actualization, the existence, of the principle, i.e., of the unofficial class as of the principle of civil society. If, however, the principle must be abandoned, then it is self-evident that still more the schisms within this principle are non-existent for the political state.

'It is only in this way', says Hegel in concluding the paragraph, 'that there is a genuine link between the particular which is effective in the state and the universal.' But here Hegel confuses the state as the whole of a people's existence with the political state. That particular is not the particular *in*, but rather *outside* the state, namely, the political state. It is not only not the particular which is effective in the state, but also the ineffectiveness [*Unwirklichkeit*] of the state. What Hegel wants to establish is that the classes of civil society are political classes; and in order to prove this he asserts that the classes of civil society are the particularity of the political state, that is to say, that civil society is political society. The expression, 'The particular *in* the state', can here only mean the particularity of the state. A bad conscience causes Hegel to choose the vague expression. Not only has he himself developed just the opposite, but he even ratifies it in this paragraph by characterizing civil society as the 'un-official class'. His statement that the particular is 'linked' to the universal is very cautious. The most dissimilar things can be linked. But here we are not dealing with a gradual transition but with a transubstantiation, and it is useless to ignore deliberately this cleft which has been jumped over and yet manifested by the very jump.

In the Remark Hegel says: 'This runs counter to another prevalent idea' etc. We have just shown how this prevalent idea is consequently and inevitably a necessary idea of the people's present development, and how Hegel's idea, despite its also being very prevalent in certain circles, is nevertheless untrue.

Returning to this prevalent idea Hegel says: 'This atomistic and abstract point of view vanishes at the stage of the family' etc. etc. 'The state, how-ever, is' etc. This point of view is undeniably abstract, but it is the abstrac-tion of the political state as Hegel himself develops it. It is atomistic too, but it is the atomism of society itself. The point of view cannot be concrete when the object of the point of view is abstract. The atomism into which civil society is driven by its political act results necessarily from the fact that the commonwealth [*das Gemeinwesen*], the communal being [*das kommunistische Wesen*], within which the individual exists, is [reduced to] civil society separated from the state, or in other words, that the political state is an abstraction of civil society.[1]

This atomistic point of view, although [it][2] already vanishes in the

---

[1] Marx first wrote *Kommune*, then crossed it out and substituted *Gemeinwesen*. The latter term appears to have been chosen both to avoid using *Kommune* twice in the same sentence and, more importantly, because it serves to signify at once both the commonwealth, or the socio-political body, and the universal nature of man, the social or communal being. Rubel holds that Marx also uses the expression *kommunistische Wesen* here to signify man's social being. Cf. Avineri, *The Social and Political Thought*, pp. 34–5; and Rubel, *Essai*, p. 74.

[2] German editors' addition.

family, and perhaps (??) also in civil society, recurs in the political state precisely because the political state is an abstraction of the family and civil society. But the reverse is also true. By expressing the strangeness [*das Befremdliche*] of this occurrence Hegel has not eliminated the estrangement [*die Entfremdung*].

The circles of association in civil society, Hegel continues, are already communities. To picture these communities as once more breaking up into a mere conglomeration of individuals as soon as they enter the field of politics, i.e., the field of the highest concrete universality, is *eo ipso* to hold civil and political life apart from one another and as it were to hang the latter in the air, because its basis could then only be the abstract individuality of caprice and opinion, and hence it would be grounded on chance and not on what is absolutely stable and justified.

This picturing [of these communities as breaking up] does not hold civil and political life apart; it is simply the picturing of an actually existing separation.

Nor does this picturing hang political life in the air; rather, political life is the life in the air, the ethereal region of civil society.

Now we turn to the representative and the Estate systems.

It is a development of history that has transformed the political classes into social classes such that, just as the Christians are equal in heaven yet unequal on earth, so the individual members of a people are equal in the heaven of their political world yet unequal in the earthly existence of society. The real transformation of the political classes into civil classes took place under the absolute monarchy. The bureaucracy asserted the idea of unity over against the various states within the state. Nevertheless, even alongside the bureaucracy of the absolute executive, the social difference of the classes remained a political difference, political within and alongside the bureaucracy of the absolute executive. Only the French Revolution completed the transformation of the political classes into social classes, in other words, made the class distinctions of civil society into merely social distinctions, pertaining to private life but meaningless in political life. With that, the separation of political life and civil society was completed.

At the same time the classes of civil society were likewise transformed: civil society underwent a change by reason of its separation from political society. Class in the medieval sense remained only within the bureaucracy itself, where civil and political positions are immediately identical. Over against this stands civil society as unofficial class. Here class distinction is no longer one of need and of labor as an independent body. The sole general, superficial and formal distinction which remains is that of town and country. But within civil society itself the distinctions take shape in changeable, unfixed spheres whose principle is arbitrariness. Money and education are the prevalent criteria. Yet it's not here, but in the critique of Hegel's treatment of civil society that this should be developed. Enough said. Class in civil society has neither need—and therefore a natural impulse—nor politics for its principle. It is a division of the masses whose development is unstable and whose very structure is arbitrary and in no sense an organization.

The sole characteristic thing is that the lack of property, and the class in need of immediate labor, of concrete labor, forms less a class of civil society than the basis upon which the spheres of civil society rest and move. The sole class in which political and civil positions coincide is that of the members of the executive power. The present social class already manifests a distinction from the former class of civil society by the fact that it does not, as was formerly the case, regard the individual as a communal individual, as a communal being [ein Gemeinwesen]; rather, it is partly chance, partly labor, etc., of the individual which determines whether he remains in his class or not, a class which is, further, only an external determination of this individual; for he neither inheres in his work nor does the class relate to him as an objective communal being organized according to firm laws and related firmly to him. Moreover, he stands in no actual relation to his substantial activity, to his actual class. The medical man, for instance, forms no particular class in civil society. One businessman belongs to a class different than that of another businessman, i.e., he belongs to another social position. Just as civil society is separated from political society, so within itself civil society is separated into class and social position, even though some relations obtain between the two. The principle of the civil class, or of civil society, is enjoyment and the capacity to enjoy. In his political role the member of civil society rids himself of his class, of his actual private position; by this alone does he acquire significance as man. In other words, his character as a member of the state, as a social being, appears to be his human character. For all of his other characteristics in civil society appear to be unessential to the man, the individual; that is, they appear to be external characteristics which are indeed necessary to his existence within the whole, i.e., as being a bond with the whole, but a bond that he can just as well throw off. (Present civil society is the accomplished principle of individualism: individual existence is the final end, while activity, labor, content, etc., are merely means.)

The Estate-constitution, when not a tradition of the Middle Ages, is the attempt, partly within the political sphere itself, to thrust man back into the limitation of his private sphere, to make his particularity his substantial consciousness and, by means of the political character of class difference, also to make him once more into a social being.

The actual man is the private man of the present-day political constitution.

In general, the significance of the estate is that it makes difference, separation, subsistence, things pertaining to the individual as such.[1] His manner of life, activity, etc. is his privilege, and instead of making him a functional member of society, it makes him an exception from society. The fact that this difference is not only individual but also established as community, estate, corporation, not only fails to abolish the exclusiveness of its nature, but is rather its expression. Instead of the particular function being a function of society, the particular function is made into a society for itself.

Not only is the estate based on the separation of society as the governing principle, but it separates man from his universal nature; it makes him an animal whose being coincides immediately with its determinate character. The Middle Ages constitutes the animal history of mankind, its zoology.

Modern times, civilization, commits the opposite mistake. It separates man's objective essence from him, taking it to be merely external and material. Man's content is not taken to be his true actuality.

Anything further regarding this is to be developed in the section on 'Civil Society'.

Now we come to

§ 304. The Estates, as an element in political life, still retain in their own significance[2] the class distinctions already present in the lower spheres of civil life.

We have already shown that the class distinctions already present in the lower spheres of life have no significance for the political spheres, or if so, then only the significance of private, hence non-political, distinctions. But according to Hegel here they do not even have their already present significance (their significance in civil society). Rather, the Estates as an element in political life affirms its essence by embodying these distinctions within itself; and, thus immersed in political life, they receive a significance of their 'own' which belongs not to them but to this element.

---

[1] Following Lieber and Furth: 'Der *Stand* hat überhaupt die Bedeutung, dass der *Unterschied*, die *Trennung*, das *Bestehn*, des einzelnen ist.' (*Werke* has: '...dass der *Unterschied*, die *Trennung*, das *Bestehn* des Einzelnen ist'. An alternate reading would be: '...the significance of the *Estate* is that it treats the individual's *existence* as one of *distinction* and *separation*'.)

[2] Here Marx misquotes Hegel, writing 'seiner eignen Bedeutung', instead of Hegel's 'seiner eignen Bestimmung'. Earlier (p. 74 above) he quoted Hegel correctly.

As long as the organization of civil society remained political, and the political state and civil society were one, this separation, this duplication of the estates' significance was not present. The estates did not signify one thing in the civil world and something other in the political world. They acquired no [additional] significance in the political world, but signified only themselves. The duality of civil society and the political state, which the Estate-constitution purports to resolve through a reminiscence, appears within that constitution itself, in that class difference (the differentiation within civil society) acquires in the political sphere a significance different than in the civil sphere. There is apparent identity here: the same subject, but in an essentially different determination, and thus in fact a double subject. And this illusory identity (surely an illusory identity because, in fact, the actual subject, man, remains constantly himself, does not lose his identity in the various determinations of his being; but here man is not the subject, rather he is identified with a predicate—the class—and at the same time it is asserted that he exists in this definite determination and in another determination, that he is, as this definite, exempted and restricted thing, something other than this restricted thing) is artificially maintained through that reflection [mentioned earlier], by at one time having civil class distinction as such assume a character which should accrue to it only in the political sphere, and at another time reversing things and having the class distinction in the political sphere acquire a character which issues not from the political sphere but from the subject of the civil sphere. In order to present the one limited subject, the definite class (the class distinction), as the essential subject of both predicates, or in order to prove the identity of the two predicates, both are mystified and developed in an illusory and vague dimorphism [*Doppelgestalt*].

Here the same subject is taken in different meanings, but the meaning is not a self-determination [of the subject]; rather, it is an allegorical determination foisted on the subject. One could use the same meaning for a different concrete subject, or another meaning for the same subject. The significance that civil class distinction acquires in the political sphere is not its own, but proceeds from the political sphere; and even here it could have a different significance, as was historically the case. The reverse is also true. This is the uncritical, the mystical way of interpreting an old worldview in terms of a new one, through which it becomes nothing but an unhappy hybrid in which the form betrays the meaning and the meaning the form, and neither does the form achieve significance, thus becoming actual form, nor the significance become form, thus becoming actual significance. This uncritical spirit, this mysticism, is the enigma of the modern constitution (κατ᾽ ἐξοχὴν the Estate-constitution) as well as the mystery of Hegelian philosophy, especially the *Philosophy of Right* and the *Philosophy of Religion.*

The best way to rid oneself of this illusion is to take the significance as what it is, i.e., as the actual determination, then as such make it the subject, and consider whether its ostensibly proper subject is its actual predicate, i.e., whether this ostensibly proper subject expresses its [the actual determination's] essence and true actualization.

The position of the classes (the Estates as an element in political life)[1] is abstract to begin with, i.e., in contrast with the whole principle of monarchy or the crown, their position is that of an extreme—empirical universality. This extreme opposition implies the possibility, though no more, of harmonization, and the equally likely possibility of set hostility. This abstract position changes into a rational relation (into a syllogism, see Remark to Paragraph 302) only if the middle term between the opposites comes into existence.

We have already seen that the Estates, in common with the executive power, form the middle term between the principle of monarchy and the people, between the will of the state existing as one and as many empirical wills, and between empirical singularity and empirical universality. Just as he had to define the will of civil society as empirical universality, so Hegel had to define the sovereign will as empirical singularity; but he does not articulate the antithesis in all of its sharpness.

Hegel continues:

From the point of view of the crown, the executive already has this character (see Paragraph 300). So, from the point of view of the classes, one moment in them must be adapted to the task of existing as in essence the moment of mediation.

The true antitheses, however, are the sovereign and civil society. And as we have already seen, the Estates have the same significance from the people's point of view as the executive has from the point of view of the sovereign. Just as the executive emanates in an elaborate circular system, so the people condenses into a miniature edition; for the constitutional monarchy can get along well only with the people *en miniature.* The Estates, from the point of view of civil society, are the very same abstraction of the political state as is the executive from the sovereign's point of view. Thus it appears that the mediation has been fully achieved. Both extremes have left their obstinacy behind, each has imparted the spirit of its particular essence into a fusion with that of the other; and the legislature, whose elements are the executive as well as the Estates, appears not to be that which must first allow this mediation to come to existence, but

[1] Marx's insertion.

to be itself the already existing mediation. Also, Hegel has already [§ 302] declared the Estates in common with the executive to be the midde term between the people and the sovereign (the same way the Estates are the middle term between civil society and the executive, etc.). Thus the rational relation, the syllogism, appears to be complete. The legislature, the middle term, is a *mixtum compositum* of both extremes: the sovereign principle and civil society, empirical singularity and empirical universality, subject and predicate. In general, Hegel conceives of the syllogism as middle term, to be a *mixtum compositum*. We can say that in his development of the rational syllogism all of the transcendence and mystical dualism of his system becomes apparent. The middle term is the wooden sword, the concealed opposition between universality and singularity.

To begin with, we notice in regard to this whole development that the mediation Hegel wants to establish here is not derived from the essence of the legislature, from its own character, but rather with regard to an existence lying outside its essential character. It is a construction of reference. The legislature is chiefly developed with regard only to a third [party]. Hence, it is primarily the construction of its formal existence which receives all the attention. The legislature is constructed very diplomatically. This results from the false, illusory κατ' ἐξοχὴν political position given to the legislature in the modern state (whose interpreter is Hegel himself). What follows immediately is that this is no true state, because in it the determinate functions of the state, one of which is the legislature, must not be regarded in and for themselves, not theoretically, but rather practically; they must not be regarded as independent powers, but as powers bound up with an opposite, and this in accordance with the rules of convention rather than by the nature of things.

Thus the Estates, in common with the executive, should actually be the middle term between the will of empirical singularity, i.e., the sovereign, and the will of empirical universality, i.e., civil society. But in fact their position is really 'abstract to begin with, i.e., in contrast with the whole principle of monarchy or the crown, their position is that of an extreme— empirical universality. This extreme opposition implies the possibility, though no more, of harmonization, and the equally likely possibility of set hostility'. In other words their position, as Hegel quite rightly remarks, is an abstract position.

It appears at first that neither the extreme of empirical universality nor the principle of monarchy or the crown, i.e., the extreme of empirical singularity, are opposed to one another. For from the point of view of civil society the Estates are delegated just as the executive is from the point of view of the sovereign. Just as the principle of the crown ceases, in the delegated executive power, to be the extreme of empirical singularity, surrendering its self-determined will and lowering itself to the finitude of knowledge, responsibility, and thought, so civil society appears in the Estates to be no longer an empirical universality, but a very definite whole which has political and administrative sense and temper, and no less a sense for the interests of individuals and particular groups (§ 302). Civil society, in its miniature edition as the Estates, has ceased to be empirical universality. Rather, it has been reduced to a delegated committee of very definite number. If the sovereign assumes empirical universality in the executive power, then civil society assumes empirical singularity or particularity in the Estates. Both have become a particular.

The only opposition which remains possible appears to be that between the two emanations, between the executive- and the Estate-elements within the legislature. It appears, therefore, to be an opposition within the legislature itself. And these elements which mediate 'in common' seem quite prone to get into one another's hair. In the executive element of the legislature the inaccessable empirical singularity of the sovereign has come down to earth in a number of limited, tangible, responsible personalities; and in the Estates, civil society has exalted itself into a number of political men. Both sides have lost their inaccessibility. The crown—the inaccessible, exclusive, empirical One—has lost its obstinacy, while civil society—the inaccessible, vague, empirical All—has lost its fluidity. In the Estates on the one hand, and the executive element of the legislature on the other, which together would mediate between civil society and the sovereign, the opposition thus appears to have become, first of all, a refereed opposition, but also an irreconcilable contradiction.

As for this mediation, it is therefore, as Hegel rightly argues, all the more necessary that the middle term between the opposites comes into existence; for it is itself much more the existence of the contradiction than of the mediation.

That this mediation will be effected by the Estates seems to be maintained by Hegel without any foundation. He says:

> From the point of view of the crown, the executive already has this character (see Paragraph 300). So, from the point of view of the classes, one moment in them must be adapted to the task of existing as in essence the moment of mediation.

But we have already seen that Hegel arbitrarily and inconsistently posits the sovereign and the Estates as opposed extremes. As the executive has this character from the point of view of the crown, so the Estates have it from the point of view of civil society. Not only do [the Estates] stand, in common with the executive, between the sovereign and civil society, but also between the executive in general and the people (§ 302). They do more on behalf of civil society than the executive does on behalf of the crown, which is itself in opposition to the people. Thus they have accomplished their full measure of mediation. Why make these asses bear still more? Why should they always be made the donkey-bridge, even between themselves and their own adversaries? Why must they always perform the self-sacrifice? Should they cut off one of their hands when both are needed to withstand their adversary, the executive element of the legislature?

In addition, Hegel first has the Estates arise from the Corporations, class distinctions, etc., lest they be a mere empirical universality; and now he reverses the process, and makes them mere empirical universality in order to have class distinction arise from them! Just as the sovereign is mediated with c[ivil]¹ society through the executive, so society is mediated with the executive through the Estates—the executive thus acting as society's Christ, and the Estates as its priests.

Now it appears all the more that the role of the extremes—the crown (empirical singularity) and civil society (empirical universality)—must be that of mediating as the middle term between the opposites; all the more because 'it is one of the most important discoveries of logic that a specific moment which, by standing in an opposition, has the position of an extreme, ceases to be such and is a moment in an organic whole by being at the same time the mean' (Remark to § 302). Civil society appears to be unable to play this role, for civil society as itself, as an extreme, occupies no seat in the legislature. The other extreme, the sovereign principle, exists as an extreme within the legislature, and thus apparently must be the mediator between the Estate- and the executive-elements. And it appears to have all the qualifications; for, on the one hand, the whole of the state, and therefore also civil society, is represented within it, and, more specifically, it has empirical singularity of will in common with the Estates, since empirical universality is actual only as empirical singularity. Furthermore, the sovereign principle does not merely oppose civil society as a kind of formula, as state-consciousness, the way the executive does. It is itself the state; it has the material, natural moment in common with civil society. On the other hand, it is the head and the representative of the executive. (Hegel, who inverts everything, makes the executive the representative, the emanation, of the sovereign. When he considers the idea whose existence the sovereign is supposed to be,

¹ German editors' addition.

Hegel has in mind not the actual idea of the executive, the executive as idea, but rather the subject of the Absolute Idea which exists corporeally in the sovereign; hence the executive becomes a mystical continuation of the soul existing in his body—the sovereign body.)

The sovereign, then, had to be the middle term in the legislature between the executive and the Estates; but, of course, the executive is the middle term between him and the Estates, and the Estates between him and civil society. How is he to mediate between what he himself needs as a mean lest his own existence become a onesided extreme? Now the complete absurdity of these extremes, which interchangeably play now the part of the extreme and now the part of the mean, becomes apparent. They are like Janus with two-faced heads, which now show themselves from the front and now from the back, with a diverse character at either side. What was first intended to be the mean between two extremes now itself occurs as an extreme; and the other of the two extremes, which had just been mediated by it, now intervenes as an extreme[1] (because of its distinction from the other extreme) between its extreme and its mean. This is a kind of mutual reconciliation society. It is as if a man stepped between two opponents, only to have one of them immediately step between the mediator and the other opponent. It is like the story of the man and wife who quarreled and the doctor who wished to mediate between them, whereupon the wife soon had to step between the doctor and her husband, and then the husband between his wife and the doctor. It is like the lion in *A Midsummer Night's Dream* who exclaims: 'I am the lion, and I am not the lion, but Snug.'[2] So here each extreme is sometimes the lion of opposition and sometimes the Snug of mediation. When the one extreme cries: 'Now I am the mean', then the other two may not touch it, but rather only swing at the one that was just the extreme. As one can see, this is a society pugnacious at heart but too afraid of bruises to ever really fight. The two who want to fight arrange it so that the third who steps between them will get the beating, but immediately one of the two appears as the third, and because of all this caution they never arrive at a decision. We find this system of mediation in effect also where the very man who wishes to beat an opponent has at the same time to protect him from a beating at the hands of other opponents, and because of this double pursuit never manages to execute his own business. It is remarkable that Hegel, who reduces this absurdity of mediation to its abstract logical, and hence pure and irreducible, expression, calls it at the same time the

---

[1] Following Lieber and Furth: '...tritt nun wieder als Extrem...' (*Werke* has '...tritt nun wieder als Mitte...')

[2] v. i. 221–30.

speculative mystery of logic, the rational relationship, the rational syllogism. Actual extremes cannot be mediated with each other precisely because they are actual extremes. But neither are they in need of mediation, because they are opposed in essence. They have nothing in common with one another; they neither need nor complement one another. The one does not carry in its womb the yearning, the need, the anticipation of the other. (When Hegel treats universality and singularity, the abstract moments of the syllogism, as actual opposites, this is precisely the fundamental dualism of his logic. Anything further regarding this belongs in the critique of Hegelian logic.)

This appears to be in opposition to the principle: *Les extrêmes se touchent.* The North and South Poles attract each other; the female and male sexes also attract each other, and only through the union of their extreme differences does man result.

On the other hand, each extreme is its other extreme. Abstract spiritualism is abstract materialism; abstract materialism is the abstract spiritualism of matter.

In regard to the former, both North and South Poles are poles; their essence is identical. In the same way both female and male gender are of one species, one nature, i.e., human nature. North and South Poles are opposed determinations of one essence, the variation of one essence brought to its highest degree of development. They are the differentiated essence. They are what they are only as differentiated determinations; that is, each is *this* differentiated determination of the one same essence. Truly real extremes would be Pole and non-Pole, human and non-human gender. Difference here is one of existence, whereas there [i.e., in the case of Pole and non-Pole, etc.,] difference is one of essence, i.e., the difference between two essences.

In regard to the second [i.e. where each extreme is its other extreme], the chief characteristic lies in the fact that a concept (existence, etc.) is taken abstractly, and that it does not have significance as independent but rather as an abstraction from another, and only as this abstraction. Thus, for example, spirit is only the abstraction from matter. It is evident that precisely because this form is to be the content of the concept, its real essence is rather the abstract opposite, i.e., the object from which it abstracts taken in its abstraction—in this case, abstract materialism.

Had the difference within the existence of one essence not been confused, in part, with the abstraction given independence (an abstraction not from another, of course, but from itself) and, in part, with the actual opposition of mutually exclusive essences, then a three-fold error could have been avoided, namely: (1) that because only the extreme is true, every abstraction and one-sidedness takes itself to be the truth, whereby a principle appears to be only an abstraction from another instead of a totality in itself; (2) that the decisiveness of actual opposites, their formation into extremes, which is nothing other than their self-knowledge as well as their inflammation to the decision to fight, is thought to be something which should be prevented if possible, in other words, something harmful; (3) that their mediation is attempted. For no matter how firmly both extremes appear, in their existence, to be actual and to be extremes, it still lies only in the essence of the one to be an extreme, and it does not have for the other the meaning of true actuality. The one infringes upon the other, but they do not occupy a common position. For example, Christianity, or religion in general, and philosophy are extremes. But in fact religion is not a true opposite to philosophy, for philosophy comprehends religion in its illusory actuality. Thus, for philosophy—in so far as it seeks to be an actuality—religion is dissolved in itself. There is no actual duality of essence. More on this later.

The question arises, why does Hegel need a new mediation on the side of the Estates at all? Or does he share with [others][1] 'the popular, but not dangerous prejudice, which regards the Estates principally from the point of view of their opposition to the executive, as if that were their essential attitude'? (Remark to § 302.)

The fact of the matter is simply this: On the one hand we have seen that it is only in the legislature that civil society as the element of the Estates, and the power of the crown as the element of the executive have taken on the spirit of actual, immediately practical opposition.

On the other hand, the legislature is the totality. In it we find [1] the deputation of the sovereign principle, i.e., the executive; (2) the deputation of civil society, i.e., the Estates; but in addition, (3) the one extreme as such, i.e., the sovereign principle; while the other extreme, civil society, does not exist in it as such. It is only because of this that the Estates become the extreme to the sovereign principle, when civil society really should be. As we have seen, only as Estates does civil society organize itself into a political existence. The Estates are its political existence, its transubstantiation into the political state. Again as we have seen, only the legislature is, therefore, the actual political state in its totality. Here, then, there is (1) sovereign principle, (2) executive, (3) civil society. The Estates are the civil society of the political state, i.e., the legislature. The extreme to the sovereign, which civil society was supposed to have been, is therefore the Estates. (Because civil society is the non-actuality of political existence,

---

[1] German editors' addition.

the political existence of civil society is its own dissolution, its separation from itself.) Therefore it also constitutes an opposition to the executive.

Hegel, therefore, again designates the Estates as the extreme of empirical universality, which is actually civil society itself. (Hence he unnecessarily allows the Estates, as an element in political life, to proceed from the Corporations and different classes. This procedure would make sense only if the distinct classes as such were in fact the legislative classes, if, accordingly, the distinction of civil society—i.e., its civil character—were *re vera* the political character. We would then not have a legislature of the state as a whole, but rather a legislature of the various estates, Corporations, and classes over the state as a whole. The estates [or classes] of civil society would receive no political character, but would rather determine the political state. They would make their particularity a power determining the whole. They would be the power of the particular over the universal. And we would not have one legislature, but several, which would come to terms among themselves and with the executive. However, Hegel has in mind the Estates in the modern sense, namely the actualization of state citizenship, or of the Bourgeois. He does not want the actual universal, the political state, to be determined by civil society, but rather civil society to be determined by the state. Thus while he accepts the Estates in their medieval form, he gives them the opposite significance, namely, that of being determined by the political state. The Estates as representatives of the Corporations, etc., would not be empirical universality, but rather empirical particularity, i.e., the particularity of the empirical!) The legislature, therefore, needs mediation within itself, that is to say, a concealment of the opposition. And this mediation must come from the Estates because in the legislature the Estates lose their significance of being the representation of civil society and become the primary element, the very civil society of the legislature. The legislature is the totality of the political state and, precisely because of this, the contradiction of the political state brought forcibly to appearance. Thus it is also its established dissolution. Entirely different principles collide within it. To be sure, it appears to be the opposition between the two elements, that of the sovereign principle and that of the Estates, and so forth. But in fact it is the antinomy of political state and civil society, the self-contradiction of the abstract political state. The legislature is the established revolt. (Hegel's chief mistake consists in the fact that he conceives of the contradiction in appearance as being a unity in essence, i.e., in the Idea; whereas it certainly has something more profound in its essence, namely, an essential contradiction. For example here, the contradiction in the legislature itself is nothing other than the contradiction of the political state, and thus also the self-contradiction of civil society.

Vulgar criticism falls into an opposite dogmatic error. Thus, for example, it criticizes the constitution, drawing attention to the opposition of the powers etc. It finds contradictions everywhere. But criticism that struggles with its opposite remains dogmatic criticism, as for example in earlier times, when the dogma of the Blessed Trinity was set aside by appealing to the contradiction between 1 and 3. True criticism, however, shows the internal genesis of the Blessed Trinity in the human mind. It describes the act of its birth. Thus, true philosophical criticism of the present state constitution not only shows the contradictions as existing, but clarifies them, grasps their essence and necessity. It comprehends their own proper significance. However, this comprehension does not, as Hegel thinks, consist in everywhere recognizing the determinations of the logical concept, but rather in grasping the proper logic of the proper object.[1])

As Hegel expresses it, the position of the political Estates relative to the sovereign implies the possibility, though no more, of harmonization, and the equally likely possibility of set hostility.

The possibility of hostility is implied everywhere different volitions meet. Hegel himself says that the possibility of harmonization is the possibility of hostility. Thus, he must now construct an element which is both the impossibility of hostility and the actuality of harmonization. For him, such an element would be the freedom of decision and thought in face of the sovereign will and the executive. Thus it would no longer be an element belonging to the Estates as an element in political life. Rather, it would be an element of the sovereign will and the executive, and would stand in the same opposition to the actual Estates as does the executive itself.

This demand is already quite muted by the conclusion of the paragraph:

> From the point of view of the crown, the executive already has this character (see Paragraph 300). So, from the point of view of the classes, one moment in them must be adapted to the task of existing as in essence the moment of mediation.

The moment which is dispatched from the estates [or classes] must have a character the reverse of that which the executive has from the

---

1 Marx's distinction here between 'true' and 'dogmatic' criticism is a distinction between the criticism of an object which focuses on its historical character and includes an account of its genesis, and an analysis which focuses on contradictions in the concept of the object. Marx later uses the same distinction in his attack on Proudhon, in a letter to P. V. Annenkov (28 December 1846); *Werke* IV, pp. 552–6; English in *The Poverty of Philosophy* (Moscow, n.d.), pp. 77–83.

point of view of the sovereign, since the sovereign and the estates are opposite extremes. Just as the sovereign democratizes himself in the executive, so this estate element must monarchize itself in its deputation. Thus what Hegel wants is a moment of sovereignty issuing from the estates. Just as the executive has an estate-moment on behalf of the sovereign, so there should also be a sovereign-moment on behalf of the estates.

The actuality of harmonization and the impossibility of hostility converts into the following demand: 'So, from the point of view of the classes, one moment in them must be adapted to the task of existing as in essence the moment of mediation.' Adapted to the task! According to § 302 the Estates as a whole have this task. It should not say 'task' but rather 'certainty'. And what kind of task is this anyway which exists as in essence the moment of mediation—being in 'essence' Buridan's ass?

The fact of the matter is simply this:

The Estates are supposed to be the mediation between the crown and the executive on the one hand, and the crown and the people on the other. But they are not this, but rather the organized political opposition to civil society. The legislature in itself is in need of mediation, and indeed a mediation coming from the Estates, as has been shown. The presupposed moral harmonization of the two wills, the will of the state as sovereign will and the will of the state as the will of civil society, does not suffice. Indeed only the legislature is the organized, total political state; yet, precisely in it appears, because it is in its highest degree of development, the open contradiction of the political state with itself. Thus, the appearance of a real identity of the sovereign and Estate wills must be established. Either the Estates must be established as the sovereign will or the sovereign will established as the Estates. The Estates must establish themselves as the actuality of a will which is not the will of the Estates. The unity which is non-existent in essence (otherwise it would have to prove itself by the Estates' efficacy and not by their mode of existing) must at least be present in existence, or else an existing instance of the legislature (of the Estates) has the task of being the unity of what is not united. This moment of the Estates, the Chamber of Peers, the Upper House, etc., is the highest synthesis of the political state in the organization just considered. With that, however, Hegel does not achieve what he wants, namely, the actuality of harmonization and the impossibility of set hostility; rather, the whole thing remains at the point of the possibility of harmonization. However, it is the established illusion of the internal unity of the political state (of the sovereign will and that of the Estates, and furthermore of the principle of the political state and that of civil society), the illusion of this unity as material principle, that is to say, such that not only two opposed principles unite but that the unity is that of one nature or existential ground. The Estates, as this moment, are the romanticism of the political state, the dreams of its substantiality or internal harmony. They are an allegorical existence.

Whether this illusion is an effective illusion or a conscious self-deception depends now on the actual *status quo* of the relationship between the Estate- and sovereign-elements. As long as the Estates and the crown in fact harmonize, or get along together, the illusion in its essential unity is an actual, and thus effective illusion. But on the other hand, should the truth of the illusion become manifest, then it becomes a conscious lie and a ridicule.

§ 305. The principle of one of the classes of civil society is in itself capable of adaptation to this political position. The class in question is the one whose ethical life is natural, whose basis is family life, and, so far as its livelihood is concerned, the possession of land. Its particular members attain their position by birth, just as the monarch does, and, in common with him, they possess a will which rests on itself alone.

We have already demonstrated Hegel's inconsistencies: (1) conceiving of the Estates in their modern abstraction from civil society etc., after having them proceed from Corporations; (2) determining them now once again according to the class distinction of civil society, after having already determined the political Estates as such to be the extreme of empirical universality.

To be consistent one would have to examine the political Estates by themselves as a new element, and then construct out of them the mediation which was demanded in § 304.

But now we see how Hegel reintroduces civil class distinction and, at the same time, makes it appear that it is not the actuality and particular nature of civil class distinction which determines the highest political sphere, the legislature, but rather the reverse, that civil class distinction declines to a pure matter which the political sphere forms and constructs in accordance with its need, a need which arises out of the political sphere itself.

The principle of one of the classes of civil society is in itself capable of adaptation to this political position. The class in question is one whose ethical life is natural. (The agricultural class.)

What, then, does this principle capability, or capability in principle of the agricultural class consist in?

Its basis is family life, and, so far as its livelihood is concerned, the possession of land. Its particular members attain their position by birth, just as the monarch does, and, in common with him, they possess a will which rests on itself alone.

The will which rests on itself alone is related to its livelihood, i.e., the possession of land, to its position by birth which it has in common with the monarch, and to family life, as its basis.

Livelihood as possession of land and a will which rests on itself alone are two quite different things. One should rather say a will which rests on ground and soil. One should rather speak of a will resting on the disposition of the state, not of one resting on itself but in the whole. The possession of land takes the place of the disposition, or the possession of political spirit.

Furthermore, in regard to family life as basis, the social ethical life of civil society appears to occupy a higher position than this natural ethical life. Moreover, family life is the natural ethical life of the other classes, of the civil as well as the agricultural class of civil society. But the fact that 'family life' is, in the case of the agricultural class, not only the principle of the family but also the basis of this class' social existence in general, seems to disqualify it for the highest political task; for this class will apply patriarchal laws to a non-patriarchal sphere, and will think and act in terms of child or father, master and servant, where the real questions are the political state and political citizenship.

Regarding the monarch's position by birth, Hegel has not developed a patriarchal but rather a modern constitutional king. His position by birth consists in his being the bodily representative of the state and in being born as king, or in the kingdom being his family inheritance. But what does this have in common with family life as the basis of the agricultural class; and what does natural ethical life have in common with position by birth as such? The king has this in common with a horse, namely, just as the horse is born a horse so the king is born a king.

Had Hegel made the class distinction, which he already accepted, a political distinction, then the agricultural class as such would already be an independent part of the Estates; and if it is as such a moment of mediation with the principality, why would the construction of a new mediation be necessary? And why separate it off from the actual moment of the Estates, since this moment achieves its abstract position *vis-à-vis* the crown only because of this separation? After he has developed the political Estates as a specific element, as a transubstantiation of the unofficial class into state citizenship, and precisely because of this has found the mediation to be a necessity, by what right does Hegel dissolve this organism once more into the distinction of the unofficial class, and thus into the unofficial class, and then derive from it the political state's mediation with itself?

In any case, what an anomaly, that the highest synthesis of the political state is nothing but the synthesis of landed property and family life!

In a word:

If civil classes as such are political classes, then the mediation is not needed; and if this mediation is needed, then the civil class is not political, and thus also not this mediation. The member of the agricultural class is not as such, but as state citizen, a part of the political Estates; while in the opposite case (i.e., [where he],[1] as member of the agricultural class, is state citizen, or as state citizen is member of this class), his state citizenship is membership in the agricultural class; and then he is not, as member of this class, a state citizen, but is as state citizen a member of this class!

Here, then, we find one of Hegel's inconsistencies within his own way of viewing things; and such an inconsistency is an accommodation. The political Estates in the modern sense, which is the sense developed by Hegel, constitute the fully established separation of civil society from its unofficial class and its distinctions. How can Hegel make the unofficial class the solution of the antinomies which the legislature has within itself? Hegel wants the medieval system of Estates, but in the modern sense of the legislature; and he wants the modern legislature, but within the framework of the medieval system of Estates! This is syncretism at its worst.

The beginning of § 304 reads:

> The Estates, as an element in political life, still retain in their own function the class distinctions already present in the lower spheres of civil life.

But in their own function, the Estates, as an element in political life, retain this distinction only by annulling it, negating it within themselves, abstracting themselves from it.

Should the agricultural class—or, as we will hear later, the empowered agricultural class, aristocratic landed property—become as such, and as described, the mediation of the total political state, i.e., of the legislature within itself, then it is certainly the mediation of the political Estates with the crown, in the sense of being the dissolution of the political Estates as an actual political element. Not the agricultural class, but class, the unofficial class, the analysis (reduction) of the political Estates into the unofficial class, constitutes here the reestablished unity of the political state with itself. (The mediation here is not the agricultural class as such, but rather its separation from the political Estates in its quality as civil unofficial class; that is, its unofficial class [reality] gives it a separate position within the political Estates, whereupon the other section of the political Estates is also given the position of a particular unofficial class, and, therefore, it

_____
[1] German editors' addition.

ceases to represent the state citizenship of civil society.) Here then, the political state no longer exists as two opposed wills; rather, on the one side stands the political state (the executive and the sovereign), and on the other side stands civil society in its distinction from the political state (the various classes). With that, then, the political state as a totality is abolished.

The other sense of the duplication of the political Estates within themselves as a mediation with the crown is, in general, this: the internal separation of the political Estates, their own inner opposition, is a re-established unity with the crown. The fundamental dualism between the crown and the Estates as an element in the legislature is neutralized by the dualism within the Estates themselves. With Hegel, however, this neutralization is effected by the political Estates separating themselves from their political element.

We will return later to the subject of possession of land as livelihood, which is supposed to accord with sovereignty of will, i.e., the sovereignty of the crown, and to family life as the basis of the agricultural class, which is supposed to accord with the position by birth of the crown. What is developed here in § 305 is the principle of the agricultural class which is in itself capable of adaptation to this political position.

§ 306 deals with the adaption to political position and significance; it reduces to the following: 'Their wealth becomes inalienable, entailed, and burdened by primogeniture. Thus, primogeniture would be the adaption of the agricultural class to politics.

Primogeniture is grounded, so it says in the Addition, on the fact that the state should be able to reckon not on the bare possibility of political inclinations, but on something necessary. Now an inclination for politics is of course not bound up with wealth, but there is a relatively necessary connexion between the two, because a man with independent means is not hemmed in by external circumstances and so there is nothing to prevent him from entering politics and working for the state.

First sentence: The state is not content with the bare possibility of political inclinations, but should be able to reckon on something necessary.

Second sentence: An inclination for politics is of course not bound up with wealth; that is, the inclination for politics in those of wealth is a bare possibility.

Third sentence: But there is a relatively necessary connexion, namely, a man with independent means etc. finds nothing to prevent him from working for the state; that is, the means provide the possibility of political inclinations. But according to the first sentence, this possibility precisely does not suffice.

In addition, Hegel has failed to show that possession of land is the sole independent means.

The adaption of its means to independence is the adaption of the agricultural class to political position and significance. In other words, independent means is its political position and significance.

This independence is further developed as follows:

Its wealth is independent of the state's capital. 'State's capital' here apparently means the government treasury. In this respect the universal class, as essentially dependent on the state, stands in opposition.

As it says in the Preface [to Hegel's *Philosophy of Right*]:

Apart from anything else philosophy with us is not, as it was with the Greeks for instance, pursued in private like an art, but has an existence in the open, in contact with the public, and especially, or even only, in the service of the state.

Thus, philosophy is also essentially dependent upon the government treasury.

Its ['the agricultural class'] wealth is independent of the uncertainty of business, the quest for profit, and any sort of fluctuation in possessions. From this aspect it is opposed by the business class as the one which is dependent on needs and concentrated on their satisfaction.

This wealth is independent of favor, whether from the executive or the mob.

Finally, it is even fortified against its own wilfulness, because those members of this class who are called to political life are not entitled, as other citizens are, either to dispose of their entire property at will, or to the assurance that it will pass to their children, whom they love equally, in similarly equal divisions.

Here the oppositions have taken on an entirely new and materialistic form such as we would hardly expect to find in the heaven of the political state.

In sharpest terms, the opposition, as Hegel develops it, is the opposition of private property and wealth.

The possession of land is private property κατ' ἐξοχὴν, true private property. Its exact private nature is prominent (1) as independence from state capital, from favor from the executive, from property existing as universal property of the political state, a particular wealth which, alongside of other wealth, is in accordance with the construction of the political state; (2) as independence from the need of society or the social wealth, from favor from the mob. (Equally significant is the fact that a share in state capital is understood as favor from the executive just as a share in the social wealth is understood as favor from the mob.) Neither the wealth of the universal class nor that of the business class is true private property, because such wealth is occasioned, in the former case directly, in the latter case indirectly, by the connexion with the universal wealth, or property as social property; both are a participation in it, and therefore both are mediated through favor, that is, through the contingency of will. In opposition to that stands the possession of land as sovereign private property, which has not yet acquired the form of wealth, i.e., property established by the social will.

Thus, at its highest point the political constitution is the constitution of private property. The highest political inclination is the inclination of private property. Primogeniture is merely the external appearance of the internal nature of the possession of land. Because it is inalienable, its social nerves have been severed and its isolation from civil society is secured. By not passing on to the children whom they love equally, it is independent even of the smallest society, the natural society, the family. By having withdrawn from the volition and laws of the family it thus safeguards its rough nature of private property against the transition into family wealth.

In § 305, Hegel declared the class of landed property to be capable of adaption to the political position because family life would be its basis. But he himself has declared love to be the basis, the principle, the spirit of family life. The class whose basis is family life thus lacks the basis of family life, i.e., love, as the actual and thus effective and determining principle. It is spiritless family life, the illusion of family life. In its highest form of development, the principle of private property contradicts the principle of the family. Family life in civil society becomes family life, the life of love, only in opposition to the class of natural ethical life, [which is, according to Hegel] the class of family life. This latter is, rather, the barbarism of private property against family life.

This, then, would be the sovereign splendor of private property, of possession of land, about which so many sentimentalities have recently been uttered and on behalf of which so many multi-colored crocodile tears have been shed.

It does not help Hegel to say that primogeniture would be merely a requirement of politics and would have to be understood in its political position and significance. Neither does it help him to say: 'The security and stability of the agricultural class may be still further increased by the institution of primogeniture, though this institution is desirable only from the point of view of politics, since it entails a sacrifice for the political end of giving the eldest son a life of independence.' There is a certain decency of mind in Hegel. He does not want primogeniture in and for itself, but only in reference to something else, not as something self-determined but as something determined by another, not as an end but as a means for justifying and constructing an end. In fact, primogeniture is a consequence of the exact possession of land; it is petrified private property, private property (*quand même*) in the highest independence and sharpness of its development. What Hegel presents as the end, the determining factor, the *prima causa*, of primogeniture is, instead, an effect, a consequence of the power of abstract private property over the political state, while Hegel presents primogeniture as the power of the political state over private property. He makes the cause the effect and the effect the cause, the determining that which has been determined and that which has been determined the determining.

What then is the content of political adaption, of the political end: what is the end of this end, what is its substance? Primogeniture, the superlative of private property, sovereign private property. What kind of power does the political state exercise over private property in primogeniture? Does the state isolate it from the family and society and bring it to its abstract autonomy? What then is the power of the political state over private property? Private property's own power, its essence brought to existence. What remains to the political state in opposition to this essence? The illusion that it determines when it is rather determined. Indeed, it breaks the will of the family and of society, but merely in order to give existence to the will of private property lacking family and society, and to acknowledge this existence as the highest existence of the political state, as the highest ethical existence.

Let us consider the various elements as they relate here in the legislature to the total state, the state having achieved actuality, consistency, and consciousness, i.e., to the actual political state [in connexion][1] with the ideal or what ought be, with the logical character and form of these elements.

(Primogeniture is not, as Hegel says, a chain on the freedom of private rights; it is rather the freedom of private rights which has freed itself from all social and ethical chains.) (The highest political construction is the construction of abstract private property.)

Before we make this comparison we should first consider more closely one statement of the paragraph, namely, that because of primogeniture the wealth of the agricultural class, possession of land, private property, 'is even fortified against its own wilfulness, because those members of this class who are called to political life are not entitled, as other citizens are,

---

[1] German editors' addition.

to dispose of their entire property at will'.

We have already indicated how the social nerves of private property are severed because of the inalienability of landed property. Private property (landed property) is fortified against the owner's own wilfulness by having the sphere of his wilfulness suddenly changed from a universal human sphere into the specific wilfulness of private property. In other words, private property has become the subject of the will, and the will is merely the predicate of private property. Private property is no longer a determined object of wilfulness, but rather wilfulness is the determined predicate of private property. Yet let us compare this with what Hegel himself says about the sphere of private rights:

§ 65. The reason I can alienate my property is that it is mine only in so far as I put my will into it...[1] provided always that the thing in question is a thing external by nature.

§ 66. Therefore those goods, or rather substantive characteristics, which constitute my own private personality and the universal essence of my self-consciousness are inalienable and my right to them is imprescriptible. Such characteristics are my personality as such, my universal freedom of will, my ethical life, my religion.

Therefore in primogeniture landed property, exact private property, becomes an inalienable good, thus a substantive characteristic which constitutes the very private personality and universal essence of self-consciousness of the class of noble entailed estates, its personality as such, its universal freedom of will, its ethical life, its religion. Thus it is also consistent to say that where private property, landed property, is inalienable, universal freedom of will (to which also belongs free disposition of something alienable, like landed property) and ethical life (to which also belongs love as the actual spirit of the family, the spirit which is also identified with the actual law of the family) are alienable. In general then, the inalienability of private property is the alienability of universal freedom of will and ethical life. Here it is no longer the case that property is in so far as I put my will into it, but rather my will is in so far as it is in property. Here my will does not own but is owned. This is precisely the romantic itch of the nobility of primogeniture, namely, that here private property, and thus private wilfulness in its most abstract form—the totally ignorant, unethical, crude will—appears to be the highest synthesis of the political state, the highest renunciation of wilfulness, the hardest and most self-sacrificing struggle with human weakness; for what appears here to be human weakness is actually the humanizing, the humanization of private property.

1 Marx's ellipsis.

Primogeniture is private property which has become a religion for itself, which has become absorbed in itself, enchanted with its autonomy and nobility. Just as primogeniture is derived from direct alienation, so too it is derived from the contract. Hegel presents the transition from property to contract in the following manner:

§ 71. Existence as determinate being is in essence being for another;...[1] One aspect of property is that it is an existent as an external thing, and in this respect property exists for other external things and is connected with their necessity and contingency. But it is also an existent as an embodiment of will, and from this point of view the 'other' for which it exists can only be the will of another person. This relation of will to will is the true and proper ground in which freedom is existent. —The sphere of contract is made up of this mediation whereby I hold property not merely by means of a thing and my subjective will but by means of another person's will as well and so hold it in virtue of my participation in a common will.

(In primogeniture it has been made a state law to hold property not in one common will, but merely by means of a thing and my subjective will.) While Hegel here perceives in private rights the alienability and dependence of private property on a common will as its true idealism, in state rights, on the other hand, he praises the imaginary nobility of independent property as opposed to the uncertainty of business, the quest for profit, any sort of fluctuation in possessions, and dependence on the state's capital. What kind of state is this that cannot even tolerate the idealism of private rights? And what kind of philosophy of right is this in which the independence of private property has diverse meanings in the spheres of private and state rights?

Over against the crude stupidity of independent private property, the uncertainty of business is elegiac, the quest for profit solemn (dramatic), fluctuation in possessions a serious *fatum* (tragic), dependence on the state's capital ethical. In short, in all of these qualities the human heart pulses throughout the property, which is the dependence of man on man. No matter how it may be constituted it is human toward the slave who believes himself to be free, because the sphere that limits him is not society but the soil. The freedom of this will is its emptiness of content other than that of private property.

To define monstrosities like primogeniture as a determination of private property by the state is absolutely unavoidable if one interprets an old world view in terms of a new one, if one attributes to a thing, as in this case to private property, a double meaning, one in the court of abstract right and an opposed one in the heaven of the political state.

[1] Marx's ellipsis.

Now we come to the comparison mentioned earlier.

§ 257 says:

> The state is the actuality of the ethical Idea. It is ethical mind *qua* the substantial will manifest and revealed to itself...[1] The state exists immediately in custom, immediately in individual self-consciousness...[1] while self-consciousness in virtue of its sentiment towards the state finds in the state, as its essence and the end and product of its activity, its substantive freedom.

§ 268 says:

> The political sentiment, patriotism pure and simple, is assured conviction with truth as its basis...[1] and a volition which has become habitual. In this sense it is simply a product of the institutions subsisting in the state, since rationality is actually present in the state, while action in conformity with these institutions gives rationality its practical proof. This sentiment is, in general, trust (which may pass over into a greater or lesser degree of educated insight), or the consciousness that my interest, both substantive and particular, is contained and preserved in another's (i.e., in the state's) interest and end, i.e., in the other's relation to me as an individual. In this way, this very other is immediately not another in my eyes, and in being conscious of this fact I am free.

Here, the actuality of the ethical Idea appears as the religion of private property (because in primogeniture private property relates to itself in a religious manner, so it happens that in our modern times religion in general has become a quality inherent in landed property, and that all of the writings on the nobility of primogeniture are full of religious unction. Religion is the highest thought form of this brutality.) The substantial will manifest and revealed to itself changes into a will dark and broken on the soil, a will enraptured precisely with the impenetrability of the element to which it is attached. The assured conviction with truth as its basis, which is political sentiment, is the conviction standing on 'its own ground' (in the literal sense). The political volition which has become habitual no longer remains simply a product [of the institutions subsisting in the state], but rather an institution subsisting outside the state. The political sentiment is no longer trust but rather the reliance, the consciousness that my interest, both substantive and particular, is independent of another's (i.e., the state's) interest and end, i.e., in the other's relation to me as an individual. This is the consciousness of my freedom from the state.

The maintenance of the state's universal interest etc. was (§ 289) the task of the executive. In it resided the consciousness of right and the developed intelligence of the mass of the people (§ 297). It actually makes the Estates superfluous, for even without the Estates they [i.e., the highest

---

[1] Marx's ellipses.

civil servants] are able to do what is best, just as they also continually have to do while the Estates are in session (Remark to § 301). The universal class, or, more precisely, the class of civil servants, must, purely in virtue of its character as universal, have the universal as the end of its essential activity [§ 303].

And how does the universal class, the executive, appear now? As essentially dependent upon the state, as wealth dependent upon the favor of the executive. The very same transformation has occurred within civil society, which earlier achieved its ethical life in the Corporation. It is a wealth dependent upon the uncertainty of business etc., upon the favor of the mob.

What then is the quality which ostensibly specifies the owners of entailed estates? And what, in any case, constitutes the ethical quality of an inalienable wealth? Incorruptibility. Incorruptibility appears to be the highest political virtue, an abstract virtue. Yet, incorruptibility in the state as constructed by Hegel is something so uncommon that it has to be built up into a particular political power; which precisely proves[1] that incorruptibility is not the spirit of the political state, not the rule but the exception, and is constructed as such. The owners of entailed estates are corrupted by their independent property in order that they be preserved from corruption. While according to the idea dependence upon the state and the feeling of this dependence is supposed to be the highest political freedom, here the independent private person is constructed; because political freedom is the private person's feeling of being an abstract, dependent person, whereas he feels and should feel independent only as a citizen. Its capital is independent alike of the state's capital, the uncertainty of business, etc. In opposition to it stands the business class, which is dependent on needs and concentrated on their satisfaction, and the civil servant class, which is essentially dependent upon the state. Here, therefore, independence from the state and civil society and this actualized abstraction of both, which in reality is the crudest dependence on the soil, forms in the legislature the mediation and the unity of both. Independent private wealth, i.e., abstract private wealth and the corresponding private person, are the highest political construction of the state. Political independence is constructed as independent private property and the person of this independent private property. We shall see in the following paragraph what the situation is *re vera* regarding this independence and incorruptibility, and the political sentiment arising from them.

---

[1] Following Lieber and Furth: '...also eben dadurch beweist, dass...' (*Werke* has: '...also eben dadurch bewusst, dass...').

The fact that primogeniture is inherited, or entailed wealth speaks for itself. More about this later. The fact that it accrues to the first-born is, as Hegel notes in the Addition, purely historical.

§ 307. The right of this section of the agricultural class is thus based in a way on the natural principle of the family. But this principle is at the same time reversed owing to hard sacrifices made for political ends, and thereby the activity of this class is essentially directed to those ends. As a consequence of this, this class is summoned and entitled to its political vocation by birth without the hazards of election.

Hegel has failed to develop the way in which the right of this agricultural class is based on the natural principle of the family, unless by this he understands that landed property exists as entailed or inherited wealth. That, however, establishes no right of this class in the political sense, but only the birthright of the owners of entailed estates to landed property. 'This', i.e., the natural principle of the family, is 'at the same time reversed owing to hard sacrifices made for political ends'. We have certainly seen how the natural principle of the family is reversed; this, however, is no hard sacrifice made for political ends, but rather the actualized abstraction of private property. But with this reversal of the natural principle of the family the political ends are likewise reversed, 'thereby (?) the activity of this class is essentially directed to those ends'—because private property received independence?—and 'as a consequence of this, this class is summoned and entitled to its political vocation by birth without the hazards of election'.

Here then participation in the legislature is an innate human right. Here we have born legislators, i.e., born mediation of the political state with itself. Innate human rights have been mocked, especially on behalf of the owners of entailed estates. Isn't it even more humorous that one particular group of men is entrusted with the right to the highest honor, the legislature? In Hegel's treatment of the summons to the legislator, to the representative of state citizenship, there is nothing more ridiculous than his opposing summons by birth to summons by the hazards of election. As if election, the conscious product of civil trust, would not stand in a completely different necessary connexion with the political ends than does the physical accident of birth. Hegel everywhere falls from his political spiritualism into the crassest materialism. At the summit of the political state it is always birth that makes determinate individuals into embodiments of the highest political tasks. The highest political activities coincide with individuals by reason of birth, just like an animal's position, character, way of life, etc. are immediately inborn. In its highest functions the state acquires an animal actuality. Nature takes revenge on Hegel for the disdain he showed it. If matter is supposed to constitute no longer anything for itself over against the human will, the human will no longer retains anything for itself except the matter.

The false identity, the fragmentary and sporadic identity of nature and spirit, body and soul, appears as incarnation. Since birth gives man only an individual existence and establishes him merely as a natural individual, and since the functions of the state—as for instance the legislature, etc.— are social products, i.e., births of society and not procreations of the natural individual, then what is striking and miraculous is precisely the immediate identity, the sudden coincidence, of the individual's birth with the individual as individuation of a certain social position, function, etc. In this system, nature immediately creates kings, peers, etc. just as it creates eyes and noses. What is striking is to see as immediate product of the physical species what is only the product of the self-conscious species. I am man by birth, without the agreement of society; yet only through universal agreement does this determinate birth become peer or king. Only the agreement makes the birth of this man the birth of a king. It is therefore the agreement, not birth, that makes the king. If birth, in distinction from other determinations, immediately endows man with a position, then his body makes him this determined social functionary. His body is his social right. In this system, the physical dignity of man, or the dignity of the human body (with further elaboration, meaning: the dignity of the physical natural element of the state), appears in such a form that determinate dignities, specifically the highest social diginities, are the dignities of certain bodies which are determined and pre-destined by birth to be such. This is, of course, why we find in the aristocracy such pride in blood and descent, in short, in the life history of their body. It is this zoological point of view which has its corresponding science in heraldry. The secret of aristocracy is zoology.

Two moments in hereditary primogeniture are to be stressed:

(1) That which is permanent is entailed wealth, landed property. This is the preserving moment in the relation—the substance. The master of the entailed estate, the owner, is really a mere accident. Landed property anthropomorphizes itself in the various generations. Landed property always inherits, as it were, the first born of the house as an attribute linked to it. Every first born in the line of land owners is the inheritance, the property, of the inalienable landed property, which is the predestined substance of his will and activity. The subject is the thing and the predicate is the man. The will becomes the property of the property.

(2) The political quality of the owner of the entailed estate is the political quality of his inherited wealth, a political quality inhering in his inherited

wealth. Here, therefore, the political quality appears also as the property of landed property, as a quality which is ascribed directly to the bare physical earth (nature).

Regarding the first point, it follows that the owner of the entailed estate is the serf of the landed property, and that in the serfs who are subordinated to him there appears only the practical consequence of the theoretical relationship with landed property in which he himself stands. The depth of German subjectivity appears everywhere as the crudity of a mindless objectivity.

Here we must analyze (1) the relation between private property and inheritance, (2) the relation between private property, inheritance, and, thereby, the privilege of certain generations to participate in political sovereignty, (3) the actual historical relation, or the Germanic relation.

We have seen that primogeniture is the abstraction of independent private property. A second consequence follows from this. Independence, autonomy, in the political state whose construction we have followed so far, is private property, which at its peak appears as inalienable landed property. Political independence thus flows not *ex proprio sinu* of the political state; it is not a gift of the political state to its members, nor is it the animating spirit [of the political state]. Rather, the members of the political state receive their independence from a being which is not the being of the political state, from a being of abstract private right, namely, from abstract private property. Political independence is an accident of private property and not the substance of the political state. The political state—and within it the legislature, as we have seen—is the unveiled mystery of the true value and essence of the moments of the state. The significance that private property has in the political state is its essential, its true significance; the significance that class distinction has in the political state is the essential significance of class distinction. In the same way, the essence of the sovereign and of the executive come to appearance in the legislature. It is here, in the sphere of the political state, that the individual moments of the state relate to themselves as to the being of the species, the 'species-being', because the political state is the sphere of their universal character, i.e., their religious sphere. The political state is the mirror of truth for the various moments of the concrete state.

Thus, if independent private property in the political state, in the legislature, has the significance of political independence, then it *is* the political independence of the state. Independent private property, or actual private property is then not only the support of the constitution but the constitution itself. And isn't the support of the constitution nothing other than the constitution of constitutions, the primary, the actual constitution?

Hegel himself was surprised about the immanent development of a science, the derivation of its entire content from the concept in its simplicity (Remark to § 279), when he was constructing the hereditary monarch, and made the following remark:

> Hence it is the basic moment of personality, abstract at the start in immediate rights, which has matured itself through its various forms of subjectivity, and now—at the stage of absolute rights, of the state, of the completely concrete objectivity of the will —has become the personality of the state, its certainty of itself.

That is, in the political state it comes to appearance that abstract personality is the highest political personality, the political basis of the entire state. Likewise, in primogeniture, the right of this abstract personality, its objectivity, abstract private property, comes into existence as the highest objectivity of the state, i.e., as its highest right.

The state is hereditary monarch; abstract personality means nothing other than that the personality of the state is abstract, or that it is the state of abstract personality, just as the Romans developed the rights of the monarch purely within the norms of private rights, or private rights as the highest norm of state, or political rights.

The Romans are the rationalists, the Germans the mystics of sovereign private property.

Hegel calls private rights the rights of abstract personality, or abstract rights. And indeed they have to be developed as the abstraction, and thus the illusory rights, of abstract personality, just as the moral doctrine developed by Hegel is the illusory existence of abstract subjectivity. Hegel develops private rights and morals as such abstractions, from which it does not follow, for him, that the state or ethical life of which they are the presuppositions can be nothing but the society (the social life) of these illusions; rather, he concludes that they are subalternate moments of this ethical life. But what are private rights except the rights of these subjects of the state, and what is morality except their morality? In other words, the person of private rights and the subject of morals are the person and the subject of the state. Hegel has been widely criticized for his development of morality. He has done nothing but develop the morality of the modern state and modern private rights. A more complete separation of morality from the state, its fuller emancipation, was desired. What did that prove except that the separation of the present-day state from morals is moral, that morals are non-political and that the state is not moral? It is rather a great, though from one aspect (namely, from the aspect that Hegel declares the state, whose presupposition is such a morality, to be the realistic idea of ethical life) an unconscious service of Hegel to have assigned to modern morality its true position.

In the constitution, wherein primogeniture is a guarantee, private property is the guarantee of the political constitution. In primogeniture, it appears that this guarantee is a particular kind of private property. Primogeniture is merely a particular existence of the universal relationship of private property and the political state. Primogeniture is the political sense of private property, private property in its political significance, that is to say, in its universal significance. Thus the constitution here is the constitution of private property.

With the Germanic peoples, where we encounter primogeniture in its classical formation, we also find the constitution of private property. Private property is a universal category, the universal bond of the state. Even the universal functions appear as the private property sometimes of a Corporation, sometimes of an estate.

Trade and business in their particular nuances were the private property of particular Corporations. Royal offices, jurisdiction, etc., were the private property of particular estates. The various provinces were the private property of individual princes etc. Service for the realm was the private property of the ruler. The spirit was the private property of the spiritual authority.[1] One's loyal activity was the private property of another, just as one's right was, once again, a particular private property. Sovereignty, here nationality, was the private property of the Emperor.

It has often been said that in the Middle Ages every form of right, of freedom, of social existence, appears as a privilege, an exception from the rule. The empirical fact that all these privileges appear in the form of private property could thus not have been overlooked. What is the universal reason for this coincidence? Private property is the species-existence of privilege, of right as an exception.

Where the sovereigns, as in France for instance, attacked the independence of private property, they directed their attention more to the property of the Corporations than to that of individuals. But in attacking the private property of the Corporations they attacked private property as Corporations, i.e., as the social bond.

In the feudal reign it almost appears that the power of the crown is the power of private property, and that the mystery of the nature of the universal power, the power of all spheres of the state, is deposited in the sovereign.

---

[1] '...das Privateigentum der Geistlichkeit'. We take him to mean that man's spiritual life was the exclusive province of the Church.

(The powerfulness of the state is expressed in the sovereign as the representative of the power of the state. The constitutional sovereign, therefore, expresses the idea of the constitutional state in its sharpest abstraction. On the one hand he is the idea of the state, the sanctified majesty of the state, and precisely as *this* person. At the same time he is a pure imagination; as person and as sovereign he has neither actual power nor actual function. Here, the separation of the political and the actual, the formal and the material, the universal and the particular person, of man and social man, is expressed in its highest contradiction.)

Private property is a child of Roman intellect and Germanic heart. At this point it will be valuable to undertake a comparison of these two extreme developments. This will help solve the political problem as discussed.[1]

The Romans were the first to have formulated the right of private property, i.e., the abstract right, the private right, the right of the abstract person. The Roman conception of private right is private right in its classical formulation. Yet nowhere with the Romans do we find that the right of private property was mystified as in the case of the Germans. Nowhere does it become right of the state.

The right of private property is *jus utendi et abutendi*, the right of wilfulness in disposing of a thing. The main interest of the Romans lay in developing the relationships, and in determining which ones resulted in abstract relations of private property. The actual basis of private property, the property, is a *factum*, an unexplainable *factum*, and *no* right. Only through legal determinations, which the society attributes to the factual property, does it receive the quality of rightful property, private property.

Regarding the connexion between the political constitution and private property with the Romans, it appears that:

(1) Man (as slave), as is generally the case with ancient peoples, is the object of private property.

This is nothing specific.

(2) Conquered countries are treated as private property, *jus utendi et abutendi* being asserted in their case.

(3) In their history itself, there appears the struggle between the poor and the rich (Patricians and Plebians) etc.

In other respects, private property as a whole, as with the ancient classical peoples in general, is asserted to be public property, either as the

---

[1] End of manuscript p. 129. At this point in the manuscript begins the material of *Bogen* XXXIV, manuscript pp. 130–2 which begins with Marx's notation, (*ad XII*), and which is found in our pp. 39–40 in accord with all of the German editions.

republic's expenditure—as in good times—or as luxurious and universal benefaction (baths, etc.) towards the mob.

Slavery finds its explanation in the rights of war, the rights of occupation: men are slaves precisely because their political existence is destroyed. We especially stress two relationships in distinction from the Germans.

(1) The imperial power was not the power of private property, but rather the sovereignty of the empirical will as such, which was far from regarding private property as the bond between itself and its subjects; on the contrary, it dealt with private property as it did with all other social goods. The imperial power, therefore, was nothing other than factually hereditary. The highest formation of the right of private property, of private right, indeed belongs to the imperial epoch; however, it is a consequence of the political dissolution rather than the political dissolution being a consequence of private property. Furthermore, when private right achieved full development in Rome, state right was abolished, [or] was in the process of its dissolution, while in Germany the opposite was the case.

(2) In Rome, state honors are never hereditary; that is to say, private property is not the dominant category of the state.

(3) Contrary to German primogeniture etc., in Rome the wilfulness of the testator appears to be the derivative of private property. In this latter antithesis lies the entire difference between the German and the Roman development of private property.

(In primogeniture it appears that private property is the relationship to the function of the state which is such that the existence of the state is something inhering in, or is an accident of, direct private property, i.e., landed property. At its highest levels the state appears as private property, whereas private property should appear as property of the state. Instead of making private property a civil quality, Hegel makes political citizenship, existence, and sentiment a quality of private property.)

§ 308. The second section of the Estates comprises the fluctuating element in civil society. This element can enter politics only through its deputies; the multiplicity of its members is an external reason for this, but the essential reason is the specific character of this element and its activity. Since these deputies are the deputies of civil society, it follows as a direct consequence that their appointment is made by the society as a society. That is to say, in making the appointment, society is not dispersed into atomic units, collected to perform only a single and temporary act, and kept together for a moment and no longer. On the contrary, it makes the appointment as a society, articulated into associations, communities, and Corporations, which although constituted already for other purposes, acquire in this way a connexion with politics. The existence of the Estates and their assembly finds a constitutional guarantee of its own in the fact that this class is entitled to send deputies at the summons of the crown, while members of the former class are entitled to present themselves in person in the Estates (see Paragraph 307).

Here we find a new distinction within civil society and the Estates: the distinction between a fluctuating element and an immutable element (landed property). This distinction has also been presented as that of space and time, conservative and progressive, etc. On this, see Hegel's previous paragraphs. Incidentally, by means of the Corporations, associations, etc., Hegel has made the fluctuating element of society also a stable element.

The second distinction consists in the fact that the first element of the Estates as developed above, the owners of entailed estates, are, as such, legislators; that legislative power is an attribute of their empirical, personal existence; that they act not as deputies but as themselves; whereas in the second element of the Estates election and selection of deputies take place.

Hegel gives two reasons why this fluctuating element of civil society can enter the political state, or legislature, only through deputies. Hegel himself calls the first reason—namely, the multiplicity of its members—external, thereby relieving us of the need of giving the same reply.

But the essential reason, he says, is the specific character of this element and its activity. Political occupation and activity are alien to its specific character and activity.

Hegel replays his old song about these Estates being deputies of civil society. Civil society must make the appointments as a society. Rather, civil society must do this as what it is *not*, because it is unpolitical society, and is supposed to perform here a political act as something essential to it and arising from it. With that it is 'dispersed into atomic units', and 'collected to perform only a single and temporary act, and kept together for a moment and no longer'. First of all, its political act is a single and temporary act, and can therefore only appear as such in being carried out. It is an ecstacy, an act of political society which causes a stir, and must also appear as such. Secondly, Hegel was not disturbed by the fact—indeed, he argued its necessity—that civil society materially (merely as a second society deputized by it) separates itself from its civil actuality and establishes itself as what it is not. How can he now formally dispose of this?

He thinks that society's associations etc., which are constituted already for other purposes, acquire a connexion with politics because society in its Corporations etc. appoints the deputies. But either they acquire a significance which is not their significance, or their connexion as such is political, in which case it does not just 'acquire' the political tinge, as developed above, but rather in it politics acquires its connexion. By designating only this part of the Estates as that of the deputy, Hegel has unwittingly stated the nature of the two Chambers (at the point where they actually have the relationship to one another he indicated). The Chamber of Deputies and the Chamber of Peers (or whatever they be called) are not, in the present case, different instances of the same principle) but derive from two essentially different principles and social positions. Here the Chamber of Deputies is the political constitution of civil society in the modern sense, while the Chamber of Peers is the political constitution of civil society in the sense proper to the Estates. The Chamber of Peers and the Chamber of Deputies are opposed here as the Estate- and the political-representation of civil society. The one is the existing estate principle of civil society, the other is the actualization of civil society's abstract political existence. It is obvious, therefore, that the latter cannot come into existence again as the representation of the estates, Corporations, etc., for it simply does not represent civil society's existence *qua* estate, but rather its political existence. It is further obvious, then, that only the estate element of civil society, i.e., sovereign landed property or the hereditary nobility, is seated in the former Chamber, for it is not *one* estate among others. Rather, the estate principle of civil society as an actually social, and thus political, principle now exists only in that one element. It is *the* estate. Civil society, then, has in the Chamber of the estates the representative of its medieval existence, and in the Chamber of Deputies the representative of its political (modern) existence. The only advance beyond the Middle Ages consists in the fact that estate politics has been reduced to a particular political existence alongside the politics of citizenship. The empirical political existence Hegel has in mind (England) has, therefore, a meaning entirely other than the one he imputes to it.

The French Constitution also constitutes an advance in this regard. To be sure, it has reduced the Chamber of Peers to a pure nullity; but within the principle of constitutional kingship as Hegel has pretended to develop it, this Chamber can by its very nature be merely an empty vanity, the fiction of a harmony between the sovereign and civil society, or of the legislature or political state with itself, and a fiction, moreover, which has the form of a particular and thereby once more opposed existence.

The French have allowed the peers to retain life tenure in order to express their independence from both the régime and the people. But they did away with the medieval expression—hereditariness. Their advance consists in their no longer allowing the Chamber of Peers to proceed from actual civil society, but in creating it in abstraction from civil society. They have the choice of peers proceed from the existing political state, from the sovereign, without binding him to any other civil quality. In this constitution the honor of being a peer actually constitutes a class in civil society which is purely political, created from the standpoint of the abstraction of the political state; but it appears to be more a political decoration than an actual class endowed with particular rights. During the Restoration the Chamber of Peers was a reminiscence, while the Chamber of Peers resulting from the July Revolution is an actual creature of constitutional monarchy.

Since in modern times the idea of the state could appear only in the abstraction of the merely political state, or in the abstraction of civil society from itself and its actual condition, it is to the credit of the French that they have marked and produced this abstract actuality, and thereby have produced the political principle itself. The abstraction for which they are blamed is, then, a genuine consequence and product of a patriotism rediscovered, to be sure, only in an opposition, but in a necessary opposition. The merit of the French in this regard, then, is to have established the Chamber of Peers as the unique product of the political state, or in general, to have made the political principle in its uniqueness the determining and effective factor.

Hegel also remarks that in the deputation, as he constructs it, the existence of the Estates and their assembly finds a constitutional guarantee of its own in the fact that the Corporations etc. are entitled to send deputies. Thus, the guarantee of the existence of the Estates' assembly, their truly primitive existence, becomes the privilege of the Corporations etc. With this, Hegel reverts completely to the medieval standpoint and has abandoned entirely his abstraction of the political state as the sphere of the state as state, the actually existing universal.

In the modern sense, the existence of the Estates' assembly is the political existence of civil society, the guarantee of its political existence. To question the existence of the Estates' assembly is to question the existence of the state. Whereas patriotism, the essence of the legislature, finds its guarantee in independent private property according to Hegel, so the existence of the legislature finds its guarantee in the privileges of the Corporations.

But the one element in the Estates is much more the political privilege of civil society, or its privilege of being political. Therefore, that element can never be the privilege of a particular civil mode of civil society's existence, and can still less find its guarantee in that mode, because it is supposed to be, rather, the universal guarantee.

Thus Hegel is everywhere reduced to giving the political state a precarious actuality in a relationship of dependence upon another, rather than describing it as the highest, completely existing actuality of social existence; he is reduced to having it find its true existence in the other sphere rather than describing it as the true existence of the other sphere. The political state everywhere needs the guarantee of spheres lying outside it. It is not actualized power, but supported impotence. It is not the power over these supports, but the power of the support. The support is the seat of power.

What kind of lofty existent is it whose existence needs a guarantee outside itself, and which is supposed to be at the same time the universal existence—and thus the actual guarantee—of this very guarantee. In general, in his development of the legislature Hegel everywhere retreats from the philosophical standpoint to that other standpoint which fails to examine the matter in its own terms.

If the existence of the Estates requires a guarantee, then they are not an actual, but merely a fictitious political existence. In constitutional states, the guarantee for the existence of the Estates is the law. Thus, their existence is a legal existence, dependent on the universal nature of the state and not on the power or impotence of individual Corporations or associations; their existence is the actuality of the state as an association. (It is precisely here that the Corporations, etc., the particular spheres of civil society, should receive their universal existence for the first time. Again, Hegel anticipates this universal existence as the privilege and the existence of these particular spheres.)

Political right as the right of Corporations etc. completely contradicts political right as political, i.e., as the right of the state and of citizenship, for political right precisely should not be the right of this existence as a particular existence, not right as this particular existence.

Before we proceed to the category of election as the political act by which civil society decides upon its political choice, let us examine some additional statements from the Remark to this paragraph.

To hold that every single person should share in deliberating and deciding on political matters of general concern on the ground that all individuals are members of the state, that its concerns are their concerns, and that it is their right that what is done should be done with their knowledge and volition, is tantamount to a proposal to put the democratic element without any rational form into the organism of the state, although it is only in virtue of the possession of such a form that the state is an organism at all. This idea comes readily to mind because it does not go beyond the abstraction of 'being a member of the state', and it is superficial thinking which clings to abstractions. [§ 308][1]

---

[1] German editors' addition.

First of all, Hegel calls being a member of the state an abstraction, although according to the idea, [and therefore] the intention of his own doctrinal development, it is the highest and most concrete social determination of the legal person, of the member of the state. To stop at the abstraction of 'being a member of the state' and to conceive of individuals in terms of this abstraction does not therefore seem to be just superficial thinking which clings to abstractions. That the abstraction of 'being a member of the state' is really an abstraction is not, however, the fault of this thinking but of Hegel's line of argument and actual modern conditions, which presuppose the separation of actual life from political life and make the political quality an abstraction of actual participation in the state.

According to Hegel, the direct participation of all in deliberating and deciding on political matters of general concern admits the democratic element without any rational form into the organism of the state, although it is only in virtue of the possession of such a form that the state is an organism at all. That is to say, the democratic element can be admitted only as a formal element in a state organism that is merely a formalism of the state. The democratic element should be, rather, the actual element that acquires its rational form in the whole organism of the state. If the democratic element enters the state organism or state formalism as a particular element, then the rational form of its existence means a drill, an accommodation, a form, in which it does not exhibit what is characteristic of its essence. In other words, it would enter the state organism merely as a formal principle.

We have already pointed out that Hegel develops merely a state formalism. For him, the actual material principle is the Idea, the abstract thought-form of the state as a subject, the absolute Idea which has in it no passive or material moment. In contrast to the abstraction of this Idea the determinations of the actual, empirical state formalism appear as content; and hence the actual content (here actual man, actual society, etc.) appear as formless inorganic matter.

Hegel had established the essence of the Estates in the fact that in them empirical universality becomes the subject of the actually existing universal. Does this mean anything other than that matters of political concern 'are their concerns, and that it is their right that what is done should be done with their knowledge and volition'? And should not the Estates precisely constitute their actualized right? And is it surprising then that all seek the actuality of what is theirs by right?

To hold that every single person should share in deliberating and deciding on political matters of general concern...

In a really rational state one could answer, 'Not every single person should share in deliberating and deciding on political matters of general concern', because the individuals share in deliberating and deciding on matters of general concern as the 'all', that is to say, within and as members of the society. Not all individually, but the individuals as all.

Hegel presents himself with the dilemma: either civil society (the Many, the multitude) shares through deputies in deliberating and deciding on political matters of general concern or all [as][1] individuals do this. This is no opposition of essence, as Hegel subsequently tries to present it, but of existence, and indeed of the most external existence, quantity. Thus, the basis which Hegel himself designated as external—the multiplicity of members—remains the best reason against the direct participation of all. The question of whether civil society should participate in the legislature either by entering it through deputies or by the direct participation of all as individuals is itself a question within the abstraction of the political state or within the abstract political state; it is an abstract political question.

It is in both cases, as Hegel himself has developed this, the political significance of 'empirical universality'.

In its proper form the opposition is this: the individuals participate as all, or the individuals participate as a few, as not-all. In both cases allness remains merely an external plurality or totality of individuals. Allness is no essential, spiritual, actual quality of the individual. It is not something through which he would lose the character of abstract individuality. Rather, it is merely the sum total of individuality. One individuality, many individiualities, all individualities. The one, the many, the all—none of these determinations changes the essence of the subject, individuality.

All as individuals should share in deliberating and deciding on political matters of general concern; that is to say, then, that all should share in this not as all but as individuals.

The question appears to contradict itself in two respects.

The political matters of general concern are the concern of the state, the state as actual concern. Deliberation and decision is the effectuation of the state as actual concern. It seems obvious then that all the members of the state have a relationship to the state as being their actual concern. The very notion of member of the state implies their being a member of the state, a part of it, and the state having them as its part. But if they are an integral part of the state, then it is obvious that their social existence is already their actual participation in it. They are not only integral parts of the state, but the state is their integral part. To be consciously an integral

---

[1] German editors' addition.

part of something is to participate consciously in it, to be consciously integral to it. Without this consciousness the member of the state would be an animal.

To say 'political matters of general concern' makes it appear that matters of general concern and the state are something different. But the state is the matter of general concern, thus really the matters of general concern.

Participation in political matters of general concern and participation in the state are, therefore, identical. It is a tautology [to say] that a member of the state, a part of the state, participates in the state, and that this participation can appear only as deliberation or decision, or related forms, and thus that every member of the state shares in deliberating and deciding (if these functions are taken to be the functions of actual participation in the state) the political matters of general concern. If we are talking about actual members of the state, then this participation cannot be regarded as a 'should'; otherwise we would be talking about subjects who should be and want to be members of the state, but actually are not.

On the other hand, if we are talking about definite concerns, about single political acts, then it is again obvious that not all as individuals accomplish them. Otherwise, the individual would be the true society, and would make society superfluous. The individual would have to do everything at once, while society would have him act for others just as it would have others act for him.

The question whether all as individuals should share in deliberating and deciding on political matters of general concern is a question that arises from the separation of the political state and civil society.

As we have seen, the state exists merely as political state. The totality of the political state is the legislature. To participate in the legislature is thus to participate in the political state and to prove and actualize one's existence as member of the political state, as member of the state. That all as individuals want to participate integrally in the legislature is nothing but the will of all to be actual (active) members of the state, or to give themselves a political existence, or to prove their existence as political and to effect it as such. We have further seen that the Estates are civil society as legislature, that they are its political existence. The fact, therefore, that civil society invades the sphere of legislative power *en masse*, and where possible totally, that actual civil society wishes to substitute itself for the fictional civil society of the legislature, is nothing but the drive of civil society to give itself political existence, or to make political existence its actual existence. The drive of civil society to transform itself into political society, or to make political society into the actual society, shows itself as the drive for the most fully possible universal participation in legislative power.

Here, quantity is not without importance. If the augmentation of the Estates is a physical and intellectual augmentation of one of the hostile forces—and we have seen that the various elements of the legislature oppose one another as hostile forces—then the question of whether all as individuals are members of the legislature or whether they should enter the legislature through deputies is the placing in question of the representative principle within the representative principle, i.e., within that fundamental conception of the political state which exists in constitutional monarchy. (1) The notion that the legislature is the totality of the political state is a notion of the abstraction of the political state. Because this one act is the sole political act of civil society, all should participate and want to participate in it at once. (2) All as individuals. In the Estates, legislative activity is not regarded as social, as a function of society, but rather as the act wherein the individuals first assume an actually and consciously social function, that is, a political function. Here the legislature is no derivative, no function of society, but simply its formation. This formation into a legislative power requires that all members of civil society regard themselves as individuals, that they actually face one another as individuals. The abstraction of 'being a member of the state' is their 'abstract definition', a definition that is not actualized in the actuality of their life.

There are two possibilities here: either the separation of the political state and civil society actually obtains, or civil society is actual political society. In the first case, it is impossible that all as individuals participate in the legislature, for the political state is an existent which is separated from civil society. On the one hand, civil society would abandon itself as such if all [its members] were legislators; on the other hand, the political state which stands over against it can tolerate it only if it has a form suitable to the standards of the state. In other words, the participation of civil society in the political state through deputies is precisely the expression of their separation and merely dualistic unity.

Given the second case, i.e., that civil society is actual political society, it is nonsense to make a claim which has resulted precisely from a notion of the political state as an existent separated from civil society, from the theological notion of the political state. In this situation, legislative power altogether loses the meaning of representative power. Here, the legislature is a representation in the same sense in which every function is representative. For example, the shoemaker is my representative in so far as he fulfills a social need, just as every definite social activity, because it is a species-activity, represents only the species; that is to say, it represents a determination of my own essence the way every man is the representative of the other. Here, he is representative not by virtue of something other than himself which he represents, but by virtue of what he is and does.

Legislative power is sought not for the sake of its content, but for the sake of its formal political significance. For example, executive power, in and for itself, has to be the object of popular desire much more than legislative power, which is the metaphysical political function. The legislative function is the will, not in its practical but in its theoretical energy. Here, the will should not preempt the law; rather, the actual law is to be discovered and formulated.

Out of this divided nature of the legislature—i.e., its nature as actual lawgiving function and at the same time representative, abstract-political function—stems a peculiarity which is especially prevalent in France, the land of political culture.

(We always find two things in the executive: the actual deed and the state's reason for this deed, as another actual consciousness, which in its total organization is the bureaucracy.)

The actual content of legislative power (so long as the prevailing special interests do not come into significant conflict with the *objectum quaestionis*) is treated very much *à part*, as a matter of secondary importance.

A question attracts particular attention only when it becomes political, that is to say, either when it can be tied to a ministerial question, and thus becomes a question of the power of the legislature over the executive, or when it is a matter of rights in general, which are connected with the political formalism. How come this phenomenon? Because the legislature is at the same time the representation of civil society's political existence; because in general the political nature of a question consists in its relationship to the various powers of the political state; and finally, because the legislature represents political consciousness, which can manifest itself as political only in conflict with the executive. There is the essential demand that every social need, law, etc., be investigated and identified politically, that is to say, determined by the whole of the state in its social sense. But in the abstract political state this essential demand takes a new turn; specifically, it is given a formal change of expression in the direction of another power (content) besides its actual content. This is no abstraction of the French, but rather the inevitable consequence of the actual state's existing merely as the political state formalism examined above. The opposition within the representative power is the κατ' ἐξοχὴν political existence of the representative power. Within this representative constitution, however, the question under investigation takes a form other than that in which Hegel considered it. It is not a question of whether civil society should exercise legislative power through deputies or through all as individuals. Rather, it is a question of the extension and greatest possible universalization of voting, of active as well as passive suffrage. This is the real point of dispute in the matter of political reform, in France as well as in England.

Voting is not considered philosophically, that is, not in terms of its proper nature, if it is considered in relation to the crown or the executive. The vote is the actual relation of actual civil society to the civil society of the legislature, to the representative element. In other words, the vote is the immediate, the direct, the existing and not simply imagined relation of civil society to the political state. It therefore goes without saying that the vote is the chief political interest of actual civil society. In unrestricted suffrage, both active and passive, civil society has actually raised itself for the first time to an abstraction of itself, to political existence as its true universal and essential existence. But the full achievement of this abstraction is at once also the transcendence [*Aufhebung*] of the abstraction. In actually establishing its political existence as its true existence civil society has simultaneously established its civil existence, in distinction from its political existence, as inessential. And with the one separated, the other, its opposite, falls. Within the abstract political state the reform of voting advances the dissolution [*Auflösung*] of this political state, but also the dissolution of civil society.

We will encounter the question of the reform of voting later under another aspect, namely, from the point of view of the interests. We will also discuss later the other conflicts which arise from the two-fold character of the legislature (being at one time the political representative or mandatory of civil society, at another time rather primarily the political existence of civil society and a specific existent within the political formalism of the state).

In the meantime we return to the Remark to our paragraph [308].

The rational consideration of a topic, the consciousness of the Idea, is concrete and to that extent coincides with a genuine practical sense. The concrete state is the whole, articulated into its particular groups. The member of a state is a member of such a group, i.e., of a social class, and it is only as characterized in this objective way that he comes under consideration when we are dealing with the state.

We have already said all that is required concerning this.

His (the member of a state's)[1] mere character as universal implies that he is at one and the same time both a private person and also a thinking consciousness, a will which wills the universal. This consciousness and will, however, lose their emptiness and

---

[1] Marx's insertion.

acquire a content and a living actuality only when they are filled with particularity, and particularity means determinacy as particular and a particular class status; or, to put the matter otherwise, abstract individuality is a generic essence, but has its immanent universal actuality as the generic essence next higher in the scale.

Everything Hegel says is correct, with the restriction (1) that he assumes particular class status and determinacy as particular to be identical, (2) that this determinacy, the species, the generic essence next higher in the scale must also actually, not only implicitly but explicitly, be established as the species or specification of the universal generic essence. But in the state, which he demonstrates to be the self-conscious existence of the moral spirit, Hegel tacitly accepts this moral spirit's being the determining thing only implicitly, that is, in accordance with the universal Idea. He does not allow society to become the actually determining thing, because for that an actual subject is required, and he has only an abstract, imaginary subject.

§ 309. Since deputies are elected to deliberate and decide on *public* affairs, the point about their election is that it is a choice of individuals on the strength of confidence felt in them, i.e., a choice of such individuals as have a better understanding of these affairs than their electors have and such also as essentially vindicate the universal interest, not the particular interest of a society or a Corporation in preference to that interest. Hence their relation to their electors is not that of agents with a commission or specific instructions. A further bar to their being so is the fact that their assembly is meant to be a living body in which all members deliberate in common and reciprocally instruct and convince each other.

(1) The deputies are supposed to be something other than agents with a commission or specific instructions, for they are supposed to be such as essentially vindicate the universal interest, not the particular interest of a society or a Corporation in preference to that interest. Hegel has constructed the representatives primarily as representatives of the Corporations etc., in order subsequently to reintroduce the other political determination, namely, that they are not to vindicate the particular interest of the Corporation etc. With that he abolishes his own determination, for he completely separates [the representatives], in their essential character as representatives, from their Corporation-existence. In so doing he also separates the Corporation from itself in its actual content, for it is supposed to vote not from its own point of view but from the state's point of view; that is to say, it is supposed to vote in its non-existence as Corporation. Hegel thus acknowledges the material actuality of the thing he formally converts into its opposite, namely, the abstraction of civil society from itself in its political act; and its political existence is nothing but this abstraction. Hegel gives as reason that the representatives are elected

precisely to the activity of public affairs; but the Corporations are not instances of public affairs.

(2) The point about their election is supposed to be that it is a choice of individuals on the strength of confidence felt in them, i.e., a choice of such individuals as have a better understanding of these affairs than their electors have; from which, once again, it is supposed to follow that the relationship which the deputies have to their electors is not that of agents.

Only by means of a sophism can Hegel declare that these individuals understand these affairs 'better' and not 'simply'. This conclusion [namely, that they understand these affairs better] could be drawn only if the electors had the option of deliberating and deciding themselves about public affairs *or* of delegating definite individuals to discharge these things, i.e., precisely if deputation, or representation, did not belong essentially to the character of civil society's legislature. But in the state constructed by Hegel, deputation, or representation, constitutes precisely the legislature's specific essence, precisely as realized.

This example is characteristic [of the way] Hegel proposes the thing half intentionally, and imputes to it in its narrow form the sense opposed to this narrowness.

Hegel gives the proper reason last. The deputies of civil society constitute themselves into an assembly, and only this assembly is the actual political existence and will of civil society. The separation of the political state from civil society appears as the separation of the deputies from their mandators. From itself, society delegates to its political existence only the elements.

The contradiction appears two-fold:

(1) Formal. The delegates of civil society are a society whose members are connected by the form of instruction or commission with those who commission them. They are formally commissioned, but once they are actual they are no longer commissioned. They are supposed to be delegates, and they are not.

(2) Material. [This is] in regard to the interests. We will come back to this point later. Here, we find the opposite of the formal contradiction. The delegates are commissioned to be representatives of public affairs, but they really represent particular affairs.

What is significant is that Hegel here designates trust as the substance of election, as the substantial relation between electors and deputies. Trust is a personal relationship. Concerning this, it says further in the Addition [to § 309]:

Representation is grounded on trust, but trusting another is something different from giving my vote myself in my own personal capacity. Hence majority voting runs counter to the principle that I should be personally present in anything which is to be obligatory on me. We have confidence in a man when we take him to be a man of discretion who will manage our affairs conscientiously and to the best of his knowledge, just as if they were his own.

§ 310. The guarantee that deputies will have the qualifications and disposition that accord with this end—since independent means attains its right in the first section of the Estates—is to be found so far as the second section is concerned—the section drawn from the fluctuating and changeable element in civil society—above all in the knowledge of the organization and interests of the state and civil society, the temperament, and the skill which a deputy acquires as a result of the actual transaction of business in managerial or official positions, and then evinces in his actions. As a result, he also acquires and develops a managerial and political sense, tested by his experience, and this is a further guarantee of his suitability as a deputy.

First, the Upper Chamber, that of independent private property, was constructed for the sake of the Crown and the executive as a guarantee against the disposition of the Lower Chamber as the political existence of empirical universality; and now Hegel further requires a new guarantee which is supposed to guarantee the disposition of the Lower Chamber itself.

First, trust, the guarantee of the elector, was the guarantee of the deputy. Now this trust itself further requires the guarantee of the deputy's ability.

Hegel would rather have liked to make the Lower Chamber one of pensioned civil servants. He requires of the deputy not only political sense but also managerial, bureaucratic sense.

What he really wants here is that the legislature be the real governing power. He expresses this such that he twice requires the bureaucracy, once as representation of the Crown, at another time as representative of the people.

Even if officials are allowed to be deputies in constitutional states, this is only because there is on the whole an abstraction from class, from the civil quality, and the abstraction of state citizenship predominates.

With this Hegel forgets that he allowed representation to proceed from the Corporations, and that the executive directly opposes these. In this forgetfulness, which persists likewise in the following paragraph, he goes so far that he creates an essential distinction between the deputies of the Corporations and those of the classes.

In the Remark to this paragraph it says:

Subjective opinion, naturally enough, finds superfluous and even perhaps offensive the demand for such guarantees, if the demand is made with reference to what is called the 'people'. The state, however, is characterized by objectivity, not by a subjective opinion and its self-confidence. Hence it can recognize in individuals only their objectively recognizable and tested character, and it must be all the more careful on this point in connexion with the second section of the Estates, since this section is rooted in interests and activities directed towards the particular, i.e., in the sphere where chance, mutability, and caprice enjoy their right of free play.

Here, Hegel's thoughtless inconsistency and managerial sense become really disgusting. At the close of the Addition to the preceding paragraph [i.e., § 309] it says:

The electors require a guarantee that their deputy will further and secure this general interest (the task of the deputies described earlier).[1]

This guarantee for the electors has underhandedly evolved into a guarantee against the electors, against their self-confidence. In the Estates, empirical universality was supposed to come to the moment of subjective formal freedom. Public consciousness was supposed to come to existence in that moment as the empirical universality of the opinions and thoughts of the Many. (§ 301.)

Now these opinions and thoughts must give proof beforehand to the executive that they are *its* opinions and thoughts. Unfortunately, Hegel here speaks of the state as a finished existence, although he is precisely now in the process of finishing the construction of the state within the Estates. He speaks of the state as a concrete subject which does not take offence at subjective opinion and its self-confidence, and for which the individuals have first made themselves recognizable and tested. The only thing he still lacks is a requirement that the Estates take an examination in the presence of the honorable executive. Here, Hegel goes almost to the point of servility. It is evident that he is thoroughly infected with the miserable arrogance of the world of Prussian officialdom which, distinguished in its bureaucratic narrow-mindedness, looks down on the self-confidence of the subjective opinion of the people regarding itself. Here, the state is at all times for Hegel identical with the Executive.

To be sure, in a real state mere trust or subjective opinion cannot suffice. But in the state which Hegel constructs the political sentiment of civil society is mere opinion precisely because its political existence is an abstraction from its actual existence, precisely because the state as a whole is not the objectification of the political sentiment. Had Hegel wished to be consistent, he would have had to work much harder to construct the Estates in conformity with their essential definition (§ 301) as the explicit existence of public affairs in the thought etc. of the Many, and thus nothing less than fully independent of the other presuppositions of the political state.

Just as Hegel earlier called the presupposing of bad will in the executive etc. the view of the rabble, so just as much and even more is it the view of

---

[1] Marx's insertion.

the rabble to presuppose bad will in the people. Hegel has no right to find it either superfluous or offensive when, among [the doctrines of] the theorists he scorns, guarantees are demanded in reference to what is called the state, the *soi-disant* state, the executive, when guarantees are demanded that the sentiment of the bureaucracy be the sentiment of the state.

§ **311.** A further point about the election of deputies is that, since civil society is the electorate, the deputies should themselves be conversant with and participate in its special needs, difficulties, and particular interests. Owing to the nature of civil society, its deputies are the deputies of the various Corporations (see Paragraph 308), and this simple mode of appointment obviates any confusion due to conceiving the electorate abstractly and as an agglomeration of atoms. Hence the deputies *eo ipso* adopt the point of view of society, and their actual election is therefore either something wholly superfluous or else reduced to a trivial play of opinion and caprice.

First of all, Hegel joins the election in its determination as legislature (§ 309, 310) to the fact that civil society is the electorate, i.e., he joins the legislature to its representative character, through a simple 'further'. And just as thoughtlessly he expresses the enormous contradictions which lie in this 'further'.

According to § 309 the deputies should essentially vindicate the universal interest, not the particular interest of a society or a Corporation in preference to that interest.

According to § 311 the deputies proceed from the Corporations, represent these particular interests and needs, and avoid confusion due to abstract conceptions—as if the universal interest were not also such an abstraction, an abstraction precisely from their Corporation, etc., interests.

According to § 310 it is required that, as a result of the actual transaction of business etc., they have acquired and evinced a managerial and political sense. In § 311 a Corporation and civil sense is required.

In the Addition to § 309 it says, representation is grounded on trust. According to § 311 the actual election, this realization of trust, its manifestation and appearance, is either something wholly superfluous or else reduced to a trivial play of opinion and caprice.

That on which representation is grounded, its essence, is thus either something wholly superfluous, etc. for representation. Thus in one breath Hegel establishes the absolute contradictions: Representation is grounded on trust, on the confidence of man in man, and it is not grounded on trust. This is simply a playing around with formalities.

The object of the representation is not the particular interest, but rather man and his state citizenship, i.e., the universal interest. On the other hand, the particular interest is the matter of the representation, and the spirit of this interest is the spirit of the representative.

In the Remark to this paragraph, which we examine now, these contradictions are still more glaringly carried through. At one time representation is representation of the man, at another time of the particular interest of particular matter.

It is obviously of advantage that the deputies should include representatives of each particular main branch of society (e.g. trade, manufactures, &c., &c.)—representatives who are thoroughly conversant with it and who themselves belong to it. The idea of free unrestricted election leaves this important consideration entirely at the mercy of chance. All such branches of society, however, have equal rights of representation. Deputies are sometimes regarded as 'representatives'; but they are representatives in an organic, rational sense only if they are representatives not of individuals or a conglomeration of them, but of one of the essential spheres of society and its large-scale interests. Hence representation cannot now be taken to mean simply the substitution of one man for another; the point is rather that the interest itself is actually present in its representative, while he himself is there to represent the objective element of his own being.

As for popular suffrage, it may be further remarked that especially in large states it leads inevitably to electoral indifference, since the casting of a single vote is of no significance where there is a multitude of electors. Even if a voting qualification is highly valued and esteemed by those who are entitled to it, they still do not enter the polling booth. Thus the result of an institution of this kind is more likely to be the opposite of what was intended; election actually falls into the power of a few, of a caucus, and so of the particular and contingent interest which is precisely what was to have been neutralized.

Both Paragraphs 312 and 313 are taken care of by our earlier comments, and are worth no special discussion. So we simply put them down as is:

§ 312. Each class in the Estates (see Paragraphs 305–8) contributes something peculiarly its own to the work of deliberation. Further, one moment in the class-element has in the sphere of politics the special function of mediation, mediation between two existing things. Hence this moment must likewise acquire a separate existence of its own. For this reason the assembly of the Estates is divided into two houses.

O Jerum!

§ 313. This division, by providing chambers of the first and second instance, is a surer guarantee for ripeness of decision and it obviates the accidental character which a snap-division has and which a numerical majority may acquire. But the principal advantage of this arrangement is that there is less chance of the Estates being in direct opposition to the executive; or that, if the mediating element is at the same time on the side of the lower house, the weight of the lower house's opinion is all the stronger, because it appears less partisan and its opposition appears neutralized.*

* Here, on page 4 of the *Bogen* numbered XL by Marx, the manuscript ends. At the top of the first page of the following *Bogen*, which is otherwise blank, Marx wrote:
Contents
Concerning Hegel's Transition and Explication

A CONTRIBUTION TO THE CRITIQUE OF HEGEL'S 'PHILOSOPHY OF RIGHT'

INTRODUCTION

BY

KARL MARX

'Zur Kritik der Hegel'schen Rechts-Philosophie. Einleitung'. In *Deutsch-französische Jahrbücher* (Paris, 1844), pp. 71–85; edited by Karl Marx and Arnold Ruge. Probable date of composition, September 1843–January 1844; originally intended as an introduction to a proposed revision of the *Kritik des Hegelschen Staatsrechts*(§§ 261–313). A brief account of the circumstances of composition and a list of early accounts and reviews of the work, as well as a list of editions and translations, is in Andréas, 'Marx et Engels et la gauche hégélienne', pp. 377–88.

For Germany, the critique of religion is essentially completed; and the critique of religion is the prerequisite of every critique.

Error in its profane form of existence is compromised once its celestial *oratio pro aris et focis* has been refuted. Man, who has found only his own reflection in the fantastic reality of heaven, where he sought a supernatural being, will no longer be disposed to find only the semblance of himself, only a non-human being, here where he seeks and must seek his true reality.

The foundation of irreligious criticism is this: man makes religion; religion does not make man. Religion is, in fact, the self-consciousness and self-esteem of man who has either not yet gained himself or has lost himself again. But man is no abstract being squatting outside the world. Man is the world of man, the state, society. This state, this society, produce religion, which is an inverted world-consciousness, because they are an inverted world. Religion is the general theory of this world, its encyclopedic compendium, its logic in popular form, its spiritualistic *point d'honneur*, its enthusiasm, its moral sanction, its solemn complement, its universal basis of consolation and justification. It is the fantastic realization of the human being because the human being has attained no true reality. Thus, the struggle against religion is indirectly the struggle against that world of which religion is the spiritual aroma.

The wretchedness of religion is at once an expression of and a protest against real wretchedness. Religion is the sigh of the oppressed creature, the heart of a heartless world and the soul of soulless conditions. It is the opium of the people.

The abolition of religion as the illusory happiness of the people is a demand for their true happiness. The call to abandon illusions about their condition is the call to abandon a condition which requires illusions. Thus, the critique of religion is the critique in embryo of the vale of tears of which religion is the halo.

Criticism has plucked the imaginary flowers from the chain, not so that man shall bear the chain without fantasy or consolation, but so that he shall cast off the chain and gather the living flower. The critique of religion disillusions man so that he will think, act, and fashion his reality as a man who has lost his illusions and regained his reason, so that he will revolve about himself as his own true sun. Religion is only the illusory sun about which man revolves so long as he does not revolve about himself.

It is the task of history, therefore, once the other-world of truth has vanished, to establish the truth of this world. It is above all the task of philosophy, which is in the service of history, to unmask human self-alienation in its secular forms, once its sacred form has been unmasked. Thus, the critique of heaven is transformed into the critique of the earth, the critique of religion into the critique of law, the critique of theology into the critique of politics.

The following exposition[1]—which is a contribution to this task—does not deal directly with the original, but with a copy, i.e., with the German philosophy of the state and of right, simply because it deals with Germany.

If we were to begin with the German *status quo* itself, even in the only appropriate way, which is negatively, the result would still be an anachronism. For even the negation of our political present is already a dusty fact in the historical junkroom of modern nations. If I negate powdered wigs, I still have unpowdered wigs. If I negate the German conditions of 1843, I am according to French chronology barely in the year 1789, and still less at the center of the present day.

Indeed, German history prides itself on a development which no other nation has previously achieved or will ever imitate in the historical firmament. We have shared in the restorations of modern nations without ever having shared in their revolutions. We have been restored, first because other nations ventured a revolution, and second because other nations endured a counter-revolution; in the first case because our leaders were afraid, and in the second case because they were not. Led by our shepherds, we have only once been in the company of liberty, and that was on the day of its interment.

One school of thought, which justifies the infamy of today by the infamy of yesterday, a school which interprets every cry of the serf under the knout as a cry of rebellion once the knout is time-honored, ancestral, and historical, a school to which history shows only its *a posteriori* as did the God of Israel to his servant Moses—the Historical

[1] That is, the projected revision of the *Critique of Hegel's 'Philosophy of Right'* (§§ 261–313).

School of Law—might well have invented German history were it not itself an invention of German history. A Shylock, but a servile Shylock, it swears by its bond, its historical bond, its Christian–Germanic bond, for every pound of flesh cut from the heart of the people.

On the other hand, good-natured enthusiasts, German nationalists by sentiment and enlightened radicals by reflection, seek our history of freedom beyond our history in the primeval Teutonic forests. But then how does our history of freedom differ from that of the wild boar, if it is only to be found in the forests? Besides, as the saying goes: what is shouted into the forests echoes back from the forest. So peace to the primeval Teutonic forests!

But war upon the conditions in Germany! By all means! They are beneath the level of history, beneath all criticism; yet they remain an object of criticism just as the criminal who is beneath the level of humanity remains an object of the executioner. In its struggle against them criticism is no passion of the brain, but is rather the brain of passion. It is not a scalpel but a weapon. Its object is its enemy, which it wishes not to refute but to destroy. For the spirit of these conditions is already refuted. They are not, in themselves, objects worthy of thought, but rather existences equally despicable and despised. Criticism itself needs no further self-clarification regarding this object, for criticism already understands it. Criticism is no longer an end in itself, but now simply a means. Indignation is its essential pathos, denunciation its principal task.

It is a matter of describing the stifling pressure of all the social spheres on one another, the universal, passive ill-feeling, the recognized yet misunderstood narrow-mindedness, all framed in a system of government which, living by the conservation of all this wretchedness, is itself wretchedness in government.

What a spectacle! The infinite division of society into the most diverse races confronting one another with their petty antipathies, bad conscience and crude mediocrity, and which, precisely because of their mutual ambiguous and suspicious disposition, are treated by their masters without distinction, though with differing formalities, as merely tolerated existences. And they are to recognize and acknowledge the very fact that they are dominated, ruled and possessed as a concession from Heaven! On the other hand there are the masters themselves, whose greatness is in inverse proportion to their number!

Criticism dealing with this situation is criticism in hand-to-hand combat; and in this kind of combat one does not bother about whether the opponent is noble, or of equal rank, or interesting; all that matters is to strike him. It is a question of permitting the Germans not a single moment of illusion or resignation. The burden must be made still more oppressive by adding to it a consciousness of it, and the shame made still more shameful by making it public. Every sphere of German society must be described as the *partie honteuse* of German society, and these petrified conditions must be made to dance by singing to them their own melody. The nation must be taught to be terrified of itself in order to give it courage. In this way an imperative need of the German nation will be fulfilled, and the needs of nations are themselves the final causes of their satisfaction.

This struggle against the limited content of the German *status quo* is not without interest even for the modern nations; for the German *status quo* is the overt perfection of the *ancien régime*, and the *ancien régime* is the hidden defect of the modern state. The struggle against the political present in Germany is the struggle against the past of the modern nations, who are still continually troubled by the reminiscences of this past. It is instructive for them to see the *ancien régime*, which experienced its moment of tragedy in their history, play its comic role as a German ghost. Its history was tragic so long as it was the privileged power in the world and freedom was a personal fancy; in short, so long as it believed, and necessarily so, in its own justification. So long as the *ancien régime*, as the existing world-order, struggled against a new world coming into existence, it was guilty of a world-historical, but not a personal, error. Its decline was, therefore, tragic.

The present German régime, on the other hand—an anachronism, a flagrant contradiction of universally recognized axioms, the nullity of the *ancien régime* revealed to the whole world—only imagines that it believes in itself, and asks that the world imagine this also. If it believed in its own nature, would it hide that nature under the appearance of an alien nature, and seek its preservation in hypocrisy and sophistry? The modern *ancien régime* is nothing but the humbug of a world order whose real heroes are dead. History is thorough, and passes through many phases when it conveys an old form to the grave. The final phase of a world-historical form is its comedy. The Greek gods, already once mortally wounded, tragically, in Aeschylus' *Prometheus Bound*, had to die once more, comically, in the dialogues of Lucian. Why does history proceed in this way? So that mankind will separate itself happily from its past. We claim this happy historical destiny for the political powers of Germany.

Meanwhile, the moment modern political and social actuality is subjected to criticism, the moment, therefore, criticism focuses on genuine human problems, either it finds itself outside the German *status quo* or it must treat its object under a different form. For example, the relationship of industry, of the world of wealth in general, to the political world is a major problem of modern times. Under what form does this problem begin to occupy the Germans? Under the form of protective tariffs, the system of prohibitions, national economy. German chauvinism has passed from men to matter, and so one fine morning our cavaliers of cotton and heroes of iron found themselves metamorphosed into patriots. Thus, in Germany the sovereignty of monopoly within the nation has begun to be recognized through its being invested with sovereignty *vis-à-vis* other nations. In Germany, therefore, we now begin with what in France and England is the end of a development. The old decayed state of affairs against which these nations are in theoretical revolt, and which they still bear only as chains are borne, is welcomed in Germany as the dawning of a glorious future as yet hardly daring to proceed from a cunning [*listigen*][1] theory to a pitiless practice. While in France and England the problem reads: political economy or the mastery of society over wealth; in Germany it reads: national economy or the mastery of private property over nationality. Thus, in France and England it is a question of abolishing monopoly, which has progressed to its final consequences, while in Germany it is a question of proceeding on to the final consequences of monopoly. There it is a question of the solution, here only a question of the collision. This is an adequate example of the German form of modern problems, an example of how our history, like a raw recruit, has until now only done extra drill on old historical matters.

If the whole of German development were at the level of German political development, a German could participate in contemporary problems no more than can a Russian. But if the single individual is not limited by the boundaries of the nation, still less is the nation as a whole liberated by the liberation of one individual. That a Scythian [Anacharsis] was numbered among the Greek philosophers did not enable the Scythians to advance a step toward Greek culture.

Fortunately, we Germans are not Scythians.

Just as ancient peoples lived their past history in their imagination, in mythology, so we Germans have lived our future history in thought, in philosophy. We are philosophical contemporaries of the present day without being its historical contemporaries. German philosophy is the ideal prolongation of German history. If, then, we criticize the *œuvres posthumes* of our ideal history, philosophy, instead of the *œuvres incomplètes* of our actual history, our criticism centers on the very questions of which the present age says: that is the question. What for advanced nations is

---

[1] A punning reference to Friedrich List (1789–1846) whose economic theory was published under the title *Das nationale System der politischen Œkonomie* (1840).

a practical break with modern political conditions is in Germany, where these conditions themselves do not yet exist, essentially a critical break with their philosophical reflection.

German philosophy of right and the state is the only German history that is *al pari* with official modern times. Thus, the German nation is obliged to connect its dream history with its present circumstances, and subject to criticism not only these circumstances but also their abstract continuation. Its future can be restricted neither to the direct negation of its real, nor to the direct fulfillment of its ideal, political and juridical circumstances; for the direct negation of its real circumstances is already there in its ideal circumstances, and it has almost outlived the direct fulfilment of these in its contemplation of neighboring nations. The practical political party in Germany is right, therefore, in demanding the negation of philosophy. Its error lies not in the demand, but in limiting itself to the demand which it neither does nor can fulfil. It believes that it can achieve this negation by turning its back on philosophy, averting its gaze, and murmuring a few irritable and trite phrases about it. In its narrow outlook it does not even count philosophy a part of German actuality, or it considers philosophy to be beneath the level of German practical life and its attendant theories. You [of the practical party] demand that actual germs of life be the point of departure, but you forget that the German nation's actual germs of life have until now sprouted only in its cranium. In short, you cannot transcend philosophy without actualizing it.

The same error, but with the elements reversed, was committed by the theoretical political party, which originated in philosophy.

This party saw in the present struggle only the critical struggle of philosophy against the German world. It failed to note that previous philosophy itself belongs to this world and is its complement, even if only an ideal complement. Critical of its counterpart, it remained uncritical of itself: it took its point of departure from the presuppositions of philosophy, and either accepted the conclusions reached by philosophy or else presented as directly philosophical demands and results drawn from elsewhere; even though these—assuming their validity—are obtainable only through the negation of previous philosophy, i.e., of philosophy as philosophy. We reserve until later a fuller account of this party. Its basic defect reduces to this: it believed that it could actualize philosophy without transcending it.

The criticism of the German philosophy of right and of the state, which was given its most logical, profound and complete expression by Hegel, is at once the critical analysis of the modern state and of the reality connected with it, and the definite negation of all the past forms of consciousness in German jurisprudence and politics, whose most distinguished and most general expression, raised to the level of a science, is precisely the speculative philosophy of right. If it was only in Germany that the speculative philosophy of right was possible—this abstract and extravagant thought about the modern state, whose reality remains in another world (even though this is just across the Rhine)—the German thought-version [*Gedankenbild*] of the modern state, on the other hand, which abstracts from actual man, was only possible because and in so far as the modern state itself abstracts from actual man, or satisfies the whole man only in an imaginary way. In politics the Germans have thought what other nations have done. Germany was their theoretical conscience. The abstract and presumptive character of its thinking was in step with the partial and stunted character of their actuality. If, then, the *status quo* of the German political system expresses the perfection of the *ancien régime*, the thorn in the flesh of the modern state, the *status quo* of German political thought expresses the imperfection of the modern state, the damaged condition of the flesh itself.

As the determined adversary of the prevailing mode of German political consciousness, criticism of the speculative philosophy of right does not remain within itself, but proceeds on to tasks for whose solution there is only one means—*praxis*.

The question arises: can Germany attain a praxis *à la hauteur des principes*, that is to say, a revolution that will raise it not only to the official level of modern nations, but to the human level which will be the immediate future of these nations?

The weapon of criticism certainly cannot replace the criticism of weapons; material force must be overthrown by material force; but theory, too, becomes a material force once it seizes the masses. Theory is capable of seizing the masses once it demonstrates *ad hominem*, and it demonstrates *ad hominem* once it becomes radical. To be radical is to grasp matters at the root. But for man the root is man himself. The manifest proof of the radicalism of German theory, and thus of its practical energy, is the fact of its issuing from a resolute positive transcendence [*Aufhebung*] of religion. The critique of religion ends in the doctrine that man is the supreme being for man; thus it ends with the categorical imperative to overthrow all conditions in which man is a debased, enslaved, neglected, contemptible being—conditions which cannot be better described than by the Frenchman's exclamation about a proposed tax on dogs: 'Poor dogs! They want to treat you like men!'

Even from the historical point of view, theoretical emancipation has a specific practical importance for Germany. Germany's revolutionary past is precisely theoretical: it is the Reformation. As at that time it was a monk, so now it is the philosopher in whose brain the revolution begins.

Luther, to be sure, overcame servitude based on devotion, but by replacing it with servitude based on conviction. He shattered faith in authority by restoring the authority of faith. He transformed the priests into laymen by changing the laymen into priests. He liberated man from external religiosity by making religiosity that which is innermost to man. He freed the body of chains by putting the heart in chains.

But if Protestantism was not the real solution it at least posed the problem correctly. Thereafter it was no longer a question of the laymen's struggle with the priest outside of him, but of his struggle with his own inner priest, his priestly nature. And if the Protestant transformation of the German laity into priests emancipated the lay popes—the princes together with their clergy, the privileged and the philistines—so the philosophical transformation of the priestly Germans into men will emancipate the people. But just as emancipation is not limited to the princes, so the secularization of property will not be limited to the confiscation of church property, which as practiced especially by hypocritical Prussia. At that time, the Peasant War, the most radical event in German history, foundered because of theology. Today, when theology itself has foundered, the most unfree thing in German history, our *status quo*, will be shattered by philosophy. On the eve of the Reformation official Germany was the most abject servant of Rome. On the eve of its revolution Germany is the abject servant of those who are inferior to Rome, of Prussia and Austria, of petty squires and philistines.

However, a major difficulty appears to stand in the way of a radical German revolution.

Revolutions require a passive element, a material basis. Theory will be realized in a people only in so far as it is the realization of their needs. Will the enormous discrepancy between the demands of German thought and the answers of German actuality be matched by a similar discrepancy between civil society and the state, and within civil society itself? Will theoretical needs be directly practical needs? It is not enough that thought strive to actualize itself; actuality must itself strive toward thought.

But Germany has not passed through the middle state of political emancipation at the same time as the modern nations. The very stages it has surpassed in theory it has not yet reached in practice. How is Germany, with a *salto mortale*, to surmount not only its own limitations, but also those of the modern nations, limitations which it must actually experience and strive for as the liberation from its own actual limitations? A radical revolution can only be a revolution of radical needs, whose preconditions and birthplaces appear to be lacking.

But if Germany accompanied the development of modern nations only with the abstract activity of thought, without taking an active part in the actual struggles of this development, it has still shared the pains of this development without sharing its pleasures or its partial satisfaction. The abstract activity on the one hand corresponds to the abstract pain on the other. One day Germany will find itself at the level of European decadence before it has ever achieved the level of European emancipation. It will be like a fetishist suffering from the illnesses of Christianity.

If we examine the German governments we find that the circumstances of the time, the situation in Germany, the viewpoint of German culture, and finally their own lucky instinct, all drive them to combine the civilized deficiencies of the modern political world, whose advantages we do not enjoy, with the barbaric deficiencies of the *ancien régime*, which we enjoy in full measure; so that Germany must participate more and more, if not in the rationality, at least in the irrationality of the political forms that transcend its *status quo*. For example, is there any country in the world which shares as naively as so-called constitutional Germany all the illusions of the constitutional régime without any of its realities? Wasn't it somehow necessarily a German government brain-wave to combine the torments of censorship with those of the French September Laws [of 1835], which presuppose the freedom of the press! Just as the gods of all nations were found in the Roman Pantheon, so the sins of all state-forms are to be found in the Holy Roman German Empire. That this eclecticism will attain an unprecedented level is assured by the politico-aesthetic *gourmanderie* of a German king [Frederick William IV], who intends to play all the roles of royalty—the feudal as well as the bureaucratic, absolute as well as constitutional, autocratic as well as democratic—if not in the person of the people at least in his own person, if not for the people at least for himself. Germany, as the deficiency of the political present constituted into an individual system, will be unable to demolish the specific German limitations without demolishing the general limitations of the political present.

It is not a radical revolution, universal human emancipation, that is a utopian dream for Germany, but rather a partial, merely political revolution, a revolution that leaves the pillars of the edifice standing. What is the basis of a partial, merely political revolution? It is this: a section of civil society emancipates itself and achieves universal dominance; a determinate class undertakes from its particular situation the universal emancipation of society. This class emancipates the whole society, but only on the condition that the whole society shares its situation; for example, that it has or can obtain money and education.

No class of civil society can play this role unless it arouses in itself and in the masses a moment of enthusiasm, a moment in which it associates, fuses, and identifies itself with society in general, and is felt and recognized to be society's general representative, a moment in which its demands and rights are truly those of society itself, of which it is the social head and heart. Only in the name of the universal rights of society can a particular class lay claim to universal dominance. To take over this liberating position, and therewith the political exploitation of all the spheres of society in the interest of its own sphere, revolutionary energy and spiritual self-confidence do not suffice. For a popular revolution and the emancipation of a particular class to coincide, for one class to stand for the whole of society, another class must, on the other hand, concentrate in itself all the defects of society, must be the class of universal offense and the embodiment of universal limits. A particular social sphere must stand for the notorious crime of the whole society, so that liberation from this sphere appears to be universal liberation. For one class to be the class *par excellence* of liberation, another class must, on the other hand, be openly the subjugating class. The negative general significance of the French nobility and clergy determined the positive general significance of the bourgeoisie, the class standing next to and opposing them.

But every class in Germany lacks the consistency, the keenness, the courage, and the ruthlessness which would mark it as the negative representative of society. Moreover, every class lacks that breadth of soul which identifies it, if only for a moment, with the soul of the people; that genius which animates material force into political power; that revolutionary boldness which flings at its adversary the defiant phrase: I am nothing and I should be everything. The principle feature of German morality and honor, not only in individuals but in classes as well, is that modest egoism which asserts its narrowness and allows narrowness to be asserted against it. The relationship of the different spheres of German society is, therefore, not dramatic, but epic. Each of them begins to be aware of itself and to establish itself with its particular claims beside the others, not as soon as it is oppressed, but as soon as circumstances independent of its actions create a lower social stratum against which it can in turn exert pressure. Even the moral self-esteem of the German middle class is based merely on the consciousness of being the general representative of the philistine mediocrity of all the other classes. It is, therefore, not only the German kings who ascend the throne *mal à propos*. Each sphere of civil society suffers its defeat before it celebrates its victory, erects its own barrier before it overthrows its opposing barrier, asserts its narrow-minded nature before it can assert its generosity, so that the opportunity of playing a great role has passed before it ever actually existed, and each class, at the moment it begins to struggle with the class above it, is involved in the struggle with the class beneath. Hence, the princes are in conflict with the king, the bureaucracy with the nobility, the bourgeoisie with all of them, while the proletariat is already beginning its struggle against the bourgeoisie. The middle class hardly dares to conceive of the idea of emancipation from its own point of view, and already the development of social conditions and the progress of political theory show that this point of view itself is antiquated, or at least questionable.

In France it is enough to be something in order to desire to be everything. In Germany no one may be anything unless he renounces everything. In France partial emancipation is the basis of universal emancipation. In Germany universal emancipation is the *conditio sine qua non* for any partial emancipation. In France it is the actuality, in Germany the impossibility, of gradual emancipation which must give birth to full freedom. In France every national class is politically idealistic and considers itself above all to be not a particular class but the representative of the needs of society overall. The role of the emancipator thus passes in a dramatic movement to the different classes of the French nation, until it finally reaches the class which actualizes social freedom no longer on the basis of presupposed conditions which are at once external to man yet created by human society, but rather organizing all the conditions of human existence on the basis of social freedom. In Germany, on the other hand, where practical life is as little intellectual as intellectual life is practical, no class of civil society has the need and the capacity for universal emancipation until it is forced to it by its immediate situation, material necessity, and its very chains.

Where, then, is the positive possibility of German emancipation?

Our answer: in the formation of a class with radical chains, a class in civil society that is not of civil society, a class that is the dissolution of all classes, a sphere of society having a universal character because of its universal suffering and claiming no particular right because no particular wrong but unqualified wrong is perpetrated on it; a sphere that can claim no traditional title but only a human title; a sphere that does not stand partially opposed to the consequences, but totally opposed to the premises of the German political system; a sphere, finally, that cannot emancipate itself without emancipating itself from all the other spheres of society, thereby emancipating them; a sphere, in short, that is the complete loss of humanity and can only redeem itself through the total redemption of humanity. This dissolution of society existing as a particular class is the proletariat.

The proletariat is only beginning to appear in Germany as a result of the industrial development taking place. For it is not naturally existing poverty but artificially produced poverty, not the mass of men mechanically oppressed by the weight of society but the mass of men resulting from society's, and especially the middle class', acute dissolution that constitutes the proletariat—though at the same time, needless to say, victims of natural poverty and Christian–Germanic serfdom also become members.

When the proletariat announces the dissolution of the existing order of things it merely declares the secret of its own existence, for it *is* the *de facto* dissolution of this order of things. When the proletariat demands the negation of private property it merely elevates into a principle of society what society has advanced as the principle of the proletariat, and what the proletariat already involuntarily embodies as the negative result of society. The proletariat thus has the same right relative to the new world which is coming into being as has the German king relative to the existing world, when he calls the people his people and a horse his horse. In calling the people his private property the king merely expresses the fact that the owner of private property is king.

Just as philosophy finds its material weapons in the proletariat, so the proletariat finds its spiritual weapons in philosophy; and once the lightning of thought has struck deeply into this naive soil of the people the emancipation of the Germans into men will be accomplished.

Let us summarize:

The only practically possible emancipation of Germany is the emancipation based on the unique theory which holds that man is the supreme being for man. In Germany emancipation from the Middle Ages is possible only as the simultaneous emancipation from the partial victories over the Middle Ages. In Germany no form of bondage can be broken unless every form of bondage is broken. Germany, enamored of fundamentals, can have nothing less than a fundamental revolution. The emancipation of Germany is the emancipation of man. The head of this emancipation is philosophy, its heart is the proletariat. Philosophy cannot be actualized without the abolition [*Aufhebung*] of the proletariat; the proletariat cannot be abolished without the actualization of philosophy.

When all the intrinsic conditions are fulfilled, the day of German resurrection will be announced by the crowing of the Gallic cock.

Index

Absolute, xxx–i, xxxv; *see also* Idea
abstraction, relationships of, 89
activity, species-, xli, xliii–xliv, 119
actuality, xxii, xxiv, xxxi–xxxii, xxxvi–
  xxxvii, 7–9, 15–19, 64
Adams, H. L., lxvi
Aeschylus, *Prometheus Bound*, 134
alienation, xxx, xxxviii n., xlv–xlvi, li,
  lvii–lviii, lix, 6, 31–2, 80, 101–2
allegory, xxxii–xxxiii, 40, 94
allgemeine Stand, see class, universal
Anarchasis, 135
anarchism, lxii
Andréas, Bert, ix n., xiv, lxiv, lxvi
*Anekdota zur neuesten deutschen Philosophie
  und Publizistik* (ed. A. Ruge), x, xvi,
  xxviii, xxix
Annenkov, P. V., xxxviii n., 92 n.
anthropology, xxx, xli
appearance: and actuality, 7–9; and
  essence, 91, 107
'Archive of Atheism' ('Journal of
  Atheism'), xxi
aristocracy, xlix, 32, 96, 106
Aristotle, xix
assemblée, constituante and *constituée*,
  xxxix n., lxv, 58
Aufhebung: property, li, lvii–lvix, lxiii;
  socio-political dualism, li, lx, lxii, 121;
  bureaucracy, liv, 48; civil society, lxii,
  9; state, lxiii, lxvi, 97; family, 9;
  religion, 131, 137; philosophy, 136;
  proletariat, 142
Austria, 138
Avineri, Shlomo, xv n., xxxiv n., xxxix
  n., xlvii n., liii n., liv n., lviii n., lix
  n., lxiii n., lxvi, 79 n.

Barion, Jakob, lxvii
Bauer, Bruno, xxi
being: as Absolute Idea, xxxi; phenomenal, xxxii; species-, xli–xlii, xlv,
  li, lii, lix, lxi, 107; and state, 15; as
  Ens, 24; in and for-itself, 62–5
bellum omnium contra omnes, xlvii, lii,
  41–2
Berlin, xix–xxi, xxviii, xxxv; University of, xix
Blessed Trinity, 92
Bockmuhl, Klaus Erich, lxvii
Bonn, University of, xix, xxi
bourgeoisie, 141
Buffon, Georges Louis Leclerc de, xi
bureaucracy: and censorship, xxv, lii;
  and state, xlviii–xlvix, lii, 43, 73–4, 78,
  80, 84, 104, 120; universal class,
  xlviii–xlvix, l, lii, liv n., lv, 43, 50, 70,
  72, 104; and Estates, l, lx; and proletariat, li, lv; characteristics, lii–liii,
  43–8, 51–4, 61; and civil society, lii,
  74, 77–8; interests, lii–liii, 41; abolition of, liv, 48; qualifications, 43, 51,
  54; and people, 124; in Germany, 141
bürgerliche Gesellschaft, see civil society

capital, 75, 98, 102, 104
capitalism, xvii
Catholic Church, 48, 50, 52
censorship, x, xvi, xxv, lii, 139
Ceylon, 38
Christianity, xxiii, xxvii, 30, 80, 90, 139
citizenship, 113, 116, 125
city-state, xlv, 32
civil service, *see* bureaucracy
civil society: and Idea, xxxii, 8–9, 40;

143

CAMBRIDGE STUDIES IN THE HISTORY AND THEORY OF POLITICS

TEXTS

STUDIES